The Foreign Policy of Islamist Political Parties

The Foreign Policy of Islamist Political Parties

Ideology in Practice

Edited by
Mohamed-Ali Adraoui

EDINBURGH
University Press

Edinburgh University Press is one of the leading university presses in the UK. We publish academic books and journals in our selected subject areas across the humanities and social sciences, combining cutting-edge scholarship with high editorial and production values to produce academic works of lasting importance. For more information visit our website: edinburghuniversitypress.com

© editorial matter and organization Mohamed-Ali Adraoui, 2018
© the chapters their several authors, 2018

Edinburgh University Press Ltd
The Tun—Holyrood Road
12 (2f) Jackson's Entry
Edinburgh EH8 8PJ

Typeset in 11/15 Adobe Garamond by
Servis Filmsetting Ltd, Stockport, Cheshire

A CIP record for this book is available from the British Library

ISBN 978 1 4744 2664 0 (hardback)
ISBN 978 1 4744 2666 4 (webready PDF)
ISBN 978 1 4744 2667 1 (epub)

The right of the contributors to be identified as author of this work has been asserted in accordance with the Copyright, Designs and Patents Act 1988 and the Copyright and Related Rights Regulations 2003 (SI No. 2498).

Contents

Notes on the Contributors   vii
Foreword by Olivier Roy   ix

1 The Islamists and International Relations: A Dialetical Relationship?   1
  Mohamed-Ali Adraoui

2 The Islamists of Morocco's Party of Justice and Development and the Foreign Policy Problem: Between Structural Constraints and Economic Imperatives   20
  Haoues Seniguer

3 The Foreign Policy of Tunisia's Ennahdha: Constancy and Changes   47
  Maryam Ben Salem

4 The Foreign Policy of the Egyptian Muslim Brotherhood   70
  Tewfik Aclimandos

5 "Islam and Resistance": The Uses of Ideology in the Foreign Policy of Hamas   104
  Leila Seurat

6 A Fighting Shiism Faces the World: The Foreign Policy of
   Hezbollah   127
   Aurélie Daher

7 Identity of the State, National Interest, and Foreign Policy:
   Diplomatic Actions and Practices of Turkey's AKP since 2002 142
   Jean-Baptiste Le Moulec and Aude Signoles

Bibliography   186
Index   196

Notes on the Contributors

Tewfik Aclimandos, Lecturer at the University of Cairo, Egypt.

Mohamed-Ali Adraoui, Marie Sklodowska Curie Fellow in the Edmund A. Walsh School of Foreign Service at Georgetown University, USA, and in the Department of International Relations at the London School of Economics, United Kingdom.

Maryam Ben Salem, Assistant Professor of Political Science at the Faculty of Law and Political Sciences at Sousse University, Tunisia.

Aurélie Daher, Deakin Fellow at St Antony's College, Oxford University, United Kingdom.

Jean-Baptiste Le Moulec, PhD Independent Researcher, IREMAM, France.

Olivier Roy, Joint-Chair Professor at Robert Schuman School of Advanced Studies and Chair of Mediterranean Studies at the European University Institute in Florence, Italy.

Haoues Seniguer, Associate Professor of Political Science at the Institute of Political Studies in Lyon, France.

Leila Seurat, Max Weber Fellow at the European University Institute in Florence, Italy.

Aude Signoles, Lecturer at Sciences Po Aix-en-Provence and Senior Researcher at the IREMAM, France.

Foreword by Olivier Roy

Is it possible to speak of an "Islamist" foreign policy? The question really only makes sense since Islamist parties have had the chance to try their hands on the levers of power. While they were opposed to the notion, the response to the question can only come from their ideological corpus. There are certainly some specific ideas to be found in the texts and programs of the parties: develop a "third way" from the time when the Western and the Communist blocs between them dominated the geostrategic landscape; unite the Muslim countries with the long-term goal of reconstituting a Califate; and ultimately revive concepts elaborated by jurists of the classical age (*dār al islam* (house of Islam), *dār al harb* (house of war), and *dār al ahd* (house of truce)) that allowed for the Islamization of concepts of diplomacy and international treaties. This applies to the Sunni Islamists, as we will see, as Iran would develop its own model of diplomacy.

Apart from this ideological reference, the Islamist movement has never taken up a jihadist stance toward the West and always sought to maintain open channels of communication with Western governments. In general, it was the West that refused to regard them as legitimate oppositional movements, even though London had liberally granted them political asylum, particularly to individuals belonging to Tunisia's Ennahda and the Islamic Salvation Front (FIS).

However, by now a large share of Sunni Islamist movements (and all those studied in this book) have had experience in managing foreign relations, even if ephemeral (Egypt), exercised in a power-sharing arrangement (Tunisia, Morocco), or, in Hezbollah's case, outside any state framework. It is therefore possible today to study actual practice instead of doing an often sterile exegesis of ideological discourse.

Interestingly, despite the great diversity of cases studied, we find a number of constants: This is what gives the book an overall unity. As may be expected, all the Islamist movements have adopted a foreign policy that is more pragmatic and moderate than their discourse lets on. Even though largely toned down, the ideological corpus has not disappeared; rather, it has slipped from a referential focused on the first Muslim community of the Prophet's era into one articulated around paradigms of identity and the clash/dialogue of civilizations formulated in terms of defending national values and traditions against a corrupting and alienating Westernization. In short, we pass from a religious cleavage (Islam/people of the book/heathens) to a civilizational split (peoples of the East against the West). We move from revelation to identity, from religion to culture. Thus, Istanbul's Justice and Development Party (AKP) mayoralty in the 1990s could launch a series of meetings whose theme was the dialogue of civilizations, an initiative subsequently taken up by the AKP Government in tandem with Spain.

Turning to the practice of diplomacy, it can be summed up as a dual approach. The first is a realistic one, in the sense of the realist theory of international relations. The Islamist parties do not question the national framework nor the grand regional balances. They are invested in the state framework. Even Hezbollah does not challenge the principle of the Lebanese state. Morocco's Justice and Development Party (PJD) adopts the monarchy's position on the Western Sahara in whole cloth. Turkey's AKP does not question the Kemalist state, Turkey's European leanings or its North Atlantic Treaty Organization (NATO) membership. Nahda the entire time refers to the Tunisian nation and subscribes to the postcolonial perspective.

Nowhere do we find complete reversals of the alliances that had marked the Islamic revolution's victory in Iran (replacement of Israel's embassy by the Palestinian embassy, support for Ireland's Irish Republican Army (IRA), and support for liberation movements in Latin America against the United States). Egypt and Turkey have maintained diplomatic relations with

Israel, while Morocco has maintained links with it even without exchanging ambassadors.

At most, a change in the new elite's tropism can be noted: Many Nahda cadres speak better English than French, because they took refuge in Great Britain or studied in the United States. The same applies to Egypt and Turkey (and to Iran as well): The old Francophone and secular elites have been overtaken by a new generation of Anglophone technocrats. French seems to be loaded with "values," while English appears to be purely the language of technology. Once again, France pays in terms of influence for its willingness to identify Francophony with civilizational values, among which, of course, figures militant secularism.

But this distancing from the former metropole and fostering identity has nothing to do with an "Islamic" diplomacy that has never made the least start at concretization or even definition.

The problem for the Islamists in power, therefore, is managing the Islamic referential that is their hallmark. To renounce it, as much in foreign as in domestic policy, means losing their specificity.

As it is often the case, the false problem of double-talk poses itself: It is said that the Islamists would like nothing better than reestablishing *sharia*, or the Caliphate, but, since they cannot, they wait for more propitious times while getting their bearings. But whatever motivates this compromise, it is indeed what passes for the actual policy, corresponding as it does to Islamist practice, and this practice has a performative effect (as does diplomacy in general): Saying is doing. Communiqués, treaties, visits, protocols—all of it creates a reality precisely by identifying the Islamists with this new pragmatism—and harping on regrets, nostalgias, or ulterior motives brings nothing.

On the contrary, by adopting a policy of realism, the Islamists contribute to discrediting the Islamic utopia, or worse yet, to letting it be manipulated by others (the Salafis, for instance). They are rightfully identified with their new discourse. On the other hand, their "institutionalization" goes far and makes them full members of the political establishment, provided, of course, that an eradicating military coup does not remake them into the opposition. The Moroccan monarchy understood this better than did the Egyptian army.

As the authors show in this book, what Islamists in power do is reformulate the strategic balances by infusing them with a "supplement of soul":

Muslim solidarity for all, references to the Ottoman empire by the AKP, a rejection of a neo-colonialism that today takes more cultural than economic forms. But this incantatory quest for a possible alternative to an alliance with the West comes to a sudden end.

Instead, the Islamic references make a comeback in the discourse for domestic use, particularly toward the militants. They therefore function as pedagogical metaphors for explaining to the militants or the people what in fact arises from realism: Hamas speaks of the Prophet's use of the truce in order to justify the ceasefire with Israel; Ghannouchi points to the Medina constitution to underline that the Prophet also concluded purely pragmatic alliances; and the AKP wraps its new interventionism in the Middle East in the Ottoman tradition. Conversely, Hezbollah will mobilize the reference to a Sunni-oppressed Shiism to justify its intervention in Syria on the side of Iran. There is nothing new here: The French Revolution, like the USSR (and Iran), pursued the geostrategic tropisms of the old regimes by dressing them up in new slogans. The Islamic reference makes it possible to account for alliances that are devoid of religion. The reference to the sunna of the Prophet and the Medina constitution are rather more rhetorical instruments that allow wrapping a realist policy in a religious tradition and, indeed, justifying and legitimizing something that would have been done in any case.

On the other hand, the reference to defense of identity seems to go beyond rhetoric because it aims to ratify the break with the colonial period. It therefore seems to define an "us" (Muslims) and an "other" (the West).

But to what does the break pertain? International relations not at all, in fact, but to internal societal questions: family, decency, and education. In this sense, the apparent anti-Western sentiment of the Islamists is a kind of conservatism that is often shared, at least with part of American society. It therefore implies no new alliances or new international hostilities. As seen in the relationship between the Saudis and the Americans, having two societies that are, in fact, totally different in no way puts in question a close and durable strategic alliance.

The real break was made by Iran. The Iranian Islamists in power (thanks to a revolution and not elections, it must be stressed) engaged in a true diplomacy that broke with that of the Shah, even though, in fact, the grand geostrategic constants hardly changed: The drive to be the great Middle Eastern regional power is a constant that presupposes outflanking the conservative Arab regimes and delegitimizing Nasser-type Arab nationalism. The reverse alliance against the Arab regimes was provided by Israel under the Shah and today it is done by the Shiite Arabs. As for the violently anti-Western posture (at least to date), other than that of the Sunni Islamists, it stems from the very powerful anti-imperialist leftist component of the Iranian revolution but that does not exist among the Sunnis or no longer does. It needs to be kept in mind that the distinctiveness of the Islamic revolution is linked to three phenomena: Shiism (and therefore an organized clergy able to lead the movement), Iranian nationalism (strongly anti-Arab), and the third-world revolutionary dimension that rallied many militants to the regime. None of its elements are found among the Sunni Islamists: They do not have a monopoly on Islam and therefore see their religiosity challenged on all sides (ulemas, Salafis); they cannot rely on pan-Arabism in a crisis and so they fall back on national patriotism that precisely prevents putting in place a Sunni front against Iran; and, lastly, they are socially and politically conservative. American society (the Tea Party, the Mormons) holds more attraction for them than the Iranian or even the Saudi model.

So, is there an "Islamist" foreign policy? In this volume, the authors accurately show that no ideological model defines an Islamist foreign policy, but that there decidedly is a diplomatic practice that Islamists in a position to influence their country's foreign policy all share. In short, it is not an Islamist diplomacy, but a diplomacy of the Islamists.

This fits with the post-islamist model that me and others established years ago.

Post-Islamism is not secularization in the sense that the actors may still be religious and motivated by religion. It means that the political logic prevails on religion: regional geostrategy, national interests, necessity to find some domestic consensus contributing to secularize foreign policy.

Religion may be called to justify a shift in foreign policy or to provide more legitimacy to a decision: For instance, after the start of the war in Syria in 2011, Hezbollah decided to side with Iran and Bashar al-Assad against the mainly Sunni uprising. Its propaganda shifted from stressing pan-Arabism, pan-Islamism, and the need to fight Israel to a "defense of threatened Shias" battle cry. It used the same religious decorum but for another agenda.

Erdogan's Turkey evokes the Ottoman past to justify its more pro-active foreign policy in the Middle East, but its priority, to thwart the Kudistan Workers' Party (PKK) endeavors to create some sort of Kurdistan, either in Syria or inside Turkey itself, has nothing to do with an "Islamic" policy and is simply the pursuit of the Kemalist anti-Kurdish strategy by other means.

Seemingly, the authoritarian shift of Erdogan in 2016 is not a way to establish an Islamic state. It is more along the Orban/Putin paradigm: authoritarian and conservative regimes, using religion as an identity and a template of conservative norms that they would have promoted anyway because their constituency is conservative. Once again it does not mean that religion does not play a role: It is a factor taken into account by the regional actors, not an ideology or a blueprint of a new world order.

Post-Islamism is also a consequence of the diversification of the religious field. The Muslim Brothers have been unable to claim the monopoly of religion in politics, since the Salafis have entered the political arena during the Egyptian spring. The Muslim Brothers do not share a common agenda due to the specificity of each national case. They are more integrated into the Maghreb than in the Mashrek.

Maghreb and Mashrek are going their own ways. The first is closely associated with the West and is framing its foreign policy in some sort of north–south relationship: Morocco is thus actively reactivating the Sufi networks (*tijannya, bousheshyia*) that have linked Senegal with Morocco for centuries and are now expanding north through the diasporas. Ennahda has a good foothold among Franco-Tunisians (with respect to the two members of the Tunisian Parliament elected by the diaspora living in France, one is a Nahda member).

By contrast, Mashrek is now split by a intricate series of civil wars (Yemen, Syria) that turned as wars through proxies manipulated by the two competing regional powers, Iran and Saudi Arabia, both claiming a religious legitimacy. The Shia–Sunni divide is neither an ideological nor a religious one: Such a sectarian and relatively recent polarization expresses the conflict between Iran and Saudi Arabia for the regional leadership. It is a purely geostrategic competition for power, not a war of religion.

In this volume, the authors accurately show that no ideological model defines an Islamist foreign policy, but that there decidedly is a diplomatic practice that Islamists in a position to influence their country's foreign policy all share. In short, it is not an Islamist diplomacy, but a diplomacy of the Islamists. Herein resides this book's great originality and great contribution.

1

The Islamists and International Relations: A Dialectical Relationship?

Mohamed-Ali Adraoui

Do Islamists execute foreign policy "normally"? At first, this seemingly caustic question is nonetheless pertinent for anyone interested in how an ideological system that claims to make its mark on the fate of Muslim societies throughout the world gives effect to it. At a time when the Arab world, the historical heart of political Islam, is experiencing major upheavals with consequences not the least of which is significantly drawing closer Islamists to spheres of power, it is essential to take an interest in their worldview and the international system[1] that they espouse as well as their foreign policy ethic. How do they view the global space, translate their attempts to subject a society's structures and history to the religious norm and, when in command of a country's destiny, translate their ideology in the diplomatic domain? Also, what do the political principles relating to international relations that are inherent in the Islamist offer lead to for other actors of the international system? If this ideology raises numerous questions about its potential radicalism, one of the principal worries concerns the "revisionist"[2] potential of militant and political Islam for the international system. Starting from a rhetoric and programmatic aims targeting specific non-Muslim countries (most prominently those that comprise the West due to the colonial legacy and some countries' primacy event, although they are not exclusively targeted) against which the majority of Muslim societies are supposed to defend their identity, their values, and their interests, the international problem, nourished by numerous hotbeds of unresolved tensions, in large part explains the image projected by Islamism for Western opinion and elites. It is problematic that certain representatives of political Islam have sharpened after earning, for the most part democratically, the right to put their ideals into practice.

An examination of the links between the theorists (those who offer to determine concepts), cadres (those who are in charge of the organization and its structures), and militants (those who subscribe to the idea of using all sorts of activity, sometimes violent, to achieve a political objective) that emerged internationally over several decades from this current, is of even greater interest than the domain of relations that an actor maintains with the rest of the world and it is important on at least two counts. Starting from a phenomenological perspective, it is a question of perceiving the self as the subject of a world to which the Islamist dialectic is meant to apply.[3] Born of a desire to restore Muslims to a dignified place in the world, the latter has from the beginning made the wish to give independence, power, and unity to the matrix of believers (*al-Umma*) the core of its ambition. Preaching on the local and national levels are the first stages of a grander projection aiming for global scale. Here it is a matter of accessing the image that the actor has of himself and hopes to convey to the alterity. On the other hand, the spirit and content of a relationship to the world, and, more particularly, to a foreign policy, provide an appropriate framework for gauging the applicability of an ideology when the moment of its fitting into reality arrives. While Islam from birth has been distinguished by a transnational aim of wanting to overcome the "pathologies" of history that affected the political social structures that divided Islam and Muslims into nations, states, clans, tribes, or parties, study of the theory and practice of international relations by its followers furnishes choice material for taking the measure of the Islamist project and the potential deviations or even possible amendments when the agenda had to be put into practice.[4]

Islamism: An Attempt at a Sociohistorical Definition. The Global Scale as the Last Stage of Islamic Renewal

In the Islamist view, international relations are both a resource and a constraint. The stage represented by the supranational is part of a larger project that is supposed to join the individual Muslim to the ensemble of his coreligionists throughout the world. By mobilizing the religious for the purpose of a political grouping together of the "Muslim nation," the Islamists seek to respond, both in international thinking and ethic, to the most powerful symbol of the decline of their religion—their domination by foreign powers. In that respect, nourishing an Islamist conception of the international order (in fact, thought of more like a disorder) means necessarily thinking of the world as an action space with the goal of escaping the contemporary developments that have turned "Islam" from a politically preponderant religion into a subjected identity. In this regard, Islam is thus a political body rather than only a mere spirituality. One of the most blatant expressions of this decay, without doubt, is this religion's division into various entities (states, countries, ethnicities, and so forth) that essentially weaken the political and statist oneness that, according to the representatives of political Islam, is supposed to be its true calling.

Alone the conception of the world promulgated by the founder of the Muslim Brotherhood almost suffices to grasp the split induced by the emergence of this current nearly a century ago in the history of Muslim societies. In his *Epistles to Young Muslims*, Hassan al-Banna, the Guide, indeed is explicit about the principles that ought to govern the "Muslim nation":[5]

> The entire world is disoriented and in turmoil, and all the powers that make up the world are powerless to resolve the problems, for there is no remedy other than Islam. Be forward in pronouncing God's name, so that this world may be delivered, for all mankind is waiting for a savior, and it shall be nothing else but the message of Islam, whose torch you carry and with which you will herald to people.
>
> O young people!
>
> Assuredly, the Muslim Brotherhood's program consists of several stages whose sequence is clear. We know exactly what we want, and we know how to achieve our objectives.
>
> 1. We want an individual who is Muslim in thought and belief, in morality and feelings, in acts and in demeanor.
> 2. Next, we want a family that is Muslim in thought and belief, in morality and feelings, and in its work and behavior …

3. Next, we want a Muslim people with traits similar to those we mentioned above …
4. Next, we want a Muslim government by the people that will lead people onto the way of Islam, as Abou Bakr and Omar, the companions of the Prophet, peace be with him, did before. This is why we do not recognize any governmental organization not based on the foundation of Islam and that does not draw inspiration from these foundations. This is also why we do not recognize the political parties, nor all those traditional figures by whom the detractors and enemies of Islam forced us to be governed and contribute to their development. We therefore will work for the rebirth of Islamic government, in all its forms, and by putting in place an Islamic government based on this organization.

    Next, we want to assemble all the parties of this Islamic homeland that Western policy has striven to fracture, and which European wishes have misled and locked inside borders. We therefore reject all the international accords that transform this Islamic homeland into an ensemble of small, weak, and tattered powers that can easily be absorbed by those who want to usurp their rights. And we will not be silent before the barriers to the freedoms of these people, whom third parties have unjustly taken over. Thus, Egypt, Syria, the Hejaz, Yemen, Tripolitania, Tunisia, Algeria, Marrakesh, and every inch of land on which there is a Muslim …, all of it constitutes our great homeland that we will force ourselves to liberate, to extract from this influence, to deliver from this tyranny, and whose parts we will reassemble. If the German Reich imposes itself as protector of all those in whose veins flows German blood, by the same token the Muslim faith calls on every capable Muslim to consider himself as protector of any person that has been permeated by the Koranic apprenticeship. Islam therefore forbids replacing the community of faith with ethnic belonging. And all faith is in Islam. Does it not distill itself, in fact, into love and hate?
5. Finally, we want that the flag of Islam once again flies high in the wind in all the countries that have had the chance to welcome Islam for some time, and where the voice of the muezzin resounds … Then misfortune has wanted that the lights of Islam should retreat from these countries

which then fell back into unbelief. Thus, Andalusia, Sicily, the Balkans, the Italian coasts and as well as those of the Mediterranean are all Mediterranean Muslim colonies and they must return to Islam. Also, the Mediterranean and the Red Sea must revert to being Muslim seas, as they were before, even as Mussolini arrogated to himself the right to reconstruct the Roman Empire. That so-called ancient empire was only built on foundations of greed and passionate desires. We therefore have the right to reconstruct the Islamic Empire, which was established in justice and equality and which spread the light of the way among the people.

6. Beyond that and with that, we want to expose our Islamic message to the entire world, reach all the people, spread across all earthly horizons and subject all tyrants to it "until there is no longer any disorder and religion will be totally devoted to God." ...

Each of these stages has its own appearance, its ramifications, and the specific means for achieving it. We contented ourselves here with setting out these stages without dwelling on them nor going into the details. And it is God who will bring His help, He will be all we need, and what a Great Guarantor He is!

Let the incompetent and the cowards characterize as fiction what would for a very long time have been anchored in our consciousness, or as a "utopia that invades people's minds." This point of view is a weakness that is foreign to us and that is foreign to Islam. This is nothing more than moral exhaustion that has been planted in the heart of this community, allowing the enemies of Islam to gain a foothold in its midst. It is also the destruction of faith found in the heart, and it is the cause of the Muslims' fall. As for us, we affirm clearly and frankly that any Muslim that does not believe in this project and does not work for its realization will not find happiness in Islam. Let him therefore find another philosophy to adopt as a religion and on whose behalf he will work.

In the course of the many centuries over which this religious phenomenon has put its mark on the evolution of numerous societies, Islam, as much in its credo as its cultural and social practice, has been mobilized in various political configurations. Among these, the religious has also been able to be kept well apart from the philosophy undergirding the organizational mode of public life—unless at times when it was the object of ideologically motivated repression[6]—than called on to serve both as an exclusive identity referent and legal matrix as well as a process of legitimizing certain regimes.

However, mobilization of the religious reference on "Islamic soil" is not sufficient for defining the "Islamist" ethic, for it relates to a precise sociohistorical experience dating back to nearly a century, and echoes principles inscribed first and foremost in a perspective of redressing the Muslim condition. Islamism is therefore to be resituated in a specific temporality, that is, one composed of metanarratives and social figurations that attribute to the religious grammar not only a central place in the definition of values and collective identity, but especially a transformative social and political function by virtue of a clear finality: the subordination of all the fields organizing society to the religious norm understood in a fundamentalist sense. This teleological design is characterized by a dual method: puritan reform on the one hand, and mass militancy on the other. From here on, we will now call "Islamism" the social and political identity offer that saw the light of day nearly a century ago in the context of societies thrown into contact with Western modernity, to their disadvantage; an offer that has as one of its characteristics the quest for intellectual matrices capable of projecting them positively into the future. It relates to a current of thought structured around the Muslim religion whose ambition is to adapt in a programmatic manner a religious norm presented as orthodox. Seeking to exercise social control by introducing the sacred prescription in all spheres that make up society (family, school, the public square, the state, the media, and so on) by means of an activist ethic that mobilizes the various tools of militancy (such as participation in electoral contests and street demonstrations, setting up unions, starting newspapers, and editorial activity), Islamism aims for moral and political magistery within a framework of what is at first a national configuration but that does not lose sight of its transitional character. What follows is this attempt at a more profound definition.[7]

Islamism is religiously Salafist in the sense that it is under the sign of the "pious forefathers" (*Salaf Salih*) and as such relates to a fundamentalist conception of the Muslim religion as intimately linked to the project of reviving a model of belief and of public life that is presented as paradigmatic. Although the Salafi reference may be the subject of numerous debates—one of the most important today without question being the relationship with political militancy—everyone recognizes the prophylactic and curative dimensions of a return to the sources presented as indispensable. The "original" ethic thus is supposed to command, from the political perspective, a total unification of believers under the banner of Islam without regard for extra-religious distinguishing factors. The centrality of this "imagined solidarity,"[8] as supposedly tying all Muslims throughout the globe and making them "religiously" keen to unify in order to defeat not only their military and political adversaries, but above all metaphysical enemies, stands for the core motivation to the Islamist design.

Islamism is an explicitly gradualist ideology in how each level of identification is supposed to entail a specific mode of action. The believer, by reforming himself in the direction of a greater adherence to religious injunctions, is only the first stage of the Islamist project. It is followed by ever higher levels of projection and accomplishment legitimizing a ceaselessly growing mobilization.

Islamism is activist and militant and herein resides the primary reason for existing in a perspective of transforming the society and exercising a moral magistery as a prelude to taking power.

The conversion of values and religious norms into a political program effectively represents a fundamental break in the contemporary history of Muslim societies. To accomplish it, this ideological system distinguishes itself clearly from a unique fundamentalist ethic by introducing as the key element of its approach the resort to a mass political party, that is, an invention of— most notably Western—political modernity. With the Muslim Brotherhood, which saw the light of day in Egypt in the late 1920s, the Muslim world experienced for the first time the coming of an actor constructed around the Muslim reference aiming to control society by means of a *modern* activist ethic. Echoing the Communist experience starting in the late nineteenth century by which Europe saw its ideological and political landscape mutate, Islamism was born from a dynamic of Westernization of the politics then seen in the Islamic lands. The Muslim Brotherhood, father movement of this identity offer, then spreaded out in pursuit of achieving its aims in every Muslim country.

The confrontation to an international system that is largely a stranger to the original Islamist vision of the world order also provides substantial material for those wishing to address the issue of Post-Islamism. Whether this concept is subject to different interpretations and debates, it must be evoked in this study. Indeed, analyzing how Islamists have been conceiving and practicing diplomacy and foreign action with, at least initially, the aim to blow up a global arena that was condemned for being built upon an anti-Islam agenda as interpreted over the colonial era, raises two major concerns.

First, what is the role of interntional considerations in the evolution from an intransigent platform seeking both unification of all the Muslims throughout the world and destruction of any nation-state supposedly challenging the core belief that the Islamic identity can do nothing but generate the political independence of the *Umma* under the Caliphate-flag? Wishing to build in a first stage a 'national Islamist foreign policy' in an attempt to reinforce the key narratives of Hasan al-Banna and finally unify the whole of the Muslim-majority countries has led to consider a state of structural weakness that the Islamist ideology has been very misfit. Insisting on the need for power while trying to consolidate first the nation-state through which the initial step toward global unification was envisaged has put Islamists in a problematic situation, leading to a certain degree of revision. In this regard, playing according to the rules of real power struggles within the international system has forces to disengage to some extent from the original revolutionary mindset. Post-Islamism in this case is principally due to the objective difficulty of deeply impacting on a world order that is more likely to socialize revisionist forces than be reframed by them. Being aware of the huge cost to redefine the international system, namely a global military engagement to defeat all the opponents to the unification of Muslims worldwide, has thus led Islamists to nationalize their narrative and political commitment.

Second, when it comes to the connection between integration into the domestic political arena and the desire for a new foreign policy that is said to modify over time the global power struggle at the benefit of the *Umma*, a second problem needs to be raised. Effectively, as we consider that, since the 1980s, certain movements referring to political Islam have embraced some democratic ideals and frameworks,[9] this ideological shift certainly had significant impacts on the way that Islamists have been theorizing international relations. Thus, in addition to a realistic reaction to the difficulty to impose a new logic within the international system, internal evolutions have also produced the conditions from which certain Islamist thinkers and activists have envisaged to revise, at least partly, their original core beliefs. In other words, when identity does change on a domestic level, this has consequences on the global scale. In other words, by moving toward a post-islamist stage internally, formerly revolutionary and intransigent Islamists have been driven the same way to consider conceptual and factual shifts in their understanding of contemporary international relations. The conversion-process to democratic norms has usually created over the last two centuries greater likeliness to move away from revisionist standards.[10]

International Relations: A Preferred Field of Study for Sizing Up the Logics and Results of a Real Ideological Confrontation

From a historical perspective, a distinct trait of the Islamist movements is that they favor action at the national level. If, paradoxically, projecting on a global scale is part of the founding design of political Islam, theorists, cadres, and militants from the start conceived of the nation-state stage as key to their perspective of religious reaffirmation and acquisition of the tools of power. By virtue of a genuine strategy of "gradualism," "rise," or of militant "ascent," Islamist entrepreneurs have shown understandings that political and civilizational unification, obstructed in their eyes (largely by the fact that the Western powers would not tolerate a first-rate strategic competitor) as an objective, however compelling, ought to be delayed for now in favor of making a success of national Islamic renewal experiments first. Such a consideration is nevertheless at the heart of a structural tension in the evolution experienced by Islamist actors for several decades. This then poses a fundamental question: are the logics and finalities of the initial Islamist engagement not likely to change by accepting a transitional stage of *"first constructing the Islamic society and state in a country"*?

Would the need to deal with defending the national interest, however conceived, not compel a second look at the initial motivations, however important, that are essential to the Islamist movements' capacity for mobilization? Indeed, to subscribe to the Islamist theses like the ones just seen in various forms in the epistles of Hassan al-Banna, in theory means taking into account the interest and willingness of the "Muslim nation" wherever its members are found and regardless in what sort of political configuration. Still, any Islamist movement that accepts integration in a national political arena is pushed *nolens volens* into a different contour. The problem of budgetary choices, electoral alliances, cooperation with other states (often non-Muslim) or even the decision to go to war become as much political practices that must be carried out as a function of gauging the interests of *the state concerned* and not *of the religion* as a whole, exclusive representation of which is meant to fall to the Islamists and whose defense, prima facie, is their raison d'être. Depending on the country under consideration, from this then follows the phenomena of accommodation with other sources of identification. Certain followers of political Islam are moved by this to preach a "synthesis" between Islam and nationalism, wanting to raise up a "democratic Muslim" ethic or to seek the means yet again for a union of the majority of states throughout the world modeled on other supranational construct forms, such as the European Union (EU), based not on force but on the rule of law and adherence to shared values. These attempts at moving beyond the original ideological matrix revert to the main question for these movements: What action is called for when the level of identification changes and the field of political action is altered?

On the other hand, the nature of the international system also decisively affects the positioning of the Islamists. Since the former pre-exists in the emergence of this current, the representatives of this identity offer find themselves compelled to accommodate a system of strong constraints (such as legal, military, economical, and diplomatic) that hems in their field of action even more and, *eventually*, the ambition of remaking the global space in their image. Besides having to think along lines of a statist, not just religious logic, the Islamist forces must also deploy their anti-system and—at least discursively—revisionist ethic within a system that represents a social reality in Emile Durkheim's meaning, one whose constraining effect[11] frequently is so powerful that they are influenced more by it than the other way around. In fact, the insertion both into an international grammar strongly marked, despite real contemporary inflections,[12] by the predominant role of states, as well as the transformation on the domestic scene into a government party, induce, in a perspective of identity redefinition and search for the most efficient means of serving an ideology called to exercise power, its reformulation under the impact of diverse factors that force it to evolve.

The coming chapters all aim to address the issue of how Islamists, within one national context, have framed international relations, both as an ideological movement denying originally the legitimacy of the states they wanted to exert power upon, and a political force contemplating nevertheless to integrate into the national realm so it can be used as a transitory stage before the unification of the entire Islamic people. The main argument of these contributions deals with the extreme difficulty of identifying one specific form of Islamist foreign policy. This concept has to be first of all seen as a leitmotiv but is finally no practical reality. States promote foreign actions, not ideologies. Those doctrinal frameworks generate representations and ideals but when it comes to political practices, Islamists have, according to the cases tackled in this volume (except maybe with Egypt), either put the national interest at the top of their agenda while their discourses were still characterized by the duty to protect Islam and Muslims worldwide, or unrarely, admitted that they could not achieve the original ideology (at least under the circumstances that thay had to handle with). In other words, this collective work highlights the fact that, wherever this was possible, the state-logic has overridden the coercive part of the original ideology, allowing a significant amount of interpretation, and sometimes amendments. Ideological radicalism, to some extent, has been tamed, although numerous questions remain when it comes to the future of political Islam within societies that are increasingly boiling.

Theoretical Framework: Constructivism. Ideas Come First

The quest to interpret the history and sociology of international relations has produced analytical currents that most often compete with one another but also strive to propose the most relevant framework for making sense of interactions between the parties occupying the global space. While no grammar of international relations could suffice to exhaust the field of structures and actors of global politics, it is still possible to find a larger heuristic potential for the subject we are dealing with among the constructivist approaches.[13] Our objective being to bring the conception of the world held by the representatives of political Islam into focus as well as to examine their international and diplomatic ethic, with the main consequence being that of interesting us in the weight of ideology and the manner in which the national interest was formulated and defended (depending on the country studied), we opt to let ourselves be inspired by an epistemology centered on the dynamics of constructing a social reality.[14]

Islamism makes it its charge to serve a sacred vision of the world. This lets us call it an ideocracy whose ambition is to irrigate the total social space with the religious norm previously "purified" by an "orthodox" understanding of the dogmatic and legal corpus.

Distancing themselves from any materialist conception of the world, it is really the perceptions as well as the ideational constructions that are at the heart of their politicization. To promote its reign, the representation's proponents thus first seek to advocate a new foreign policy agenda for the countries of which they are part, but also to bring forth a new international system no longer based on the primacy of the state (for the benefit of a political grouping of Muslim societies) and that would no longer be dominated by powers perceived as non-Muslim.

Because the social reality (here a global one) is subject to a different view and definition, the Islamists come to it having to deal with two obstacles. The first is the political action framework. International relations, emerging partly as an intellectual and academic discipline starting in the nineteenth century, is tied to affirmations of the state and its prerogatives in the global space. However, because of the ambition of wanting to symbolically and, especially, politically unify the matrix of believers (*al-Umma*), Islamism slots itself ontologically into a transnational perspective, with states being viewed as a historical contingency dividing a religious community in the name of parochial interests or even ones contradicting those of "Islam." The dialectic initiated in this way is one of moving beyond the national framework after a political resocialization under Islamist impetus in majority Muslim countries, with the aim of awakening consciousness imprisoned by schemas that are foreign to "Islam" to the imperative of unifying the body of believers planet-wide.

From the perspective of numerous Islamist movements, the act of presiding over the destiny of a state therefore also has a utilitarian aspect, since it is a question of taking advantage of a "national moment" to convince of the need to globalize the *Umma* in a larger sovereignty space—a cyclical dimension, in that the experience of power is inscribed in a finite temporality at the end of which the states, already in decline today, will decay and leave the field to a civilizational authority capable of representing all believers. The second obstacle relates to a contradiction inherent in the Islamist project. How, indeed, to reconcile the time of the state and the transnational horizon? If the Islamic identity is posited as profoundly resistant to being reduced in any way to a political space that would not encompass all the faithful, how then to justify a militant action organized with the aim of addressing itself to only a part of this spectrum? In other words, how to combine the religious reference and the national framework when the Islamist forces are the bearers of an ambition for cultural and political "denationalization" of Muslims for the benefit of a single legitimate framework of identification? If the "time of the state" is supposed to be circumstantiated in time, how to exit from it and, especially, how to meet the expectations of a society defined on a country scale when the ideologically projected scale is that of the Muslim world?

Moreover, the constructivist theses (even though they may not all be unambiguous) lead us to ask ourselves about the conditions for building a social identity (a religious one in this case). No structure could be given in a manner that is ahistorical.[15] Demographics, interactions with other entities, the personal trajectories of deciders, and the interpretation of the country's history are so many elements that play a role in constructing the bundle of representations around which a collective identity and its foreign policy interest will coalesce. In this way, the act of trying to reintroduce the religious norm on the domestic level finds powerful echoes in the same project pursued on the scale of Muslim communities around the globe. Here, the interests of the states they lay claim to managing are diametrically opposed to the interests of the majority of their competitors on the domestic political scene. In addition, the constructivist approaches also permit analyzing the discourses and actions undertaken in the international relations domain in a potentially dynamic manner, since from the possible transformations of the Islamist agenda inside a specific state may develop major modifications when it comes to relations with the alterity on the global level. The conversion to certain democratic theses that some hence believe they detect in some movements of political Islam thus would explain the relativization if not abandonment—but most often the reformulation—of principles that are nevertheless fundamental in their ideology, starting with the inevitable coming of an entity that will gather together the planet's Muslims symbolically and politically.

Methodology and Principal Findings

Three principal queries structured the approach of this work. Naturally, if the subject represented by the relationship of Islamists to the world and their practice with regard to international relations is too vast to hope for producing an exhaustive work, three problems have structured this putting of the Islamist grammar into perspective when it decides to apply itself to the international object.

What is the Islamist conception of the world and of relations between the different actors making up the international system? We have seen succinctly the centrality of ambitions aimed at restoring Islam and its faithful that has been "trampled" by the conditioned exercise of politics in contemporary times, but what concrete results has it produced? More precisely, depending on which Islamist movement is studied, what vision of the world prevails in the environment in which it intends to evolve?

Next arises the necessity of taking a look at what the theorists, cadres, and militants have produced by way of thinking about the foreign policy to be carried out. If political Islam should not be considered as an unequivocal movement despite similarities in aspirations, this justifies moving into the discursive registers and structural ideas that proceed from the mouth and from under the pen of its apologists. While the volume of materials required to answer these questions is far from complete, the researcher can nevertheless rely on public pronouncements, publications, or even elements gathered during ethnographic observations.

The final problem concerns the implementation of the foreign policy agendas that we can shed light on in this way. To what extent does the revisionist potential pertain to Islamism or does it not deploy as a force opposed to the established order as well as to the rules of the game thought to be stacked against Muslims? Put differently, what is the place of the ideational factor in the construction and promotion of the national interest that the upholders of political Islam purport to represent, define, and uphold? Under this heading, what does the study of diplomacies and interpretation of decisions taken teach us when the latter have worked at the summits of a state apparatus?

The chapters that follow cover six countries in which representatives of Islamism have historically organized to assert their views and govern national affairs in greater conformity with their conception of the religion. Thus, Morocco, Tunisia, Egypt, Palestine, Lebanon, and Turkey provide venues for testing the hypotheses evoked above. The writings by cadres of the different movements studied as well as the views of militants make it possible in each case to portray the landscape of a powerful mobilizing ideology, but one whose implementation (with the notable exception of Egypt's Muslim Brotherhood), according to the individual authors, elicits considerable "revisions of the revision." To put it another way, it appears that the change of status from anti-system movement to governing party in the international affairs domain entails a redefinition, be it only a discursive one, of the original theses of political Islam. The sociological, generational, and political changes seem to have significant impact on the contours and structures of the Islamist ideology, but without its defenders having made a clean break in their approach to power, thus revamping the militant engagement motifs by reformulating their objectives and not by deliberately transforming them. This step-wise evolution as the powerful revisionist potential, domesticated in light of "reality," unquestionably occurs but this does not imply its disappearance—at least not in the symbolic sense. Depending on the tenor of the crises and tensions in which the Islamist actors come to play an active role, the allusions and references to a religious and civilizational partitioning of the global space can resurface, such as in the case of centers of conflict that they have historically focused on in their discourse on global politics—with the Palestinian cause usually ranking first among these.

Taking several case studies into account leads us to recognize that Islamism is not monolithic. As a one-century-old ideology that has impacted almost all the Islamic cultural sphere, and even beyond, this appears extremely difficult to avoid generalizations, and doing so leads the researcher to some necessary humility. All the countries concerned thus offer relevant material to address the issue of how the Islamists have framed international relations from a pluralistic point of view. Ideological similarities are still obvious, but today more to justify the persistence of some doctrinal tradition than the constancy of a precise and unalterable Islamic theory of world power.

It finally turns out that Islamism as historical experience needs to be studied more than ever from a nationalistic view. Although this does mean that the global design is abandoned, ideology and practice seem to have become two separate things, at least when it comes to the intial doctrinal framework. In most of the countries where there exists the gradualist approach in which political Islam attempts to impose itself, local and national realities have most frequently been insurmountable challenges. The fact that a national identity such as the Tunisian one does exist in parallel to the predominant faith among the Tunisian people, that is undoubtedly Islam, had made the Islamist motto questionable. The same argument could be naturally made about other nationalized Islamist experiences. In other words, it must be underlined that mobilizing in the name of a protesting form of Islam was not the same thing as ruling in the name of it. Thus, once the researcher is no longer focused on the original ideology, the plurality of the political experiences generated by Islamists seizing or sharing power at the head of one state becomes not only obvious but most probably unavoidable. In this regard, offering to go in-depth into the issue of Islamism and foreign policy compels one to admit that there has principally been so far in the foreign policies undertaken by Islamists more than one single type of foreign action led by them. In this respect, it has to be said that the initial gradualist design does represent a failure, except if one were to argue that the original squeleton has undergone constant rewording and will continue to do so.

Integration in a political system that they initially did not legitimize consequently does not signify the inability of the Islamists to acquire other registers of identification, either partisan—starting with the state whose fate they seek to safeguard—or philosophical, as in mobilizing international law or human rights, but rather the progressive and self-interested character of plural positioning as a function of the opportunities and constraints presenting themselves. If, in most of the cases, they did not seek to overturn the strategic order they inherited, they do not yet seem prepared to abandon what is often still a mobilizing discourse when it comes to certain opinions sensitive to the state of global power relationships, especially those involving "Muslim peoples." Nevertheless, this makes them run the risk of being criticized for inaction, or even "hypocrisy," when the gap between the promise of dignity regained and the reality of diplomatic practices consisting of temporizing or even concessions is judged to be too large. Also added to the accusation of "double speak" that they face from observers that doubt their desire for respecting the rules of democracy are others emanating from forces within their base that accuse them of weakness or even duplicity. In grappling with the exercise of power, this ideological offer seems bound to follow the path of all the others that preceded it with claims of remaking the world in their image: making allowances for realities over which it has very little control.

Notes

1. Barry Buzan and Richard Little, *The Idea of International Systems in World History*, Oxford, Oxford University Press, 2000.
2. Aiming at replacing the current set of rules and rights that govern interactions among states, Islamists have a line of vision aimed at getting rid of the anarchic order that is supposedly working at the detriment of "Islam" to build a new world order based on power struggles that would be fed by cultural and religious belonging. To do so, first on the "re-Islamized" nation-state level, and then on the Caliphate-level, foreign policy has to follow two objectives: first, the unification of all Muslims worldwide, and, second, the struggle of attaining this major reconfiguration against opponents within the international system. See: Sten Rynning and Jens Ringsmose, "Why are Revisionist States Revisionist? Reviving Classical Realism as an Approach to Understanding International Change," *International Politics*, January 2008, Vol. 45, no. 1, 19–39.
3. By this we understand the fact that Islamism's actors, because they define themselves by an intentionality principle (they are aware of a specific sphere of human action—politics—on which they intend to make their imprint), are distinguished mainly by the will to define the world by what they are. The Islamist subject accesses a reality that he shapes and determines by his thought. As Edmund Husserl wrote, the world "is correlated to their subjective beliefs." See: Edmund Husserl, *The Crisis of European Sciences and Transcendental Phenomenology*, Evanston, Northwestern University Press, 1970.
4. As such, our work fits into the revival of Islamism studies by asking itself more precisely, from a pragmatic angle, what these types of religious and political conceptions lead to once they have acquired the right to be applied and to serve the government's program. Here is actually the raison d'être of political Islam, which is an identity offer that, like Marxism, strives not only to interpret the world but really to transform it. See especially: Samir Amghar (ed.), *Les islamistes au défi du pouvoir. Evolutions d'une idéologie* [The Islamist Challenge to Power. Evolutions of an Ideology], Paris, Michalon, 2012.

5. The Arabic term he uses is *al-watan* and can be translated by "nation," but it also relates just as easily to the "nation-state" vision (there exists a French, German, Egyptian, or Japanese nation) that is a larger concept, ignoring borders and seeking to assemble the totality of people on Earth seen as sharing a moral, cultural, religious, or linguistic identification. When Hassan al-banna thus evokes the "Muslim nation," he is referring to this second meaning of the world. In a certain sense, he has an "international nation" in mind for his project. Hassan al-Banna, *Majmu'at rasa'il al-imam al-shahid Hassan al-Banna* [Anthology of the Epistles of the Martyr Imam Hassan al-Banna], Beirut: al-Mu'assasa al-Islamiyya, 1984, p. 79. Translation by Mohamed-Ali Adraoui.
6. Mustafa Kemal "Atatürk" certainly being one of the most striking exemplars.
7. Our proposed definition should therefore be seen as complementary to that given by Olivier Roy for whom "[the Islamists] see in Islam a political ideology and think that society's Islamization will come about through installing an Islamic state and this not solely by implementing *sharia*. From Maududi to Saïd Qotb, through Hassan al-Banna, politics and the state are the focus of their thought, not because they would perpetuate a tradition of mixing up 'religion' and 'politics' exclusive to Islam, but simply because they believe that tradition has not drawn the consequences of this affirmation of inseparability between religion and politics. This rehabilitation is carried out by taking into account modern concepts, such as those of the economy, ideology, and of institutions. They tackle the contemporary problems of society (status of women, education, poverty, technology, even drugs) in a way that is different from searching the *sharia* for juridical paradigms." *Globalized Islam: The Search for a New Ummah*, New York, Columbia University Press, 2004, p. 33.
8. This imagined solidarity "is forged spontaneously among different actors who come to a consensus by imagining, subjectively constructing, common interests and shared values betwee, themselves." See: Asef Bayat, "Islamism and Social Movement Theory," *Third World Quarterly*, 2005, Vol. 26, no. 6, 891–908.
9. Olivier Roy, *The Failure of Political Islam*, Cambridge, MA, Harvard University Press, 1994.
10. Maximilian Terhalle, "International Relations Theory and the Moderation of Revolutionary States. The Case of Iran," *International Politics*, September 2015, Vol. 52, no. 5, 589–93.
11. The international system is a "social fact" in the sense given it by Émile Durkheim who conceived of it as "all manner of acting, thinking and feeling, fixed or not, capable of exerting an external constraint on the individual; and

which is general throughout a given society, but all the while having its own existence, independent of its diverse manifestations on the individual level." Émile Durkheim, "What is a Social Fact?" in *The Rules of Sociological Method*, Ann Arbor, Michigan University Press, 1961 [1925], p. 11.

12. Bertrand Badie and Marie-Claude Smouts, *Le retournement du monde. Sociologie de la scène international* [The World Turned Upside Down. Sociology of the International Scene], Paris, Presses de Sciences Po, 1999.
13. For detail of these hypotheses and their approach, we refer to these works: Christian Reus-Smit and Duncan Snidal (eds), *The Oxford Handbook of International Relations*, Oxford, Oxford University Press, 2010; Dario Battistella, *Théories des relations internationales* [Theories of International Relations], Paris, Presses de Sciences Po, Références, 2012; and Alex Macleod, Evelyne Dufault, F. Guillaume Dufour, and David Morin, *Relations internationales. Théories et concepts* [International Relations. Theories and Concepts], Outremont, Athéna Editions, 2008.
14. "We can define 'reality' as a quality attaching to phenomena that we recognize as having an existence independent of our own will (we cannot 'wish' them), and define 'knowledge' as the certainty that the phenomena are real and possess specific traits." Peter Berger and Thomas Luckmann, *The Social Construction of Reality*, New York, Anchor Books, 1966, 7–8.
15. "Identity is, of course, a key element in subjective reality, and like any subjective reality, it finds itself in a dialectical situation in society. Identity is shaped by social processes. Once crystallized, it is preserved, modified, or even retired by social relationships. The social processes in play at the same time in the maintaining and shaping of identity are determined by the social structure. Conversely, the identities produced by the interaction of the organism, the individual consciousness, and the social structure in turn influencing the given social structure, maintaining it, transforming it, or giving it a new form. Societies have a history in whose course specific identities emerge; this history, however, is produced by people possessing a specific identity." Peter Berger and Thomas Luckmann, *op. cit.*, 235–6.

2

The Islamists of Morocco's Party of Justice and Development and the Foreign Policy Problem: Between Structural Constraints and Economic Imperatives

Haoues Seniguer

In this chapter on the international relations of the Moroccan legalist Islamic current, in this case the Party of Justice and Development (PJD), we formulate the following hypothesis: The more institutionalized this party's actors become, particularly in an authoritarian or semi-authoritarian regime like the Sherifian monarchy, the more they normalize their presence on the legal political field and the more their discourse becomes rationalized, sanitized of the residual programmatic, protesting, even revolutionary stances that they would have adopted or favored during the party's extra-parliamentary phase, or, more recently, in the Parliamentary opposition. Just as that of any other social actors, the posture of legitimist political Islam's representatives, particularly in the area of foreign affairs, is tightly interwoven with the position that they occupy on the national political stage. By this measure, and especially in an authoritarian context, relativizing "the autonomy of the national decision makers"[1] by rigorously paying heed to, on the one hand, the domestic systemic constraints on the actors, and, on the other, their country's actual geopolitical weight on the international scene, is indispensable. Thus, according to the periods and positions occupied in the internal political space, the Islamists oscillate between ideology and pragmatism or further differentiate "the morally desirable" from the "politically possible," be it in their internal (national) or external (extra-national) practice.

Still, the recency of PJD's accession to power ought to preclude making definitive statements, just as any sort of prospective statements would be hasty. In fact, this Islamist party entered the government as part of a heterogeneous coalition barely four years ago, after achieving a majority in the general election of November 25, 2011.[2] So, at most, one may venture to formulate some explanatory, by definition tentative, hypotheses that certainly take into consideration some very contemporaneous elements but still more those from the recent or more distant past. It is impossible to understand the true nature of the perception of Morocco's Islamists and sometimes of its transformations through the years, most notably in international relations, without doing a dual retrospective study. For one, it is important to adhere *in globo* to a historical vision on this subject like that formulated by one of the founding fathers of contemporary Islam, Hassan al-Banna, because it rightfully has spread through all of the Muslim world, including Morocco. Second, care must be taken to recall the different stages of these transformations as well as the circumstance under which they occurred among the Moroccan Islamists, generally following a dual dialectic that combines internal and external pressures of the political environment.

An *Islamized* Royal Diplomacy?

It would be difficult to challenge that activism in the foreign affairs component is a function of the relationship between internal forces in the political arena where social actors evolve, in this case the Islamists, and of the royal diplomacy's own positions that retain substantial discretionary resources on this subject by reason of the monarch's quality and his symbolic and material attributes. As Irene Molina Fernandez reminds us,

> foreign relations historically have belonged, and continue to belong today, at the hard nexus of state power where no step has been taken toward a separation of powers. Consequently, they are still considered, from their establishment at the start of the reign of Hassan II to be part of the sovereign's *exclusive domain*, the Ministry of Foreign Affairs—one of the sovereign's ministries whose head the King chooses directly without paying heed to the parliamentary majority … Imagining it as a pyramid, its summit would be occupied by the "central decisional unity" (the King, the Royal Cabinet and the army) which relies on a "subordinate decisional unity" (the

government and the parliament), with the political parties, the employers' and civic organizations relegated to being part of the "marginalized decisional unity."[3]

From this perspective, one of the remarkable acts of the royal foreign policy that truly consecrated or lastingly crystallized the palace's grip on this matter is the Green March of November 6, 1975, organized by the country's highest authorities to rally a crushing majority of the political class to the side of Hassan II in sustaining an active defense of Moroccan sovereignty over the Western Sahara. In this regard, the neo-Salafist leader Allal al-Fassi even spoke of a "sacred duty," and, in doing so, Islamizing what is essentially a national cause, at least a priori.[4]

The Moroccan Islamist movement, since its creation in the late 1960s, therefore has had to face two great difficulties apart from the palace locking up the social space since achieving independence in 1956. On the one hand, there are the considerable religious resources at the disposal of the Moroccan sovereign in his capacity of Commander of Believers and by virtue of his "Sherifness,"[5] which confers on him an atypical form of supplemental holiness that takes into account the postulated filiation with Muhammad the Prophet of Islam as well as his descent. Add to this the fact that Hassan II, upon inheriting the throne from his father in 1961, would exercise a "Muslim leadership" on the world Islamic stage—in other words, simultaneously *intra* and *extra muros*. Also, from the beginning, the Islamists started off symbolically handicapped in a major way that they tried, for better or worse, to compensate for, get around, and transcend. Any organization, however, that wants to endure needs to stand out on the market for symbolic and material goods. This the PJD tried to do numerous times only to fail.

Since the start of his reign, Hassan II has taken several pan-Arab and pan-Islamic initiatives right in line with actions taken by his father Mohammed V, who, for example, supported the fight for Algerian independence that his son would continue in the name of freeing colonial subjects and "Brothers."

Usually, a peculiarity attaches to Islamist foreign policy because of the primacy the language of Islam has in their political *ethos*, and, especially, because of the particular sensitivity with which they view the Palestinian problem, regarded essentially as rooted in religion.

However, in the Moroccan case, the interaction or "the connections" between "local Islam" and "global Islam," just like an early interest in the Arab-Israeli or Israeli-Palestinian conflicts, in particular, manifested themselves during the reign of Hassan II (1961–99). This is precisely what the sociologist Abdessamad Belhaj recalls:

> In its foreign policy, the regime of Hassan II made use of the Islamic factor along three axes. First, it developed an extensive cooperation with the Sunni Arab conservative front (with Saudi Arabia leading the pack). Second, it assumed the leadership of the Community of Muslim Nations in the OIC (Organization of the Islamic Conference) and of the Al-Qods committee; it also played the role of leading interlocutor in the Palestinian conflict. Lastly, it sponsored Islamism by backing establishment of the University of the Islamic Renaissance (to which international Islamist actors were invited), by hosting Hassanian religious talks (headlined by top-ranked *ulemas* and at which a traditional, tolerant Moroccan model of Islam was presented), and by working on the creation of the prestigious Hassan II mosque.[6]

To fight revolutionary socialism, an ideology spreading both to the south and north of the Mediterranean, the Moroccan monarchy, abetted in this impulse by other members of the conservative Arab club such as Saudi Arabia, instigated and in September 1969 held a "meeting of Muslim heads of state" in Rabat, "which would give birth to the Organization of the Islamic Conference as proposed by King Feisal of Saudi Arabia with energetic support from Hassan II."[7] Allal al-Fassi, a leading figure of nationalist neo-Salafism, a key player in Moroccan national liberation and unconditional defender of the throne, was one of "the founding members of the Muslim World League set up by King Feisal of Saudi Arabia to counter Nasserism."[8] In fact, this meeting of the Islamic Conference, which would eventually result in the Organisation of Islamic Cooperation's (OIC's) creation, happened after the criminal arson on August 21, 1969 of the Al-Aqsa mosque (one of Islam's three holy places after Mecca and Medina) that was blamed on Israeli extremists. It was on this occasion that the OIC and, more particularly, the Morocco of Hassan II "took up the Palestinian question, affirming the Islamity of Jerusalem, while supporting the idea of a peaceful settlement of the conflict. The decision to put the Palestinian problem on the agenda of all of the organization's summits would definitively seal the 'Islamic' dimension of the problem."[9]

It was also Hassan II who would assume the presidency of the Al-Qods Committee at its first session held at Fez in 1979. On the official website of the Moroccan foreign ministry can be found two highlighted declarations, those by Hassan II and by his son and successor Mohammed VI:

> Al-Qods As-Charif occupies a special place in the concerns of Muslims worldwide, to such an extent is this city connected with their religious faith and lays claim to a preeminent place in their civilization's political history. Cradle of divine revelations and meeting point of religions, this city in the Al-Aqsa mosque has a monument chosen by God for the first Qibla and the third Haram for believers. (Hassan II)

> In Our capacity as President of the Al-Qods Committee, We expend every effort on behalf of the international community to preserve the legal status of this wounded city. It is about nothing less than defending its civilizational identity and sacred religious symbols against the acts of aggression that menace it and especially the searches, the excavations and all the other prejudicial violations of the Al-Aqsa Mosque's sacredness to which Muslims are extremely sensitive. In parallel with Our diplomatic steps, We have opted for a pragmatic approach by virtue of which the Beït Mal Al-Qods Office takes on the responsibility under Our supervision of implementing specific projects relating to lodging, health, education and other social services on behalf of our Brothers who inhabit Al-Qods.[10] (Mohammed VI)

In practicing Islamism in many respects in place of the Islamists, by preempting some of their themes, and even by sometimes enlisting them in his mobilizations, at least until the mid-1970s, for fighting the left and extreme left at the time dominating the high schools and campuses, Hassan II thus sought to demine to a maximum the terrain for protests and conflicts in his land, that is, in the places where these mobilizations were most susceptible of taking hold: Islam and Palestine.

This Al-Qods Committee, created on June 6, 1975 and primarily overseen by the Sherifian kingdom has four principal aims: "follow the evolution of the situation in Al-Quods, watch over the implementation of resolutions adopted by the Islamic Conference on this subject, make contact with other international organisms to aid in the protection of Al-Qods, and make proposals to the member states and all organizations interested in prospective steps to assure the carrying out of these resolutions and to confront new situations."[11]

In conformity with Muslim tradition, the Arab name rather than the Western name "Jerusalem" is constantly favored, as if to underline the eternally Islamic character of the thrice-sanctified city. On the official website of the Ministry of Foreign Affairs and Cooperation, searches of "Palestine" and "Palestinian" return several notable hits.[12] In contrast, the key words "Israel," "Zionist," or "Zionism" come up empty. Only the expression "Israeli aggressions," stigmatizing the process of colonization of Palestinian territory practiced by that country, display a few hits for these key words.[13]

However, this committee[14] relates more to inter-Arab and/or inter-Islam solidarity on questions of housing, school construction, health coverage, or social assistance directed to the Palestinian populations. In other words, it relates much more to humanitarian aid than classic diplomatic activism. As such, it is not a political organ with a negotiating mandate, exerting direct or indirect pressures with a view to a negotiated settlement of the conflict. It is instead the protection of Al-Qods, both its Arab-Islamic and multi-religious character as a holy place, that the committee focuses on, thus bypassing political conflict.

In contrast, Moroccan diplomacy since the reign of Hassan II has, at different times, tried to play the role of intermediary with the aim of peacefully resolving the Israeli-Arab and Israeli-Palestinian conflict, in particular insisting on the creation of an independent Palestinian state within the 1967 borders with Al-Qods as its capital.[15]

In that case, how to explain, on the one hand, the emergence of an anti-establishment Islamist current in the kingdom and, on the other, the existence of a vision competing with that of the palace when it comes to foreign affairs, on a properly Islamic basis? Islam, it seems, would not be the only and unique distinguishing variable of the Islamist mobilization.

The Monarchy vs. the Islamists: Competing Foreign Policy Visions?

While the first structured Moroccan Islamist organization, Islamic Youth (al-shabība al-islāmiyya), was created in 1969, and then legalized in the ranks of the apostolic association Appeal to God in 1972, all the while maintaining a more discrete political profile, Hassan II, from 1958 to 1959, before he became king, totally opposed any kind of political Islam movement and of the pan-Arab leader Nasser, by declaring notably:

> At a dinner with Lebanese intellectuals, I unfortunately said: "But after all, the Arabs will never be able to solve this problem. If I were them, I would recognize Israel and integrate it into the Arab League ... It makes sense, because in any event it is a state that is not going to disappear."[16]

Instead of adopting a warlike and messianic position on the eminently conflicted Palestinian problem, in a radical break with the demands by political Islam or the traditional positions maintained by Gamal Abdel Nasser, the leader of Arab nationalism, he opted for the way of dialogue with the Jewish state. Also, well before Anwar al-Sadat who, for his part, officially recognized Israel with the Camp David accords of September 17, 1978 and that Hassan II moreover supported, the Moroccan sovereign quickly leaned toward a normalization of Arab relations with the Jewish state, rejecting the rhetoric of its destruction. His position, even though he sent troops in 1967 and 1973 to fight beside the Egyptian armed forces, basically ended up setting aside the ideological posture in favor of quite rapidly turning toward a pragmatic solution that the Islamists in all countries for a long time clearly rejected before more or less falling into line with it: "I really very much want to work with you, but you will never destroy Israel, so stop living an illusion because you will solve nothing and you will make the heads of the Arab states waste their time."[17]

Nor was the Sherifian sovereign against the idea of Jerusalem as Israel's capital. Hassan II's declarations regarding Palestine broke in at least three ways with Islamism's theses, as represented principally by the historic Muslim Brotherhood in Egypt, and their Maghrebian and Moroccan avatars in particular: rejection of the long-held perspective of a return to a pre-1967 Palestine, renunciation of the destruction of the Jewish state and armed struggle, and recognition of that state. Mohammed VI did not really cause this diplomatic line to change, with the situation in the Palestinian territories and Israeli occupation clearly not figuring among the priorities on the palace's foreign agenda.

Worse yet, Morocco would be a "discreet partner of Israel,"[18] as revealed by the Moroccan journalist Ali Amar of the online journal *Slate Afrique*. According to the WikiLeaks revelations, which confirmed the Sherifian orientations in this regard that spanned several decades, if "Rabat and Tel Aviv were in accord on diplomatic subjects, it was in business that their cooperation was more obscure." Such a partnership is not surprising if the long history of relations between the Moroccan authorities and the Jewish state is taken into account. The discreet nature or recent lack of Israeli diplomatic representation, particularly with the closure after October 2000 during the second Intifada, "of Israel's liaison office in Rabat and the departure of its diplomat, Gadi Golan, who held the rank of ambassador," is linked to the hyper-sensibility in the Arab street to the situation of the Palestinians and the repressive measures that the Israeli army employed against the Palestinian populations. The monarchy did not wish to have this relationship excessively publicized or discussed in society and "given visibility" throughout the legal political space at the risk of discrediting its discourse of solidarity with regard to Palestine and, in so doing, play into the hands of political Islam opposition actors in a quasi-legal or extra-legal situation, like the Justice and Charity movement of the late Sheikh Yassine.[19] Nevertheless, Ali Amar revealed that this type of relationship between the Moroccan and Israeli chanceries, as well as regular and multifaceted meetings between leading players of both countries, had been going on for years with the blessing of the United States. The exchanges would touch on several subject areas (tourism, technology, and military armaments) outside the sole diplomatic channel that was deemphasized due to its sensitivity:

> Despite the popular opposition to normalization with the Jewish state, conveyed by numerous anti-Israel marches in the kingdom protesting the events in Gaza, Rabat continues to maintain trade relations with Tel Aviv in a volume that is far from negligible. Many Moroccan groups regularly denounce the ties between the Jewish state and the Sherifian kingdom. *The national initiative to boycott Israel* estimates that they amount to some US$

50 million (Euro 35.3 million) annually, especially in the agro-industrial sector. Seeds and technology are transshipped through Europe to mask their Israeli origin. Some Moroccan companies import products from Spain, the Low Countries, or Denmark whose technology or inputs in reality come from Israel. In 2005, the press reported the existence of containers unloaded in Casablanca marked with the star of David or components *made in Israel* built into telecommunications equipment imported by Morocco Telecom ... Following a merger with Morocco Tours, Yambateva Travel recently opened a representative office in Marrakesh. The Israeli operation plans to take 45% of Israeli tourism in Morocco ... Rabat has opted to make military purchases from the Israeli armaments industry. The subject is so sensitive that both countries made it a state secret.[20]

In contrast, Islamists in general and the PJD in particular, which moreover previously went down a path of militants of political Islam in other, much more radical, organizations, such as Islamic Youth (1969–81), on an ideological level never have accepted the normalization of relations with the state of Israel. They are systematically careful, moreover, to avoid as much as possible using the word "Israel" as a way of acting out symbolically their absolute non-recognition of this state, therefore preferring pejorative expressions instead: "Zionist entity," "occupying power," and so forth. It is nevertheless necessary, as Walid M. Abdelnasser stresses, to "differentiate the foreign policy of a state from positions adopted by a political movement with respect to external problems."[21]

Indeed, to fully understand the type of disputes that can bring the actors of political Islam and the monarchy into conflict on the question of international relations, on the Palestinian dossier above all, it is indispensable, at least in broad outline, to interweave two perspectives: first, on the "foreign policy" and the Palestinian question, such as they have been coopted by the original matrix of contemporary Islam, in this case by the Muslim Brotherhood of the era of Hassan al-Banna (1906–49) and its immediate successors that spread throughout the Muslim world, including Morocco; second, still in relation to the subject of "international relations," on the principal stages by which the Moroccan Islamist movement was constituted, of which there are four: underground, legality, opposition, and government.

From the beginnings of the Muslim Brotherhood and of Islamism, which the former greatly inspired by also establishing activist branches[22] starting in the 1930s in Morocco, Sudan, Palestine, Lebanon, Syria, and Bahrain, as well as Europe (more during the 1970s) where they also progressively spread, the international or foreign relations of the Muslim world, in the name of Islam and its expansion through the world, were a major subject, all the more so because the colonial period was at its apogee and because the Islamists wished to reverse this historical tendency of domination by a near-hegemonic Europe on the global scene. They wanted to reverse the international balance of power to their advantage. Also, it is by first confronting the sources of contemporary political Islam that it is possible to appreciate the difference between the Moroccan Islamists, inheritors of H. al-Banna's thinking, despite their progressive theologico-political autonomization, and the Sherifian Islamic diplomacy in relation to Israel or the West more generally.

Internationalism, with the establishment of the Califate as leitmotiv for eventual unification of all Muslim nations under a central theologico-political authority, is at the heart of the ideology of the Muslim Brotherhood's founder. In addition, he dedicated a specific section of the *Collected Letters* not only to "foreign policy" (*al-siyāsiyya al-kharijiyya*) but also, in other sections, to Palestine. He posits, on a subject that touches on the international, that "Islam has held to the sovereignty of the Islamic Umma to serve as the guide to all communities, and this (as it appears) in numerous verses of the Koran. The Umma has to preserve this sovereignty, including by force."[23] According to him, it is indispensable to guard "the independence of the Umma, its liberty, its visibility, its dignity and power, to lead it toward glorious ends from which it occupies its place among nations and its noble abode among the peoples and the states …" There is a strong messianic dose in these texts by H. al-Banna that he integrates with foreign policy by hammering home that it is "at the heart of Islam as understood by the Companions and the pious predecessors."[24] For al-Banna, the Muslim Brotherhood and the Islamists, under formulations that vary with the contexts, the places, and the groups, it is a matter of "countering the Jewish domination of Palestine," in the name of the sacredness of Palestine territory because Al-Qods or Jerusalem was the "first Qibla" (direction of prayer) and for a long time (before Medina replaced it) "the second holy place" after Mecca. Palestine is considered as "the center of unity" of the Arabo-Islamic world and "the spirit of nations." Al-Banna faults the West for its "moral laxness and atheism"; it would head up a conspiracy to make the Muslim world turn its back on the sacred principles at the economic, political, and cultural levels. For only the Califate, whose abolition in 1924 would precisely be one of the causes of Palestine being colonized, and the complete temporal restoration of the sacred norms on the soil of Islam, could be the means of saving the Muslims from their "humiliating dependence with respect to the West."[25] For the Muslim Brotherhood, the loss of Palestine is closely linked to the spread of anti-Islamic, materialist ideologies in the Muslim world to the detriment of the application of the precepts of faith by these populations.

The Islamists and the International: The Three Ages of Brotherhood-style Foreign Policy

This is the ideological perspective that the members of the PJD subscribed to originally before going through some remarkable inflections. Still, it is important, in order to better understand the quality of the party's evolution when it comes to foreign affairs, to sequence the positions taken by its cadres (or its theorists) into four key periods: that of the Islamic Youth, from 1969 to 1981/2, during which the current leaders of the PJD (Abdelillah Benkirane, Abdellah Baha, Saadeddine al-Othmani, Mohamed Yatim, and Mustafa Ramid) agitated for the overthrow of the monarchy, the total application of the *shariā'a* and the restoration of the Califate; the period from 1981/2 to 1996, during which they strove for legality by abandoning their original revolutionary perspective of fighting the monarchy and in deferring *sine die* the possibility of installing the Califate; the period of inclusion in the Parliamentary opposition, from 1997/8 to 2011; and, lastly, the "governmentalization" period starting in December/January 2012. During at least the first three decades of the Islamist movement, it retained a distinctly simple if not simplistic conception of international relations as a universal apostolate meant to furnish the world with an alternative model of society governed by Islamic precepts. This utopian vision did not truly integrate geopolitical constraints and the immediate pressures of the institutional environment. A kind of mechanical relationship was postulated between returning to the pure faith by the world's Muslims, reconciliation with the teachings of Muhammad, of the pious predecessors, and the reconstitution of the Califate, with Islam and the Muslim world ultimately at center stage internationally and hegemonically at that. This was the *idealist* period: a manifest and acritical confusion over "the politically possible" and the "morally desirable."

From 1981/2 to 2011/12, the Moroccan Islamists would reason about international relations in three registers of discourse, most notably regarding relations with the West, the United States, and Israel, sometimes with variations and differences of tone, depending on the places, expressions of public support as well as the degree of pressure exerted by the throne: (1) confessionalization/communitarization or messianism in discourse; (2) a progressive rationalization of discourse, and, finally, (3) the externalization of anti-establishment discourse, that is to say, the act, for the men of the PJD in the government, of respecting the red lines drawn by the palace by subcontracting to other organs close to its base the protesting or polemical dimension and by not taking on directly the governmental responsibility of actors of political Islam. In this connection, ideological accents, be they messianic or tribunitial, alternated with pragmatic tones or succeeded one another. For a long time, and there are still some hints of it, foreign affairs in Islamist eyes in general and Moroccan ones in particular were summed up as an irreducible dualism or an Islam *versus* the West face-off. This antagonism has not completely disappeared and has been covered over with pure pragmatism.

Abdellillah Benkirane, in his book *The Islamist Movement and the Problem of Method* in a chapter titled "Western Civilization and the New International Order," returns to the crippling ontological dispute that would pit "Islam" against "the West." He writes that "the world down here has become an end in itself," "the beliefs of Muslims have been spoiled, while foreign philosophies have intruded."[26] The golden age of Islam that is to be resurrected is that of a globalized Islam, trans-border, universal, with cultural, religious content in a socio-political and economic fulfillment yet to come. The West, in a book written as recently as 1999, is relegated to a kind of essence that is irreconcilable with Islam for it would produce a "philosophical thought built upon the negation of the hereafter" and would attach itself to deliberately extending its empire. This opposition originates in Western "materialist or secular traditions" that Islam would intrinsically reject, since it denounces "publicly committing morally reprehensible acts in the public space: homosexuality, the presence of groups defending homosexuals."[27] Again according to A. Benkiran, Islam would replace for the West its former "Communist" enemy. This would be the work of "proactive lobbies, executing, colored by Zionism, naturally hostile to Islam and to Muslims"[28] that would use all informational tools to bring to a successful conclusion their projects for dominating the latter. The current prime minister, A. Benkirane, envisions that, off-stage, it would be "the Zionists," the very ones who would despoil Palestinian lands and their helpers across the world, foremost the United States, to achieve their projects of domination against Islam, Muslims, and the Arabo-Islamic world. In his view, a neo-Califate would be a means of resistance and of rebirth for the latter as matter of collective duty.[29] The idea of putting an Empire back together again is therefore never entirely excluded, even if no explicit time horizon is set. The confessionalization of the international relations concept was particularly palpable before the PJD made its debut in Parliament in 1997–8. However, we will dwell on four articles representative of this period, dating successively from 1992, 1993, 1994, and 1996. During this epoch, the future actors of the PJD still focused their propaganda on Morocco's internal situation in essentially religious terms, but also on the situation in other Muslim countries, involving particularly the activities of "Brother" Islamist movements in Algeria, Tunisia, Sudan, Afghanistan, and so forth.

In an article in the Islamist magazine *Al-Rā'ya* (The Standard), dated February 9, 1992 and titled "Zionist Defeat and Great Palestinian Gain," the author glorifies "the intensification of the blessed intifada in occupied Palestine, in the shadow of Zionist trials" and deplores "the Arab division and international conspiracy" sharpened by the West and "Zionism." The author also praises Hamas, its historical head, Ahmad Yassine, and its military arm, "the 'Azal-dīn al-Qasām phalanxes," for their offensives against the "robber authorities of the Zionist entity." He assigns five challenges to the Palestinians, including: "Privilege a decision to return to its land, as a nation and people no matter the cost (author's note: when the Palestinians were still in the refugee camps) ... no place other than occupied Palestine ... support the *intifada*, its intensification, its importance as an irreversible popular choice, rely on armed struggle as a strategic choice for confronting the usurper's occupation, and invite all the Palestinian forces to a complete national dialogue." This shows that for Morocco's political Islam actors, Palestine is on the order of a profane and sacred preoccupation at the same time.

On June 7, 1994, still in *Al-Rā'ya*, A. Benkirane, leader of the Moroccan legalist Islamist current, delivers an exposé on the "situation of the Islamic world." After the *basmallah*, the sacred ritual formula used by Muslims, he proposes a definition of this geographical space relating to essentialism, to the monolithic, in which this ensemble, while extremely diverse and fragmented, is totally identified with Islam. It would oppose the materialist, atheistic, and hegemonic West. For the leader of political Islam, the sole power capable of restoring the Islamic world to its rank is hands down the Islamist movement:

"We can affirm that its only hope resides in the Islamist movement which must continually renew itself to stay up to the historic task it is duty-bound to carry out, especially on the level of the unification of its ranks and factions, the precision of its ideas, the clarity of its project and discourse, the development of its programs, the realism of its approaches, and the effort of total renewal that it must bring to bear."

In an article in the same magazine dated February 23, 1993, titled "L'Islam and the West: Conditions for the Dialogue," A. Benkirane, with Koranic motives as his starting point, encourages dialogue with a West still viewed as completely homogeneous, while recognizing "the positive things the West has given" Muslims and "to all of humanity, despite its negative points ... colonization ..., and its attempts to inculcate in the colonized Muslim population 'ideas that break with the true religious science.'" With the future ex-Yugloslavia in advanced disintegration, he denounces "the genocide" in Bosnia and the aggression in Iraq instigated by the West. He denounces the latter's complicity in the Israeli colonization of Palestine by not sufficiently applying the Security Council resolutions, or still more, its suspected responsibility for annulling the Islamic Salvation Front's (FIS's) victory in Algeria in the early 1990s. Tasking a culturalist approach, he calls on the West to acknowledge the special "civilizational and historical identity of the Umma." He even exhorts it to "open itself to Islam without prejudice to find in it a remedy for certain civilizational sicknesses." Here we see the full apostolic expression.

Finally, in 1996, when the Islamists under their leadership stand at the gates of Parliament for the first time in their history, they grant the philosopher-historian Roger Giraud, visiting Morocco at their invitation, a prominent platform. He arrived to hold a conference on a work in which the theologico-messianic-political tone dominates: *The Founding Myths of Israeli Policy*.[30] During this forum, which is a recap *in extenso* of the text of his paper, R. Garaudy, a convert to Islam and found guilty of revisionism in France, variously explains, here also interlinking the secular, geopolitical (anti-globalism, anti-Americanism, anti-Zionism, third-worldism and so forth) and prophetic dimensions, that:

> the state of "Israel" no longer is just the proxy for a collective Western colonialism under American hegemony, it has become a major piece of an important planet-wide defense for the United States ... Because we have shown that the principal enemy is the United States and that their Israeli mercenary is the nerve center in the confrontation, converging efforts must be made, not just by Muslims, but by all third-world people and also by a formerly colonizing Europe but that is today in the process of "taking its turn as the colonized." Let us not forget that in the "Maastricht Treaty" it is repeated three times: "Europe can only be the European pillar of the Atlantic Alliance," and it is the start of a colonization, the Maastricht Treaty, the pressures by NATO, the World Trade Organization ... which is the civilian power of monotheistic market religion, that is to say, the idolatry of money, shows us very well how the process rolls on ... It is therefore necessary to refuse to pay to the International Monetary Fund these spurious debts and usurious interest ... I believe that on the political level this implies a collective retreat from all the institutions with pretensions to universality that have been turned into instruments of domination by a single one and which serve as a cover for its military aggressions ... My sisters and Brothers, the project of the future is not a utopia if everyone feels personally responsible for attaining it ... It is not a utopia, I repeat; at a moment when the British Empire was the most powerful on earth and it possessed the strongest army in the world, a very small gentleman named Gandhi jeopardized all the industries in Manchester by calling on the Indian people to provide an example ... I want to remind you what (Babeuf) wrote the day before his death by execution, when he said "When the storms have died down, when the people of the Good breathing freely

enough come to throw some flowers on my grave, then you will see realized in good time what the corrupt of today call dreams."

It is only on entering the Assembly of Representatives after the general elections of 1997–8 that the PJD's actors increasingly relativized their messianic accents in international questions by adopting a more political and rational discursive register. They thus professionalized their discourse, because now they were under a certain number of constraints, be they political in nature in terms of their actual mobilizing capability in Parliament that for a long time was limited (they had nine representatives from 1997 to 2002, 42 from 2002 to 2007, 46 from 2007 to 2011, out of a total of 325) or institutional, given the palace's centrality. The impacts of environment, circumstance, and structure progressively combined and influenced not only the party's agenda, but also, going forward, the manner of presenting their approach to international relations less and less in specifics relative to the monarchy's own demarches with which it tended to align itself. In this regard, one of the immediate conditions imposed on the Islamists when they applied for legalization was that of having to defend the "territorial integrity," that is, accept the Moroccanness of the Western Sahara provinces and, between the lines, the criminalization of the Polisario secessionists. Or by totally backing the royal account spun and broadcast on the occasion of the 1975 Green March, behind which nearly all forces of Moroccan politics and society had lined up with only a few individual exceptions. It was, moreover, a remarkable act relative to foreign policy conducted by the monarchy, which accordingly enduringly solidified its grip and its legitimacy on two levels: on the level of domestic action, and this ever since independence, and on the level of external action. This was one specific battlefield less for the Islamists.

Two reference texts produced by the PJD help to document the relativization of the Israelo-Arab/Palestinian question's centrality and the rationalizing of the discourse on this subject: The doctrinal charter, which is the party's ideological skeleton and a document distributed in the form of a booklet available in four languages (Arab, French, English, and Spanish) under the title *La politique étrangère du PJD: principes et orientations* [The Foreign Policy of the PJD: Principles and Orientations]. The charter, sixty-five pages long, does not contain a separate chapter dealing with Palestine. It is essentially an Islamo-nationalist,[31] even identitarist, reorientation that one is witness to:

> As for our party, it guards the historical identity of our people, of our state, its civilizational and historical brilliance and its struggle, just as it guards ... its traditions, its development during four decades since independence, the goals, the challenges, the internal and external constraints and the regional and global context in which our country evolves ... with a view to participating in building a modern, progressive Morocco, proud of its historical authenticity.[32]

Where this text deals with the "orientations and choices" of the party which it envisages for international relations, always in second place, the favored angle is that of "sovereignty" or of sovereignism. The document proposes "a popular diplomacy that defends Morocco's unity, its sovereignty, and the justness of its questions in international organizations." In addition, Islamic solidarity is stripped of its messianic aspect and conflictual sides, moving it more into humanitarian terrain, but, for all that, still rejecting "normalization with the Zionist entity":

> As it requires concentrating on furthering the defense of Morocco's strategic interests by economic diplomacy ... Press for reaffirming the effectiveness of the OIC ... for attaining political, economic, and cultural mutual assistance among the Islamic states with a view to achieving complementarity in these fields. Contribute to mutual assistance between the popular political and humanitarian institutions in the Arabo-Islamic world and rest of the world. (The) importance of the Palestinian problem or the Arabo-Islamic problems, by activating the role of peoples in supporting the Palestinian people until they obtain their freedom and have their rights fully restored; discontinue any form of normalization, overt or hidden ... with the Zionist entity ... by constraining the Zionist entity to respect the execution of international legal decisions.[33]

The novelty is the legalist Islamists rallying to the side of international solutions to the Israeli-Palestinian problem, when for three decades of closely following the teachings of H. al-Banna their sole perspective was armed struggle to destroy Israel. However, this recognition of international law, particularly in the case of this problem, remains variable, ambivalent, if not conflicted. In this short text of barely ten pages, the authors are careful to avoid using the noun Israel, because it would amount in their view to recognizing its existence, even if symbolically, given how much they always challenge it on the level of discourse. This is less a programmatic text than a text naming a series of external enemies like the "United States of America" hostility (*sic*) toward Morocco and to the Arab and/or homogeneous Muslim world. Without question, the PJD avoids the messianic cues characteristic of the Islamist movement in contemporary times, but after all it is content to secularize an old conspirational rhetoric. On the one side, with respect to implementing international law it appeals to the United Nations (UN), which presupposes giving at least some credit to this organization, while, on the other, it considers it to be manipulated by American power:

> Worn out by these plots, the Arab and Islamic states have turned in on themselves, being content with managing their internal affairs and, for some among them, our country included, abandoning the role they once played in consolidating and fostering Arab and Islamic solidarity. Worse, many Arab countries have reached a point where they no longer seek anything but their security under the American-Zionist aegis, which explains why many of them hasten to normalize their relations with the Zionist entity. It was under these conditions, no longer content to sit still for their supremacy on the international scene by one party, namely the United States of America, that the 9/11 attacks were perpetrated. In response, and on the pretext of the war on terror, the United States exploited these attacks to wage more wars and impose their political vision on the whole world. Worse still, the Zionist lobby in the United States, allying itself with the all-powerful conservative right wing, benefited from the 9/11 attacks by associating Islam and Muslims with terrorism and declaring a merciless war against religious teaching in the Islamic world as well as against charitable activity. This happened at the same time that this lobby mobilized all kinds of political and material support for the Zionist aggression against the Palestinian people … and missed no chance to justify the criminal Israeli policy.[34]

However, simultaneously, the Charter enumerates six "basic principles" of foreign policy: justice on the level of "all treaties, accords, and international conventions" without "prejudice ... or injustice toward any community, ethnicity, or minority whatsoever ... equal rights ... opposition to any accord that would constitute an attack on the principle of equality or which is liable to establish racial discrimination or favor the application by a state, a group, or a community of a policy of ethnic cleansing or sectarian or religious persecution ... the freedom of travel, of sojourn, of movement, of work and property ... respect for bilateral and international treaties, the recognition of the civilizational plurarity and cultural specificities" as well as "communal cooperation."[35] It is in the framework of international legality that the party's discourse, eminently rational as a consequence, inscribes itself.

While in Parliament from 1997 to 2011, the PJD globally used discursive repertoires borrowing from populism, at times concurring with an accepted or latent clash of civilization. In addition, it seemed to fulfill the classic function of protest movements that, from one moment to the next during their journey, go through a tribunitial phase, especially in the parliamentary or extra-parliamentary opposition. The Islamists also did not completely abandon a moralizing tone. Still, the movement renounced an anti-imperialist logic by admitting the cultural, ethnic, and religious specificities of nations. It was a language that no longer really squared with the califal views of earlier days, which remained an active utopia with an absolutely indeterminate due date.

If the "logics" or "field effects"[36] play out on an internal level of politics, they also play out fully on the level of internal pressures that a party may be subject to, especially under an authoritarian regime, as soon as the international interests of the persons at the top of the state apparatus (the monarchy) are taken into account. This was the case with the announcement after the attacks of September 11, 2001 of a "global war against terrorism" by the American president George W. Bush, which the Islamists virulently opposed. That is, before they rallied to some extent to the cause consequent to the royal willingness to take new steps for the fight against terrorism in Morocco following the Casablanca suicide attacks of May 16, 2003. This they did inspite of the infringements on the level of individual and collective freedoms entailed by the language of the law finally passed with the approval of the PJD, which, sometime earlier, had still denounced the "anti-Islamist" and "pro-American" plot,[37] "hiding behind the war against terrorism." Some observers branded this law as a retreat from respect of human rights and privacy.[38] In the Islamist party's final pronouncement on the vote in favor of the anti-terrorist law, it stated, for example: "Moroccans are like one hand, a solid front, monolithic in the fight against terrorism, under the noble leadership of the Commander of the faithful, His Majesty Mohammed VII, may God protect him."[39]

It must be recalled that the alignment of the legalist Islamists with the anti-terrorism law project was obligatory. This, despite its reflecting in part elements of the *USA Patriot Act* voted for by the United States Congress and signed by George W. Bush on October 26, 2001 after the attacks on New York's World Trade Center that were roundly condemned by political Islam's actors. This text provided one of the legal foundations for future military operations in Afghanistan and Iraq.

It was under fire fed by criticism of the left-wing groups, by the NGOs and part of Moroccan civil society and with the king's indulgence that the PJD, held "morally responsible" for the Casablanca attacks, finally aligned itself with those who favored the law at the outset. It is a new, blatant example of the interaction between external and internal constraints, which even the Islamists could not escape and that they, indeed, had to bend to in their political strategies.

Despite its routine anti-American and anti-Western rhetoric, on the fringes of a debate on the US–Morocco Free Trade Agreementof 2004 almost exclusively led by the palace, the PJD, from a perspective of future electoral alliances, moved closer to the liberal Popular Forces party. The Islamist party presented itself as a liberal party on the economic plane, even "ultra-liberal," deploring the "hold of the state on certain companies" termed "prejudicial to their competitiveness" and, to this end, praising the merits of the "economic opening" and "progressive integration with the global economy."[40] The legalist Islamists thus did not vote against the US–Morocco FTA, despite its political implications and its potentially negative economic impacts on the country for the greater objective profit of the United States:

> In this way the "Greater Middle East" appears to be the instrument by which the American administration intends to reconfigure all of that part of the world stretching from Pakistan to Morocco in the service of its world

view and interests. In this grouping, they have to start with some "good students" to provide an example and start a trend. Morocco—pro-Western, even pro-American, a constitutional monarchy carefully tending to its democratic façade, a fan of economic liberalism and "happy globalization"—is rapidly appearing as one of a few countries (such as Jordan and Bahrain) handpicked by the United States and which it will favor as it pursues the realization of its design.[41]

It should be understood that this anti-American rhetoric tended to be downplayed at least since the mid-1990s, even if it continues to be expressed occasionally and at the margin. Indeed, the Moroccan Islamists, in the quest for institutional integration and aware of the great sensitivity in Washington and Europe on questions of security linked to terrorist groups laying claim to Islam, sought to be anointed by the authorities and think tanks close to the American administration. In recent years, even before taking on governmental responsibilities, the members of the PJD regularly took part in the work of the Center for the Study of Islam and Democracy (CSID).[42] This institute organizes debates[43] on the compatibility of Islam and democracy, of democracy with forms of Islamism, and so forth. Mustafa al-Khalfi, the minister of communications, who also came from PJD ranks, was even a Visiting Scholar in 2005–6 at the American Congress as part of study of "American policy in the Middle East," with a "focus on efforts to promote democracy."[44]

To sum up, in order to prove their adherence to democratic principles, as consecrated in the great international texts, and simultaneously witness to its legalism both in its relations with the internal as well as external political environment, the PJD thus sought the approval of the world's greatest power, the very same United States whose whole weight rests on the Arab and Muslim world's conflicts. In doing so, the Islamists are looking for a respectability capable of inducing a "boomerang effect"[45] on national and international levels. They reckon at the same time that transnational mobilization, the accruing participation on global platforms, will create conditions of confidence with the world's great powers as well as financial institutions (the International Monetary Fund, the World Bank and so forth) with a view toward lifting the suspicions on both sides by the time of an eventual taking power by the Islamists in the present or in the course of the next few years.

The determinants—particularly, economic and political—due to the negative repercussion of the European financial crisis of 2008–9 on the Sherifien kingdom, as well as the geopolitical balance of power in which the Sherifien kingdom carries less weight than other voices of the north or south, in part had gotten the better of the PJD's traditional ideological postures. Indeed, since the Islamist party came into power and supplied the head of the government, economic relations with Europe and the United States, which remain favored partners (Turkey, the foremost Muslim client/supplier, only ranks in eleventh place),[46] for one have not diminished and, for another, trade flows with Israel have not ceased; they actually have grown since early 2012. "Moroccan imports from Israel during 2012 registered a spectacular leap of 216% while exports grew by 150%,"[47] through Israeli companies operating in the ports, in agriculture, and in security, with Abdelkader Amara, the Islamist minister holding the portfolio, not denying the reality of these activities and companies embedded in the kingdom.

That is not to say that the PJD actors would have totally abandoned the language of Islam or its critical positions vis-à-vis the West, the United States, or the "Zionist entity" as they frequently call Israel. However, the exercise of governmental power forced them all the more to euphemize their religion- and populism-accented discourse, particularly with regard to international questions. This attitude is the corollary to the distinction between political structures (PJD) and apostolic ones (Unicity and Reform Movement) conceded by the legitimist Islamists. When they had to broach the Israeli-Palestinian problem, they opted increasingly for the more specific angle of international legality than that of religion *sense stricto*.

They also did not want to enter into conflict with or be on the wrong side of Morocco's real chief diplomat, as always Mohammed VI. That is why the somewhat more radical or messianic discourse against Israel was left, among others, to the printed press, like the *Al-Tajdīd* magazine, which could be viewed as an ideological sounding board for positions that were more radical than the PJD itself could take within its own ranks. This Arabophone daily, also available online, reserved space specifically dedicated to Palestine in which, unsurprisingly, can be found texts in quantity that support the Palestinian people and call on them "to liberate their country from the Zionist occupation," all the while declaring itself systematically hostile to any kind of normalization with the Jewish state.[48] Finally, if regular exchanges and collaborations exist between the PJD and other political Islamist groups in the Arab and/or Muslim world, it is above all communitarian, fraternal, and ideological solidarity that is valued. On Palestine, the Moroccan representative of political Islam is less in favor of the route of military or armed confrontation with the Israeli state than "foremost, religious invocation, and then waging the struggle by modern electronic means, the symbolic contribution in all its forms, giving gifts to the Sherifian Al-Qods Foundation."[49] As for the words and commitments issued by Hassan II siding with Anwar al-Sadat for an Arab normalization with Israel, to our knowledge they have never officially been criticized and called into question by the legitimist Islamists, foremost among them A. Benkirane. In fact, the latter is said to have accepted the invitation by an Israeli, Ofer Bronchtein, the president of the International Forum for Peace and no less than a former advisor to Shimon Peres "during the era of the Oslo and Camp David negotiations," at the PJD's seventh national congress held in Rabat in July 2012.[50] All the same, some members of the Islamist movement declared, *a posteriori*, that this man was, in fact, in full agreement with the rights of Palestinians.

Nevertheless, the party assumes or exhibits, on this point as well as others, a certain ambivalence linked to the complications of excercising power, which regularly oblige them to put the rigid ideological positions of the past between parentheses. For the PJD is also constantly caught between ideology and realism, which imposes on it, if not entering into a community of thinking with all the actors on the political scene, at least into dialogue with as many as possible, including the Israelis, whom they generally stigmatize publicly.

By way of conclusion, we are in a position to sustain the idea according to which the legalist Islamists, engaged in a routinized policy of normalization and institutionalization, are caught in such a bundle of systemic constraints, be they of an internal or external order, that they de facto favor the pragmatic over the ideological. For the actors of political Islam do not evolve outside the national, regional, and international political realities that require them to make doctrinal, ideological, or strategic adjustments. They therefore euphemize the "morally desirable" under the guise of religious or messianic accents to further prioritize "the politically possible," which they can in addition seek to legitimize theologically. The bottom line is that the Islamists as soon as they become institutionalized tend to normalize and make themselves more banal on the domestic but also on the international stage. Does this mean that they will renounce all the fundaments of their original political culture for good? Nothing is less certain.

Notes

1. Guillaume Devin, *Sociologie des relations internationales* [Sociology of International Relations], Paris, Repères/La découverte, 2007, pp. 11–12.
2. King Mohammed VI of Morocco, after the strong reverberations felt in his country from the upheavals in Tunisia, Yemen, Egypt, Libya, Syria, and Bahrain—in order to avoid such an eventual "contagion" effect from popular protests—decided to introduce new constitutional reforms, approved by referendum on July 1, 2011 and intended to give more weight to future governments and elected parliaments. It was precisely in this context that the Party of Justice and Development, until now limited to the parliamentary opposition, for the first time carried off a win in the national elections, and this time with a relative majority of 107 seats out of 395 in the lower chamber.
3. Irene Fernandez Molina, *Le PJD et la politique étrangère de Maroc. Entre l'idéologie et le pragmatisme* [The PJD and Moroccan Foreign Policy. Between Ideology and Pragmatism], Barcelona, Edicions Bellaterra, Fundacion CIDOB, Documentos CIDOB, 2007, pp. 1–91, p. 35; emphasis in the original.
4. Gilles Perrault, *Notre ami le roi* [Our Friend the King], Paris, Éditions Gallimard, 1990, p. 238.
5. Mohamed Tozy, *Monarchie et islam politique au Maroc* [Monarchy and Political Islam in Morocco], Paris, Presses de Sciences Po, 1999.
6. Abdessamad Belhaj, "L'usage politique de l'islam: l'universel au service d'un État. Le cas du Maroc" [Political Uses of Islam: The Universal in Service of the State. The Case of Morocco], *Recherches sociologiques et anthropologiques*, 2006, Vol. 37, no. 2, posted on March 10, 2011, http://rsa.revues.org/575, accessed September 17, 2013.
7. Malika Zeghal, *Les islamistes marocains. Le défi à la monarchie* [The Moroccan Islamists. The Challenge for the Monarchy], Casablanca, Éditions Le Fennec, 2005, p. 97.
8. *Ibid.*
9. Abdessamad Belhaj, *op. cit.*

10. http://www.diplomatie.ma/ActionduMaroc/LeComitéAlQods/tabid/104/language/fr-FR/Default.aspx, accessed September 17, 2013.
11. *Ibid.*
12. http://www.diplomatie.ma/SearchResults/tabid/42/language/fr-FR/Default.aspx?Search=palestine, accessed September 17, 2013.September
13. http://www.diplomatie.ma/SearchResults/tabid/42/language/fr-FR/Default.aspx?Search=agressions+israéliennes, accessed September 17, 2013.
14. http://www.bmaq.org/fre/page/al-quds-committee, accessed September 17, 2013.
15. http://www.diplomatie.ma/ActionduMaroc/LeComitéAlQods/tabid/104/vw/1/ItemID/3261/language/fr-FR/Default.aspx, accessed September 17, 2013.
16. Hassan II, *La Mémoire d'un Roi, entretiens avec Éric Laurent* [A King's Memoirs, Conversations with Éric Laurent], Paris, Plon, 1993, p. 245.
17. *Ibid.*, p. 251.
18. http://www.slateafrique.com/37555/economie-maroc-le-partenaire-discret-d-israel, accessed 19 September 19, 2013.
19. The Moroccan Islamist Justice and Welfare movement, founded in 1973 by sheikh Abdessalam Yassine, has always rejected the principle of participation in the official political arena suspecting that the rules of the game were rigged.
20. http://www.slateafrique.com/37555/economie-maroc-le-partenaire-discret-d-israel, accessed January 10, 2014; emphasis in the original.
21. Walid M. Abdelnasser, *The Islamic Movement in Egypt. Perceptions of International Relations 1967–1981,* London/New York, The Graduate Institute of International Studies, 1994, p. 9.
22. Brynar Lia, *Society of the Muslim Brother in Egypt. The Rise of an Islamic Movement 1928–1942,* Liban, Ithaca Press, 1998, pp. 154–7.
23. Hassan al-Banna, *Ensemble des Épîtres de l'imam Hassan al-Banna* (en arabe) [Collected letters of imam Hassan al-Banna (in Arabic)], ed. Al-Shahāt Ahmad al-Tahān, Egypt, Dâr al- kalîma li al-nashr wa al-tawzî', 2005, p. 334.
24. *Ibid.*, p. 333.
25. Walid M. Abdelnasser, *The Islamic Movement in Egypt. Perceptions of International Relations 1967–1981, op. cit.*, p. 169.
26. Abdelillah Benkirane, *Le mouvement islamiste et la problématique de la méthode* (en arabe) [The Islamist Movement and the Problem of Method (in Arabic)], Casablanca, Al-najâh al-jadîda, 1999, p. 17.
27. *Ibid.*, p. 18.

28. *Ibid.*, p. 20.
29. *Ibid.*, p. 34.
30. Roger Garaudy, *Les Mythes fondateurs de la politique israélienne* [The Founding Myths of Israeli Politics], Pithiviers, Samiszdat, 1996.
31. Olivier Roy, *The Failure of Political Islam*, Cambridge, MA, Harvard University Press, 1994.
32. *PJD. La charte doctrinale et le programme général* (en arabe) [The Doctrinal Charter and General Program (in Arabic)], Rabat, PJD, s.d.
33. *Ibid.*, p. 34.
34. *La politique étrangère du PJD: Principes et orientations* [The Foreign Policy of the PJD: Principles and Directions], Rabat, Tūbbarīs, 2008, pp. 4–5.
35. *Ibid.*, pp. 7–11.
36. Pierre Bourdieu, *Questions de sociologie* [Problems of Sociology], Paris, Éditions de Minuit, 1980.
37. Khadija Mohsen-Finan and Malika Zeghal, "Opposition islamiste et pouvoir monarchique au Maroc. Le cas du Parti de la Justice et du Développement " [The Islamist Opposition and Monarchical Power in Morocco. The Case of the Party of Justice and Development], *RFSP*, 2006, Vol. 56, no. 1, 79–119, 109.
38. http://www.leconomiste.com/article/886827-le-11-September-10-ans-apres brla-loi-antiterroriste-liberticide-mais-pas-tellement, accessed September 21, 2013.
39. PJD, *Le terrorisme, positions, leçons et enseignements* [Terrorism: Positions, Lessons and Teachings], Rabat, PJD, p. 21, s.d.
40. "Lahjouji courtise le PJD" [Lahjouji woos the PJD], *Aujourd'hui le Maroc* [Morocco Today], May 24, 2004.
41. Najib Akesbi, "L'Accord de libre-échange Maroc-USA: un acte éminemment politique" [The Morocco–USA Free Trade Agreement: An Eminently Political Act], in NajibAkesbi (ed.), *Accord de libre-échange Maroc-USA* [The Morocco–USA Free Trade Agreement], Rabat, Critique économique no. 21, pp. 3–8.
42. https://www.csidonline.org/, accessed September 22, Last accessed on September 2013.
43. http://archive.constantcontact.com/fs093/1102084408196/archive/1102128 62 3072.html, accessed September 22, 2013.
44. http://carnegieendowment.org/experts/?fa=273, accessed September 22, 2013.
45. http://www.attajdid.ma/?info=7857; http://www.attajdid.ma/index.php?info= 6700; accessed 22 September 22, 2013
46. The concept comes from the Syndey Tarrow. For details, refer to: Sidney

Tarrow, "La contestation transnationale" [The Transnational Challenge, *Cultures & Conflits*, 2000, Vols 38–9, posted March 20, 2006, http://conflits.revues.org/276, accessed November 29, 2013.
47. "Competitiveness of Moroccan Exports: What is the Balance Sheet?", Kingdom of Morocco, Ministère de l'Économie et des Finances, Direction des études et des prévisions financières, May 2013, personal document.
48. http://www.yabiladi.com/articles/details/18632/parlement-l-istiqlal-tacle-normalisation-relations.html, accessed September 22, 2013.
49. "Abû Zayd al-Muqrî' al-Idrisî (ndla député du PJD): on veut qu'on oublie et qu'on efface la Palestine de notre mémoire," *Al-Tajdîd*, , April 10, 2012.
50. http://www.slateafrique.com/91355/maroc-les-islamistes-accueillent-les-israeliens-a-bras-ouverts, accessed September 24, September2013.

3

The Foreign Policy of Tunisia's Ennahdha: Constancy and Changes

Maryam Ben Salem

Several questions suggest themselves when it comes to Islamism, a particularly anxiogenic but relatively ambiguous phenomenon, despite the abundant literature devoted to it. In point of fact, the anti-establishment position taken by some Islamist parties in the Arabo-Islamic area casts doubt on their "dual discourse" oscillating between legalistic endeavors and protesting logic. It stems from the tension between the fundamentals of militant Islam (defense of the Arabo-Muslim identity) and the exigencies of the insertion into politics. This is especially the case with Tunisia's Ennahdha movement, which, since its legalistic turn starting in 1981, seeks to affirm its adoption of the democratic idiom while still maintaining its Islamist identity. After a brief period of calm in its relations to power, as the result of Zine el-Abidine Ben Ali ascending to head of state in 1987, the movement would go through a phase of violent repression that saw the imprisonment and exile of a number of its members.

The first free elections in Tunisia's history were held on October 23, 2011 to choose the members of the National Constituent Assembly (ANC), which was tasked with writing a new Tunisian constitution. The Ennahdha party, legalized in March 2011, received 41.1 per cent of the seats in this body (89 out of 2,017),[1] thus passing from the status of pariah party to that of dominant party.[2]

The movement's coming to power ratcheted up this tension, for the party no longer limited itself to its relations with "democratic" or "secular" opposition groups but extended it to international relations as if it were the head of a sovereign state.

Analyzing the foreign policy of the Ennahdha movement is of great interest since it is particularly enlightening about the process of adaptation—indeed, normalization—to the logic of power and the practice of a party until then relegated to the sphere of the opposition. One of the aspects of Ennahdha actions that raises the most questions is the equivocal character of its positioning, which would be due to the permanent tension between democratic pretensions and the project of state and societal Islamization. This ambition has registered since its genesis in the anti-globalism in reaction to the West and the identification with the Muslim Umma and no longer with the Tunisianism proclaimed by Bourguiba. During the elections for the National Constituent Assembly (NCA) in October 2011 and with its accession to power, the debate on reconciling the movement's democratic reputation reaches its fever pitch. Simultaneously with making an issue out of the religious dimension for electoral mobilization, Ennahdha is anxious to reassure, both inside the country and on the international level, the compatibility between Islamism and democracy.

The question that this chapter intends to answer is how the stance of rejecting acculturation with the colonizing West, which has constituted one of the foundations of Islamist ideology in Tunisia and, in addition, is addressed by the foreign policy adopted by the movement henceforth in power (until the 2014 elections, which saw a switch to Nidaa Tounes and his dear Beji Caïd Essebsi). Did the party try to establish a diplomacy that puts an end "to dependency, alienation, and loss"[3] by turning Tunisia toward the East, in this case the Gulf states? It calls for comparing the principles of Ennahdha's external action, particularly where the West is concerned, and the application of these principles with the previous positions taken by the movement and its members on these questions. Tackling Ennahdha's foreign policy (its principles and its execution) in light of the positions of Islamists toward the West seems fundamental to us because, more than a constituent principle of it ideology, it represents one of the motivations to adhere to the movement and an organizing element of the militant identity. This chapter thus tries to analyze the ambiguities of this movement's external action, precisely as it relates to the West, in light of the evolution of postures relative to the latter. That said, confining ourselves to an analysis of the concordance or lack thereof between the party's ideology as it appears in the official documents and declarations and the foreign policy principles applied today, seems insufficient because it amounts to signaling evolutions or contradictions, if any, without making their sources explicit. Here, the analysis of the militant careers of thirty-three of the party's cadres effected as part of our thesis work[4] furnishes material for understanding how the movement's foreign policy operationalizes the passage from an oppositional register to a position of power that requires taking into account the reality of foreign relations, on the one hand, and the movement's ideational foundations and their transformation on the other.

We therefore propose to analyze for the first time how the relationship with the West structured the militant imagination of Ennahdha members and how their positions on the problem evolved over time before the movement's legalization in 2011 (1), and then to examine the implementation of the Islamist agenda when in power as reflected in foreign policy so as to shed light on moments of rupture and of continuity with positions previously advocated (2). Finally, we question the changes in Ennahda relations with the West and its vision of the international system since the presidential and legislative elections in 2014 that led to the departure of the movement of power, at least as the main governmental force, and recent announcement of the movement on the release of political Islam (3).

The Question of Westernization and Relations with the West in Militant Careers: Constructing the Islamist Project in the Alterity

Analysis of the militant careers of Ennahdha cadres clearly brings to light an evolution on both ideological and referential levels. This is particularly true in their relationship to the West, which, as we will see, has gone through more or less sharp transformations at four milestones of their career paths (initiation, formal entry into militancy, the episode of the "great test," and the access to power phase).

The problems of deculturation and imposed Westernization appear as central in militant logic and especially during the first experiments with activism. The alterity with regard to the West and the identification with the

Umma indeed constitute as much motives for engagement as an integral part of the ideology. The analysis of tendencies to join in the Islamist movement reveals the importance of the relationship to the West in the crystallization of perception schemas that fostered drawing closer to political Islam's discourse. In observing family socializing experiences, we found that the first types of anti-Western attitudes are mainly reactions by the militants against the moral "decay" of Tunisian society. Underlying these are rules of behavior and principles inculcated since infancy through the transmission of a political vision that rejects Westernization pursued by Bourguiba for a conception of power based on Arabity and Islamity. These elective affinities between Islamist ideology and the parentally transmitted system of representations and behaviors reside essentially in the diffuse or explicit reference of these values to the Islamic ethic. Decent ways of behaving and dressing, clean language, respect for the sacred, obedience to the father, and respect for one's elders are all norms opposed to the conduct and attitudes not yet dominant but increasingly visible in the Tunisian social sphere.[5] It is also surely a matter of violation of public morality by the tourists flooding the country subsequent to the development of the tourist sector, as well as behaviors "imported from the West" and adopted by Tunisians, such as drinking alcoholic beverages, gambling, and blasphemy (looked upon as kaba'ir[6]). The conservatism cultivated by the middle class and the peasant strata favors adoption of an ethic of rehabilitating the values they were taught (such as modesty, non-mixing, and chastity) but that they experience as greatly devalued in modern post-colonial Tunisia. The indignation that these behaviors often elicited in fathers is frequently echoed and appropriated by the militants. Gradually it transforms itself into a sense of duty, that of upholding the moral order and protecting oneself against deviance, which facilitates their adhesion to the ideology of rupture that the movement extolls.

Ridha Bettayeb,[7] aged forty-seven, who joined the movement in 1980 and is still a member, held the post of political leader of the movement's engineering school section from 1980 to 1981, and then served as a member of its politburo from 1981 until June 1984:

> We felt that the Bourguiba regime had tied Tunisia to a different context, i.e., the West, than it should be, that's to say, the Islamic one, that he had

despotically imposed a way of life through coercion on the Tunisian people, and he rejected the presence of Islam by closing Zitouna University; the religious institutions played no role of any kind and were simply closed, which brought with it a great moral decline of society. My father's job forcing us to move from town to town, I saw that clearly. I was at the high school in Gafsa, and I remember studying a text there in writing class, a verse from the Koran that the professor chanted, so that all the students laughed, that's how bizarre it seemed to them. Each of us in his own way saw this exile that Islam lived in our country.

Coming from conservative families or from Youseffian[8] ones, the religious and political socialization of the militants interviewed shows the existence of tendencies that are molded or reactivated in the movement, such as: the demand for rehabilitation of the religion (the tendency to religiosity) and a propensity for protesting the political system and particularly the developmentalist and Westernizing model followed by H. Bourguiba (the tendency to protest). During the initial phase corresponding to the training stage of the new Islamist (open circle and cell), the demarcation from society's dominant values is heightened. Identification with the group implies a durable and organized affiliation to the extent that it is realized through the actors' interpersonal relationships, the sharing of norms and values, time spent together, and advocating the same cause. Yet, from the moment that the neophyte transitions to a religious status, the identification with the group also proceeds by opposition to the "pre-Islamic" society as a whole or against specific groups that it consists of, such as the Communists, the Westernized elite, the Sufis, and non-believers.

Ali Laariadh[9] was born at Ben Guerdane in 1955; he joined the Islamist Movement of Islamic Tendency (MTI) in 1972 and was the prime minister in the troika government:

> I felt that I was different from the masses; it is a very immediate feeling, this sense of being different from others, and it leads to a sort of break, influenced by certain texts we had read (S. Qutb), which assert that the Muslim must liberate himself from different ignorances, isolate himself from his environment. This is an intangible isolation: the customary values, attraction to filthy things, admire your close friend's success even if it is

> ill-gotten, regionalism and tribalism—you try to cut yourself off from them to rebuild yourself. Gradualism is not beneficial. The movement becomes the member's family while his family now represents *jahiliyya* (ignorance). As the movement's members integrate and strengthen their ties, their relationship with society becomes very difficult. We restored that very extreme orientation consisting of severely judging the society and excommunicating it; we are harsh with our Brothers, our parents.
>
> We felt close (linked), not fearing loss because we were weak and formed a small unit that feared its environment would rob it of its identity. We shut ourselves off because we needed a strength that let us break with the reality that we were living.

The Islamist novice perceives himself as a stranger in his environment. Convinced of his Islamity and knowledge, he comes to anathematize (Bourguiba's) regime that had distorted the revealed message by taking the colonizing and dominant West as a model. The rupture that results is a symbolic one rather than a physical one, based on the idea that "the Muslim is a stranger and his exile grows along with his religious knowledge and his emancipation from cultural alienation." The price of this freeing and the vindication of the Muslim culture's supremacy is a break with the Western model and its values.

Said Ferjani,[10] born in Kairouan in 1955, jointed MTI in the mid-1970s. Returning to Tunis after January 14, he held the post of counselor in one of the ministries. (This interviewee refused to furnish us with a number of details about his social background, referring us to a press account of his militant career.)

> In other words, they presented us where everything was mixed up, they told us we were wretched [Muslims], that we are pitiful and that our ideal, our model, ought to be the West. In other words, that when he [the leftist professor] taught Marx to me, it was in dogmatic fashion ... it made an impression on me, being taught Marx this way. As for me, I accuse the elite that taught us, it was the elite's fault. The left was responsible and it abused, it wanted to politicize the teaching in order to gain ground. My idol was Jean-Paul Sartre. When the talk is of freedom, you find Jean-Paul Sartre; when it is about how to aid the weak, the wretched, you encounter Karl

Marx—in the end, that is to say, there is a kind of ... dogmatic content that only wants to show you that but which does not integrate our heritage. Me, I did international studies, which is when I saw that even the West has a problem, for example, when it comes to democracy. It started in Athens, then Rome; after that, it passes directly to France and the United States and other Anglo-Saxon countries, thus London also falls into line. When I realize that and I compare it with the extraordinary meritocracy that prevailed in the Carthaginian Republic,[11] I am sorry for the West, for its subjectivity ... it is as if the West said to us "I am wisdom and knowledge" as if there was nothing before and there would be nothing after. This is a dogmatic structuring of research. While what we really need is: these sciences are human efforts, in well-defined periods there were other civilizations, without leaving out any no matter what. At present, it is the West that is weak, there is no talk any longer of its power but the world does not stop there, it transforms itself and all that. This engenders your dealing with everything in your head and in your ideas without an inferiority complex. My sense is that the educational system is in the process of inculcating in us an inferiority complex in relation to the West, as if the West is knowledge, all there is to know, the West is all development, the West is all of history, in other words, we are worth nothing either before or now.

The phase of passage to formal militantism that generally coincides with entering the university seems to reinforce the anti-Western attitudes even more. The principal transformation that takes places in this state is incorporation of the Marxist, hence Western, referential. In confronting the leftist students, the Islamists have been stigmatized as preachers without any militant, political, or even intellectual competence, given that their ideational production is confined to the religious domain. The positioning of the Islamists was a source of discredit in the militant field. The skills acquired during the novitiate phase (religious ethic, cultural capital solely grounded in religious literature) by virtue of this find themselves affected by a negative valuation within the university by leftist militants in particular, therefore bringing with it a feeling of inferiority and exclusion from the terrain that they want to occupy. The religious status, claimed to define the Ennahdha militant by differentiating him from others and constituting his very identity, is transformed into a handicap to the extent that it fails to procure for him the credibility necessary for setting himself up in a competitive relationship with the leftist students, at the time very powerful. The *nahdhaoui* is then very quickly stigmatized as a religious reactionary and lacking the qualities necessary for making him a true militant. Clashing with the leftist activists, the Islamists therefore were led to appropriate the social justice register for themselves and Communist literature of class warfare. Islamization of the Marxist referential was made possible by theorists like Baqir Essadr and Ali Chari'ati who came to replace Hassan al-Banna and Sayyid Qutb, whose writing turned out to skirt reality and lean right, if not to the extreme right.[12] Chari'ati's writing introduced to Islamist discourse words close to Communist terminology, enabling it to compete on the same ideological terrain. The ideational evolution as a consequence of the competition with the left in the university thus did not happen at the price of moving away from the Islamist referent.

The attachment to this register remained a distinguishing element in the university militant arena, but the mastery of two cultures, Islamic and Western, constituted itself as a mark of superiority over the left. Said Ferjani:

> Our movement was a Cartesian one. It makes room for a spiritual dimension. The idea contained in the letter is the following: these are two lines that we talked about. Listen to me, you representatives of the left, you secularists, we came out of the same schools, we have the same baggage, but we went you one better: what distinguishes us is that we also know and perfectly master the culture of our region, its philosophy, and its history. Therefore, we master both cultures, the two ideological references.

Rejection of the West and of its influence grew, notably with the advent of the Iranian revolution in 1979, which the Islamists interviewed regarded as the concretization of the ideal of Muslim victory over that entity.

Ajmi Lourimi,[13] born at Chott Meriem of the Sahel in 1961, today is a leading movement cadre, having joined it in the late 1970s:

> The Iranian revolution is an extraordinary event. Khomeini is an Islamic symbol that proves that Islam can make a revolution. Religion is allied with the ruling classes in the Marxist discourse, while Khomeini proved that religion is the weapon of the weak, it is a revolt against injustice. He

had given the Muslim the image that he needed to consolidate his position before others. The solution henceforth was there, in real life and was not limited to theories in books. The vision that the young have of Islam is that of an adolescent but highly charged with meaning, for his existence, for challenging the world; he has a vision, a model, it liberates all of humanity, as imam Khomeini put it, "proletarians of all countries, unite!"

This attitude toward Khomeini's Iran calls for special attention. Indeed, the references to the inauguration of the Islamic Republic crop up frequently in the interviews that the militants granted us prior to 2011, thus demonstrating the exemplary nature of the Iranian model yet left uncompromised by the Shiism. This state of things did not keep Ennahdha from showing an accentuated tropism toward the Sunni Gulf that it confirmed when it took power. The diplomatic positions taken by the troika put it systematically in opposition to Iranian interests, including on the Syrian question. It is only during the phase known as the "great ordeal," which designates the repressive episode of 1991, that took a great number of militants to exile in Europe and North America and others to prison, that a certain softening on the question of relations with the West became evident. It is revealed by the use of Western and modern concepts (civil society, peaceful transition of power, political freedoms, and independent judiciary, human rights, and so forth) that signal its distance from the traditional referential corpus.[14]

The influence of the militants in exile had a great deal to do with this shift, in particular with regard to how the movement related to the West. Their discovery in Europe or North America of values such as respect for the individual, freedom of expression and thought, and democracy that were non-existent in their native countries would, according to the interviews, reconcile the Islamists with the Western world. Societies and movements in defense of human right, including ones on the left, actually aided the exiled Islamists in obtaining political refugee status, facilitated their social integrations, or also took up the cause of imprisoned militants. In addition, the involvement of the exiled activists in defending their imprisoned peers resulted in appropriating the human rights register.

For the movement's members who remained in Tunisia and were liberated after more than a dozen years of imprisonment, cooperation with the different political tendencies in Tunisia imposed itself as a way of reentering the political scene, taking into account the movement's weakened state. A change of the referential thus was called for in order to avoid accusations of religious extremism by the government and the legal opposition parties.

It is no longer the West, that imaginary and essentialized entity, that is condemned, but the Westernization of Muslim societies by despotic regimes who exclude them from the political arena. The position of the Islamists around this problematic as a result has become ambivalent, closer to one of suspicion and eclecticism than of rejection and total denunciation. It is exactly this ambivalence that is found in the attempts made by Rached Ghannouchi, the movement's principal theoretician, to include the democratic idiom. His book entitled *Les libertés publiques dans l'État islamique* [Public Freedoms in the Islamic State], published in 1993, indeed bears on this question. However, it was not so much about demonstrating Islam's compatibility with democracy as a concept imported from the West but about proving Islam's essentially democratic character and thus once more affirming the religious referent's autonomy from Western influence.

The Islamist Agenda in External Action: The Ambiguities of "Moderate Islamism"

On taking power following the elections to the National Constituent Assembly in October 2011, the Islamist party stood out for its ability for electoral mobilization unequaled in Tunisian politics and relatively unexpected in view of its weakening during the opposition years. Two factors were decisive in its electoral victory. First, Ennahdha's financial resources allowed it to better cover the Tunisian space. In fact, many Tunisian and foreign politicians suspected the existence of funding by foreign interests, particularly from Qatar. The second factor is its marshaling of the Islamity meme during the electoral campaign, which had added value compared to competing groups.

Governing as part of a coalition, Ennahdha was set on obtaining the foreign affairs portfolio, which was given to Rafik Ben Abdesselem, the son-in-law of Rached Ghanouchi, the movement's president and longtime leader. Despite numerous challenges raised that questioned the MFA's competence, his family ties to R. Ghannouchi, and the Sheraton-gate affair,[15] R. Ben

Abdesselem remained in office until the head of the government, Hamadi Jebali, stepped down in March 2013.

The Ennahdha party's hold on foreign policy resulted in the appearance of a partisan diplomacy taking the place of state diplomacy, the majority of councilors in the Ministry of Foreign Affairs being Ennahdha militants rather than career diplomats. Moreover, during official visits abroad, the minister relied on his network of personal acqaintances and relations of the party in the Gulf countries rather than the posted Tunisian diplomatic personnel. This foreign policy monopoly by the party gives meaning to the approach taken in this chapter of investigating the militant past and the movement's history for interpretive keys to help understand the directions of Tunisian diplomacy under the Ennahdha Government.

The first evidence of rebranding of Ennahdha's anti-Western positions was manifest in the movement's official documents. In the section of Ennahdha's campaign platform of 365 points dedicated to diplomacy, there was no mention of the problem of deculturation. The article stipulating the need for Tunisia to emphasize its autonomy and sovereignty had nothing original to say. If we compare the movement's constituent platform dated June 6, 1981 to the revised statute immediately after the ninth Congress held from July 12–July 15, 2012, we note the omission of the term "Westernization"[16] and the total lack of reference to this issue:

> Contribute to asserting a foreign policy based on the country's sovereignty, unity, and independence vis-à-vis any power, to establishing international relations on the basis of mutual respect, cooperation, justice, equality and the right of peoples to decide for themselves and work to support weakened peoples and just causes and foremost among them the Palestinian cause.[17]

By comparison, the 1981 text clearly evokes Westernization and calls it into question:

> To promote the Islamic character of Tunisia so that it regains its role as the center of Islamic civilization in Africa and puts an end to the state of alienation and aberration. To renew Islamic thought in the light of Islam's origins and the exigencies of progress and its purification of the vestiges of decadent times and Westernizing influences.[18]

In practice, the Ennahdha foreign policy is, however, marked by a certain fickleness, for without being squarely hostile to the West, it also no longer subscribes to the Tunisian diplomatic tradition.

The signs of this break with tradition are everywhere. The first strong sign is the Anglicization and Arabization of all of the Ministry's dossiers. This break with the traditionally Francophone[19] and Francophile diplomacy corresponds to an expansion of Ennahdha's foreign policy with Middle Eastern countries. In this, it confirms an Arabo-Muslim grounding for the Tunisian state and its relative detachment from France and Francophony. Although this decision may be linked with the profile and course of the MFA that no longer masters the language of the former protective power, the linguistic rapprochement with the Arab countries at the expense of Francophony is symptomatic of the rejectionist attitude toward what is perceived as diplomatic and cultural interference.

The Minister of Foreign Affairs reproaches France for its intervention both in the affairs of his country and also in lesser-developed countries. He declares on the subject of the military intervention in Mali, "it is our view that the problems in Mali should be solved within Africa. We are opposed across the board to any foreign intervention," before retracting his statement the next day and praising this intervention as necessary. Also, following the declaration by Manuel Valls, the French Minister of the Interior, concerning the assassination of Chokri Belaid,[20] the French ambassador in Tunis would be called in by the head of the Tunisian Government. The Tunisian Minister of Foreign Affairs reacted as follows in explaining this summons: "The declarations of the French interior minister regarding Tunisia are cold-eyed, unfriendly, and harmful to the bilateral relations between the two countries." The version broadcast and publicly espousing of a summoning of the French amabassador, true or not, seemed to be addressed more to domestic public opinion as a way of showing[21] by this display of power that Tunisia had exited the state of servitude in relation to Western countries.

Ennahdha's reaction in this case in effect nourished a lively conflict with French policies. A pro-Ennahdha group demonstrated in front of the French embassy in Tunis, chanting the famous "get out" at the French ambassador. Accusing the French of interfering in Tunisia is evident among others in the attitudes of nahdhaouist militants and sympathizers. The accusations hurled at members of the Westernized, secular elite as "France's orphans" or "Francophone rejects" are revelatory of the association between "deculturation" and that country.

This makes it seem that Ennahdha's positions vis-à-vis the West are essentially focused on the former colonizer, which is perceived as embodying a Western culture imposed after independence. The MFA's reactions tend to confirm that Tunisia's sovereignty has to pass invariably through affirmations of its autonomy with regard to France. But beyond diplomatic discourse, the country remains Tunisia's primary trade partner, which implies a strong dependency even if setting aside all cultural aspects. Ennahdha thus finds itself in the awkward position between a geopolitical reality and a vision acquired by its militants in the course of their socialization and education in the movement, according to which the alienation of Tunisia from France under H. Bourguiba and Z. Ben Ali is the principal cause of its underdevelopment and decline.

Not seeing the same attitude on Ennahdha's part toward the United States is explained by the subtle differences in European and American positions toward the Islamists. From the movement's accession to power, it was regarded as a partner by the Americans on the express condition that it should demonstrate the compatibility between Islam and democracy. American diplomacy showed itself also less nervous than Europe with regard to the Islamists. The latter was anxious to be reassured before implementing cooperative projects that remained in suspense until the impending elections and final drafting of the constitution.[22] None of the partnership promises made at Deauville were concretized while the implementation of bilateral cooperation continued by habit despite the problem of respect for human rights under Z. Ben Ali. The United States, on the other hand, continued to support the government even after the torching of their embassy on September 14, 2012.

The second indication of a break was the intensification of bilateral relations with the Gulf countries and principally with Qatar compared to what they were before the revolution of January 14. The final declaration of the first interministerial meeting of the Friends of the Syrian People at Doha was even finalized by the MFA. Diplomatic relations with these countries were not as developed before the revolution because of the editorial criticism leveled by the *al-Jazira* network against the Ben Ali regime in Tunisia.

This shift in Tunisia's diplomacy, Western-oriented by tradition, translates the hold of the Ennahdha party on foreign relations into a model that is more nearly partisan action than state diplomacy. Although routinely denied by the movement, several accusations and documents attest to the provision of financial aid by Qatar to the movement antedating the revolution and during its electoral campaign for the October 2011 elections.[23] In addition, *al-Jazira* was the choice platform for the Ennahdha militants in exile, with the MFA having moreover overseen the research department in the TV network's research center.

In terms of policy in the neighboring region, the movement evinces a desire to revive the Maghreb Arab Union and to revitalize the Arab League but, with Qatar as the exception, foreign relations with the "Brothers" or "friends" of the region seem to lack coherence with respect to its ideology. Bilateral relations with Egypt and Libya, two countries that experienced popular revolutions and the fall of dictatorial regimes, have not evolved at all compared to what they once were. With Saudi Arabia there is not, properly speaking, any rapprochement despite a number of high-level visits nor an accord on extraditing Z. Ben Ali to Tunisia. Tensions even surfaced with the Algerian neighbor following unadroit declarations respecting this country that confirmed that the Arab spring ended up touching it also. Ennahdha was even accused by the National Liberation Front of having supported candidates from the Islamist current in the 2012 Algerian legislative elections.[24]

Concerning Iran, although it had incarnated victory over the West by its revolution as well as providing a source of inspiration for the nahdhaouian cadres during the 1980s, nothing much changed on the level of diplomatic relations. Ennahdha furnished a substitute model for the Iranian one that was more reassuring for the Western countries and as seen by Tunisian public opinion, which is one of moderate Islam or AKP-style Islamoconservatism. Indeed, during its election campaign, the movement ceaselessly cited the Turkish example as the successful embodiment of the match between Islam and democracy.

In addition, a rapprochement with this country, which is considered a solid partner along with Qatar, on the Syrian question is notable, while with Iran there is a fundamental point of divergence on this issue. Implicitly,

Ennahdha thus positions itself against Iranian interests and certain Shiite groups in the region that support the Bachard al-Assad regime.

In this connection, the decision to break diplomatic relations with Syria without consulting its neighbors constitutes an innovation in Tunisia's foreign policy, which has always followed a moderate line, particularly in the Middle East. Ennahdha's submission to Qatar seems to be at the bottom of this energetic and highly debatable posture with regard to Syria, making it the first state to break diplomatic relations with a member of the Arab League without prior consultations. The support for the "Syrian revolution" highlights the evident will to occupy a pioneering position in the Arabo-Muslim area and to promote a cascade of revolutions in the region that would let Islamist parties assume power. It is equally an opportunity for Ennahdha to mark the transition from a soft diplomacy to a foreign policy intended to be radical and based on the principles of "Muslim solidarity."

A landmark diplomatic action under the Ennahdha Government that seems to line up with its ideology and historical principles regarding foreign policy was the MFA's visit to the Gaza Strip at the head of a Tunisian delegation. This mission confirmed a specific attachment to the Arabo-Muslim identity and its support for the Palestinian cause. In fact, it was one of Ennahdha's foreign relations priorities. It was part of the movement's constitutive platform in 1981, of the revised by-laws after the ninth Congress in 1981 and it was repeated in the latest version of the preamble to the constitution dating from March 2013.

It was a first in the history of Tunisian diplomacy, which had always taken a prudent, moderate position on the Israeli–Palestinian conflict, that a minister of foreign affairs would go to Palestine during an armed conflict and show himself hostile to Israel. It nevertheless remains to specify that the delegations arriving in Gaza in a show of support for the Palestinian people would not have been able to access it without the prior authorization by the Israeli Government.

Despite this audacious *marketing* ploy, normalization of relations with Israel up to that point had not been officially condemned by Ennahdha. Attempts to write penalties into the constitution for normalization of relations with this country were headed for failure and the movement was forced to beat a retreat following European and American objections. In an interview granted to the American think tank Washington Institute for Near East Policy (WINEP) in November 2011, the movement's president was quizzed on the plan to include an article in the new Tunisian constitution criminalizing normalization with the Zionist entity. Rached Ghanouchi denied it, saying, "There is no reason to include an evolving political situation such as the Israeli–Arab countries crisis. The only country that should be named in the constitution is Tunisia." Additionally, he stated that it had only been mentioned in the Republican Accord of the High Instance of Yadh Ben Achour, in that way signaling its exteriority with regard to the movement.

The most striking element in examining specific aspects of the Tunisian Islamist movement in power is the absence of connecting threads, especially with its past. The passage from an oppositional (mobilizing) register to one of wielding power (pragmatism) makes its positions difficult to discern clearly.

Exit from Power and Exit from Political Islam: Which Consequences on Ennahdha Foreign Policy?

In 2014, Nidaa Tounes (Call for Tunisia) won the presidential and legislative elections of which Ennahdha was placed in a subaltern position with sixty-nine seats in the parliament compared with eighty-six for Nidaa Tounes (out of a total of 217 seats).[25] A coalition between Ennahdha and Nidaa was set up to avoid political instability due to the lack of a comfortable majority for Nidaa. Participating to the governmental coalition Ennahdha was granted one ministerial position (vocational training and employment) and three secretaries of state within the Habib Essid Government.

A second political crisis solved by the so called National Unity Government headed by the new chief of government Youssef Chahed increased the number of Ennahdha's ministerial positions within the Government. Ennahdha holds today three ministerial positions and three secretaries of State. Ennahda, however, remains sidelined from foreign policy. This ministerial post was assigned respectively to Taeib Baccouche (from Nidaa Tounes) and Khemais Jhinaoui (a career diplomat). The Minister of Foreign Affairs elaborates and implements the foreign policy of the Government in accordance with the guidelines and options defined by the Head of State.

Two questions come to mind with regard to this new configuration of power: the first one is to know whether Ennahda, as part of the governing coalition, continues to have an impact on the Tunisian foreign policy? The second concerns the consequences of the separation between political and religious activities on the movement's vision of the world and especially its relations to the West.

Regarding the first question, it should be noted that the Tunisian foreign policy has had some inflections in comparison with the Tunisian Diplomacy under Ennahdha's Government. The first difference concerns the Syrian issue. Ennahda and former President Moncef Marzouki positioned themselves in favor of the rebels, which led to the breaking of diplomatic ties with Damascus. This decision was qualified as a diplomatic error by the current Minister of Foreign Affairs Khemais Jhinaoui and a consular mission opened in Damascus pending full resumption of diplomatic relations with Syria. Intended to be neutral, the Tunisian position remains vague on the issue, since the resumption of relations with Damascus is conditioned by the establishment of a political solution to the Syrian crisis according to a statement from the Minister.[26]

Besides, Saudi Arabia, which has seen its influence diminish in favor of Qatar during the government of the Troika, is now rehabilitated by the Tunisian foreign policy. The rapprochement with the Saudis in particular is visible through the proliferation of high-level visits between the two countries and a kind of confused alignment with the Saudi position. The positioning of Tunisia in favor of Saudi Arabia following the severance of diplomatic relations with Iran in January 2016 is indicative of this rapprochement. The Ministry of Foreign Affairs had indeed published a press release dated January 3, 2016 in which he "calls for the need to ensure the protection of diplomatic and consular missions, while preserving their sovereignty against these attacks." More recently, the Minister of Religious Affairs who declared that Wahhabism is the source of terrorism was dismissed for "non-respect of government's imperatives and his statements that conflict with the principles of the Tunisian diplomacy."

The other remarkable element in the same vein concerns the classification of Hezbollah as a terrorist organization at the meeting of the Council of Arab Ministers of the Interior on March 2, 2016 in Tunis. Tunisia, through its Interior Minister Hedi Mahjoub, accepted the declaration of the Council—a position that was immediately rectified by the Minister of Foreign Affairs who issued a press release stating that it is not a binding decision. Even if Rached Ghanouchi is openly opposed to Hezbollah,[27] the displayed and assumed contradiction between two sovereign ministries, the Ministry of Foreign Affairs and the Ministry of Interior, is less a sign of the influence of the latter in the foreign policy than a strategy that aims to please Riyadh in order to attract Saudi investments in Tunisia, while mitigating the consequences of such a decision: alleviate the anger of national public opinion and not offend the countries of the region.

Regarding the second question, namely the decision of the movement after his tenth Congress[28] to separate political action from *daʿwa*, it should be noted that it is more a question of specialization than strict separation to the extent that the members of the movement have to specialize either in preaching or in political action. Yet, the consequences of such a decision are far from being negligible on the movements' vision of the international system and more precisely its relations to the West.

The reading that was made of this decision can be divided into two trends: on the one hand, those for whom this is an important advance of Tunisian political Islam toward democratization and secularization and, on the other, those who see a double discourse intended to deceive public opinion and political actors at national and international levels, in other words a kind of *Taqiyya* toward the West. In my view, this shift should be interpreted taking into account the specificities of militant trajectories within the movement without excluding the strictly pragmatic dimension.

Ennahda, since its very beginning, had for its main feature the existence of an initiation phase that is central in the recruitment process—a phase in which religiosity is a central motivation of membership and a major dimension of the identity of the neophyte. It is during this phase that occurs in fact the ideologization process of Islam.

Some would argue that this religious dimension initially aiming at the establishment of the *sharia* and of an Islamic State cannot be evacuated overnight. But the very logic of militant careers within the movement shows that religious motivations behind the entry into militancy are gradually giving way to secular motivations, following "a desecration process." This desecration occurs under the effect of the initiation process itself, which, at the contrary of Sufi initiation, is based on the development of the militant's Ego and contributes to the replacement of extra-worldly retribution (the search for extra-worldly salvation and the satisfaction derived from fulfilling the function of khilafa—lieutenance—the Creator) by material and symbolic rewards of activism. The different frames of interactions in which the militants evolve after the novitiate period—militancy within the university and the confrontation with the Left, prison, exile and finally, the exercise of power—are all experiences that accelerate, although to different degrees, the secularization process and adaptation of the movement to the political environment.

However, this desecration does not concern all the militants in the same way, taking into account their differentiated dispositions and social and militant trajectories. This is not strictly speaking a confrontation within the movement between militants from the outside seen as "more open" and those more radical from the inside in which the first would have taken over. The opposition is much more complex since it is related to: 1) the militants' dispositions that determine, since the initiation phase, the specialization into activism by preaching or activism through political action, and 2) activist's social experiences, including experiences of excellence during their militant careers (revolutionary for some, intellectual or religious for others) that contribute in the desecration of Islamist militancy. The layout of the movement to compromise and therefore moderation is then less the result of the dominance of outside moderates within Ennahda, than the consequence of its operating logic.

The so-called separation, unless it is mere political tactic, is not completely devoid of strategic considerations at different levels: internally and internationally.

Internally, this action seeks to protect Ennahdha from the revolt of its members who are still committed to preaching activity and to the original project, namely the Islamization of society. Besides, while maintaining its presence in the social and religious fields, the movement protects itself from accusations of instrumentalization of Islam for election purposes, since outsourcing these "services" to groups from the party and formed by members who are now somehow detached.

At the international level, and this is the question that specifically concerns us here, a general trend among Islamist movements in the Arab and Muslim region can be observed, which is the rejection of the term "Islamist" or "political Islam" in favor of a party with an Islamic background. This shift, done at the expense of ideological coherence of these movements, seeks to make Islam soluble in democracy and seems to be encouraged by Western Governmental and Non-Governmental Organizations. With this regard, the issue of terrorism makes registration as a political party with a religious reference beneficial for the movement, rather than an ideological party whose objective would ultimately be restoration of the *sharia* and the Islamic State. Tunisian Islamists, anxious not to be excluded from the circles of cooperation, have adopted the themes, and methods of training and debate promoted by international bodies.[29]

The parallel drawn with the AKP (Justice and Development Party), especially during election campaigns, was to convince the Tunisian electorate of the existence of a moderate Islamist model, able to evolve in a democratic, secular context and to achieve excellent results at the economic level. However, the comparison with the Christian Democrats since the release of political Islam shows Ennahda's will to blend into a model recognized and accepted by the West.

Under the troika government, Tunisia began to turn toward the East, thus affirming its Arabo-Muslim roots. However, this turnabout, although justified by these two unifying elements, was not without inconsistency. Qatar is at the forefront at the expense of countries that are closer ideologically, like Egypt with the Muslim Brotherhood in power, and despite the movement's organizational and ideological attachment to this other movement since its creation. Ennahdha's foreign policy also contains elements of its former posture toward the West marked by its attempts to assert equal-to-equal relations with this part of the world. The simultaneous media and strategic imperative of moderate Islam imposed a softening in the positions taken by the movement in this regard, even an abdication of its basic principles, such as normalization with Israel.

The interplay between domestic and foreign policy is not to be left out of explanations for this inconsistency. Are not shows of force toward France, however prudent, or the visit to Gaza, ways of proving to Tunisian public opinion that Tunisia's foreign policy under Ennahdha is rooted in unyielding values, namely autonomy where the West is concerned and attachment to the Arabo-Muslim identity?

Notes

1. Report of the Instance Supérieure Indépendante des Elections—ISIE, http://www.isie.tn/Ar/image.php?id=724, last accessed May 21, 2015.
2. Following the elections, the Ennahdha movement allied itself with two parties of the left: the Democratic Forum for Labor and Freedoms (DFLF) and the Congress for the Republic (CFR) in order to form the government. The ANC's presidency went to Mustapha Ben Jaafar, top leader of the DFLF and the presidency of the Republic to Moncef Marzouki, head of the CFR.
3. Constituent platform of the Movement of Islamic Tendency (Ennahdha's old name) in June 1980.
4. Maryam Ben Salem, *Le militantisme en contexte répressif. Cas du mouvement islamiste tunisien* [Militantism in a Repressive Context. The Case of the Tunisian Islamist Movement], PhD thesis in political science, under the direction of Daniel Gaxie, Université Paris 1 Panthéon Sorbonne, 2013.
5. As noted by Jean Séguy, it is difficult to demonstrate empirically that a value system dominates in a society, but also the absence of unanimity in this domain in societies, *a fortiori* in a period of transition, also makes this enterprise more difficult and therefore requires paying attention to a differentiated relationship to morality according to social classes or layers on the one hand and, on the other, to the changes in these relationships as a function of the groups frequented by the individual. Jean Séguy, "La socialisation aux valeurs utopiques" [Socialization in Utopian Values], *Archives des Sciences Sociales de la Religion*, 1980, Vol. 50, no. 1, p. 9, p. 16.
6. *Kaba'ir* is a major sin under Islam.
7. Interview conducted in 2009.
8. Designates followers of Salah Ben Youssef (1907–61), a member of the Destorian party, comrade in arms of Bourguiba, and Minister of Justice in the Chenik Government who opposed the policy of the Tunisian Republic's first president and was assassinated.
9. Interview conducted in 2007.
10. Interview conducted in 2012.
11. This reference to the Carthaginian Republic, a non-Arab and non-Muslim African power, is quite revealing about the territorial reading of the East–West conflict. It likewise denotes after all a basic knowledge of Phoenician history, Carthage, like Athens, being an aristocratic Republic.
12. According to a study by A. Hermassi, Baqir Essadr and Ali Chari'ati are high on

the list of Islamist most-read authors. Abdelbaki Hermassi, "La société tunisienne au miroir des islamistes" [Tunisian Society in the Islamist Mirror], *Monde arabe Maghreb-Machrek*, no. 103, 1984, 39–56.
13. Interview conducted in 2008.
14. Sadri Khiari, *Tunisie. Le délitement de la cité. Coercition, consentement, résistance* [Tunisia. Distintegration of the City. Coercion, Consent, Resistance], Paris, Karthala, 2003.
15. A Tunisian blogger Olfa Riahi exposed to the media an affair of misappropriated funds directly implicating the Minister of Foreign Affairs.
16. In Arabic, the term *taghrib* refers to the West *gharb* wholly in its allogene character.
17. Constituive rules of the movement after revision (ninth Congress):
18. بعث الشخصية الإسلامية لتونس حتى تستعيد مهمتها كقاعدة كبرى للحضارة الإسلامية بأفريقيا ووضع حد لحالة التبعية والاغتراب والضلال. تجديد الفكر الإسلامي على ضوء أصول الإسلام الثابتة ومقتضيات الحياة المتطورة و من تنقيته رواعصو سبر الانحطاط وآثار التغريب.البيان التأسيسي
لحركة الاتجاه الإسلامي (حركة 1981 -6 -6 لنهضة لاحقا) تونس في
19. The diplomatic correspondence of the Tunis Regency kept in the Tunisian National Archives (TNA), historical series, attests unequivocally the use of French as the language of diplomacy with foreign powers and Tunisia's own representatives abroad from the early nineteenth century on. Arabic, Ottoman Turkish, and Italian were also utilized.
20. Tunisisan politician, president of the Patriotic Democratic Movement WATAD (al-WATaniyyun al-Dimkratiyyun al-Muwahid), who was assassinated on February 6, 2013.
21. This version is questioned by a source in the Ministry of Foreign Affairs, which assures that it was meeting.
22. Source: Ministry of Foreign Affairs.
23. One accusation was leveled by the Syrian Minister of Foreign Affairs in a newspaper interview. Having met Rached Ghannouchi during a visit to the emir of Qatar, the Syrian minister asserted that the latter is supposed to have ordered disbursement of USD 150 million for supporting the Ennahdha party in its campaign for the October 23, 2011 elections.
24. Anouar Chennoufi, "Ennahdha réfute les accusations du porte-parole du parti algérien le Front de Libération Nationale (FLN)," Tunivisions, May 12, 2012, https://www.turess.com/fr/tunivisions/34660, last accessed October 9, 2016.

25. Today, Ennahdha and Nidaa have equal number of seats within the parliament (sixty-nine) given the crisis within Nidaa that led to the resignation of seventeen of its deputies.
26. Interview granted by the Minister to the Egyptian newspaper *al Ahram* on September 11, 2016.
27. In an interview with TRT Arabic, R. Ghannouchi condemned "Hezbollah's commitment to the counterrevolutionary forces in Syria and Yemen and its contribution to the destruction of the country" and stated that Ennahdha cannot be at his side given the fact that Hezbollah "has blood on his hands."
28. The congress was held in Hammamet on May 21–22, 2016.
29. Seif Soudani, "Discrète visite de Rached Ghannouchi aux États-Unis: décryptage d'une réconciliation," *Le courrier de l'Atlas*, December 7, 2011, http://www.lecourrierdelatlas.com/1396071220011Discrete-visite-de-Rached-Ghannouchi-aux-Etats-Unis-decryptage-d-une-reconciliation.html, last accessed October 12, 2016.

4

The Foreign Policy of the Egyptian Muslim Brotherhood

Tewfik Aclimandos

Foreword: Looking Back to This Study

This author stopped studying the Brotherhood by the end of 2013, for many reasons, some personal, and others related to the Egyptian situation and to work ethics—Muslim Brothers are jailed and they cannot defend their cause. This author's dislike for their ideology and their way of doing things does not prevent him from being respectful to the men, their commitment to their cause and their sacrifices.

Studying the Brotherhood tests the limits of "neutral axiology." Studying this movement raises hard questions, regarding religion, the nation state, ethics, politics, polity, security, lies and truth in politics, democracy, revolution, the relation between religion and law, the relation between religion and ideology, the relation between religion and polity, the relation with the "other," and how you study this "other." Do we have a universal political science's idiom enabling us to use the same concepts for describing widely different worlds? To claim being neutral toward these issues is lying. Defining the right distance between the movement and the researcher is impossible; managing the actual distance between them is delicate.

Our "sources" are widely different: interviews with top, middle-ranking, and modest militants; doctrinal books written by top and middle-ranking

Muslim Brothers; testimonies of former members, of dissidents, and/or of militants who disapprove of the "official line"; testimonies of their Egyptian foes who had to work with them: these foes can be secular actors, security officials, or simple people; testimonies of their "public"; and anthropological, sociological, and historical studies.

It should be clear that this is a clandestine organization, with a solid and deep-rooted "culture of clandestinity." This does not mean that it has never tried "openness"; it means that it is not organized for a "natural" relation with the "other." This culture precedes Egypt's authoritarian turn: al Banna, the great founder, the "imam," praised secrecy. He had a grand design (the caliphate and the conquest of the world), and thought that evil forces (Crusaders, international Jewry, free masonry) would do their utmost to counter it: so it had to adopt the organizational structure and way of doing things of masonry, as he imagined it. The Brotherhood would be a masonry "for the good."

Saying this means that this author considers the ideology to be relevant, to be much more relevant than thought by other colleagues and scholars. It structures the shared worldview. Of course, not all the Brothers have the same understanding of "Islam," of "takfir" issues. They disagree on democracy, on the tools to seize power, on jihad and violence. In the Brotherhood you have many different profiles. Some are more "Salafis" than the Salafis, others are simply conservative, others are liberals. Many prominent leaders consider the martyr Qutb (the main ideologue) to have developed a very dangerous worldview and to be very weak on theological issues. But even those who do not like him feel compelled to pay tribute to him, and this is significant: they will tell you that Qutb has not been properly understood; they will tell you that he does not say what he seems to be saying; they will say the last writings should not lead us to forget the previous ones; they will say his interpretation of Quran is not the work of a ulema, but remains important; and so forth. All this is true. But it underestimates the widely shared common assumptions. All the known Muslim Brothers agree to say that a Muslim society that tolerates alcohol, that does not execute the hudud (penal corporal sanctions), and that accepts the "mingling" between women and men is not really Muslim. All of them want the restoration of an imperial caliphate and the conquest (not necessarily violent) of the world. Observers who forget the powerful appeal of this goal miss the crucial point. This means that I am convinced that the "post-Islamism" paradigm, which assumes that the great narratives are dead, is most inappropriate for analyzing the Muslim Brotherhood. I do not say that post-Islamism does not exist and is an illusion. I am saying the leadership and the great majority of the membership is not post-Islamist. To claim the contrary or to think that this is a normal evolution of the movement is a huge mistake.

This leads us to specify what pragmatism is. Pragmatism means that the leadership understands that this goal cannot be reached for now. It also means many Brothers understand that societies may not be ready for now for their kind of medicine and a gradual approach is needed. It may mean a flexible approach regarding the means and the allies: for instance, the leaders understand (albeit for the wrong reasons, their fantasies about International Jewry ruling the word) that they need to placate the USA and Israel friends in Washington. Recognizing the peace treaty is not too high a price for seizing control of Egypt and other countries.

I evoked "known Muslim Brothers." We should never forget that this is a clandestine organization. Nobody has relevant and reliable data regarding the membership. Even former insiders disagree: Khalil al Anna told me, many years ago, the Brotherhood did not accept Salafists. The late Husam Tammam, Farid Abdul Khaliq and Ahmad Raif, strongly disagreed. Tammam claimed the Brotherhood, once an urban movement, became—during the Mubarak years—a rural one, with an increased hostility to Egypt's culture, produced by cities and urban people. Sure, the last years proved Cairo was irremediably hostile to the Brotherhood. But what about other cities, and most notably Alexandria?

Other experts try to draw distinctions between different generations: some would say the fracture opposes two generations, others evoke three different generations and others four. All those experts concur to demonize the oldest to which I do not agree, but few seem to consider the very real fact that none of the generations is homogeneous, or willing to admit that we simply do not have reliable data.

Some would say the Brotherhood imposes a strict discipline. Others tell us this is an illusion: the leadership never had the means to impose this. Others tell us everybody has the right to express his views, but also has to shut up when a decision is adopted. Some insiders tell us "discipline is necessary when people has different views. The great majority of the militants trust the leadership and is more homogeneous than we think." A journalist who knows the movement says we should not underestimate the fact that most of the members, including some of the top guys, are not really interested in politics. They are religious people and tend to trust those (Khayrat al Shatir) who decide.

A lot of analysts, including some pro-Islamists like Khalil al Anani, say the collapse, the failure of the Morsi presidency is to be explained by the lack of a serious agenda, the bad shape of the organization, aging and slowing and sheer incompetence. This diagnosis needs some comment: first, the Muslim Brothers had an agenda and a plan. It was simple: to seize power, exploiting the divisions and the incompetence of their foes, and the army's dependency (so they thought) on Washington's help. They simply misread the Egyptian electoral map, misunderstood the nature of clientelism (a relation grounded on mutual interest, not on ideological affinities) and did not see how deeply the Egyptian youth rebelled against all kinds of authorities, including religious authorities, and how much other Egyptians were keen on protecting their private liberties, and were committed nationalists, not interested in the kind of transnational allegiance they advocated for.

The bad shape of the organization is a polysemic claim: it can mean this organization is not working. The strongest argument for this is "despite the warning of the young militants, the leadership did not see the coming storm," but it is clear that this is not related to the existing internal channels. Instead, it was a clash of analyses. It meant that the movement no longer had the means of imposing discipline: militants were disaffected, disobedient, did not believe their leaders, had multiple allegiances (for instance, a Muslim Brother judge was first a judge and second a Muslim Brother, not the other way round). It is clear we can find evidence for such claims and evidence that disproves these claims. While admitting that I do not have scientific means to prove my claim, I do not buy this argument. We simply do not know. It may mean that the Muslim Brothers were divided on many issues and that different cliques competed for influence (Morsi, at some point, tried to emancipate himself from al Shater, but failed): this is true but not really relevant. They had a shared interest in governing Egypt. Last but not least, it may mean that the strongman al Shatir behaved as if the Brotherhood was a Leninist organization, while it was merely "Brezhnevian": too bureaucratic, too plural, paying tribute to ideology without seriously believing in it or, to be more accurate, without behaving as committed believers. There is a grain of truth in this, of course, but once again we do not have enough data to know.

The argument that "they are stupid and incompetent" is very popular in Egypt. For instance, many Leftist militants who fought the Brothers for the controls of syndicates and labour unions told this writer: "I (have) never met a competent Muslim Brother. We can meet competent Salafists who are good engineers and militants, (but) there are no competent Muslim Brothers." They were unable to explain this and tended to say: anyhow, being a Brother guarantees you clients and incomes, so there is no need to improve and to learn. I do not know. I have problems with this assessment. Suffice to say, incompetence, if real, does not explain the demise. Ideological lenses or blindness is a safer bet. Incompetence may also mean "lack of competent staff on some issues": for instance, they do not have serious economists. But this claim is not convincing: so many conservative people (having a problem with the so called "July's State") were willing to work for them. The Brotherhood simply did not co-op them. Some explained this by the need to reward members of the Brotherhood, others by a deep rooted paranoia against all those who were not members of the movement. Some, including many allies, say the problem was not with the Brotherhood, but with President Morsi. Choosing him as the presidential candidate was a huge mistake. This tends to forget that the real center of decision was not the presidency, but the Guidance bureau, and, more accurately, the strongmanship of Khayrat al Shatir. Last but not least, we are told the "deep state's" hostility paralyzed them and ultimately destroyed them. At the time of writing (February 2017), some in the Deep State claim that "letting them win the presidency was a clever trap aimed at discrediting them." But this claim is implausible. Of course, the Brotherhood had "foes" in the Deep State, but they also had allies. They were unable to capitalize on their resources and quickly antagonized every significant actor, including the Salafists and their allies.

Before the conclusion of this foreword, I present a quick allusion to the "democratic transition" and the "conversion to democracy" paradigms. I never believed in this. The smartest argument went like this: "the Muslim

Brothers have renounced the violence, but they still want power, so they are compelled to seek this though elections; they don't believe in democracy but they will have to adapt to it and progressively they will adopt democratic values." It is clear that this is too deterministic and I have written some long pages regarding the naivity of these experts who assumed that the Brothers were lying. I should point to Leslie Piquemal's work as her views are more nuanced. Many Brothers vaguely understand democracy as a nice thing, providing many resources to their movement, starting with protection and freedom to speak.[1] However, they either do not accept some basic assumptions of democracy (such as equality for all citizens, the right to free speech, and sovereignty of the people), or they think they can convince a majority to renounce to this, or that they do not really understand how this is working. Anyhow, the main consequence of their approach to democracy is a very liberal use of the main concepts, which lose any meaning. Equality means equality and inequality, civil state means non-military, and does not prevent ulemas from having a veto power on legislation. Rightly or wrongly, their discourse antagonized everybody else.

Introduction

The "Arab spring" radically transformed the regional scene. It also occurred at a time of American withdrawal. Each country was the theater of a struggle opposing different actors, most of them benefiting from external support. Different projects and alliances competed for the regional hegemony and for "the soul of the Arab spring": a Turkish/Qatari/Muslim Brotherhood project, relying on a "strategical alliance" between Erdogan's Turkey and Egypt's Morsi, funded by Qatar, a conservative project carried by the Emirates, Abdullah's Saudi Arabia, Kuwait, the Egyptian Army, Mubarak's supporters and many factions in the Deep Egyptian State, and some democratic forces, some of them funded by the Emirates. Last but not least, Iran had its clients, many of them shiites, and its own projects.

Of course, we should analyse the event with more nuance. For instance, King Salman of Saudi Arabia does not share the Emirates' and his brother's hostility to the Brotherhood. He can use them as long as they accept a second seat. The Egyptian army was not a permanent member of the "conservative alliance": it decided in 2011/12 that Egypt's stabilization needed to let the

Brotherhood seize power, and I have many serious reasons to believe this would have been an ideal solution for them, if the Brotherhood accepted to rein in its transnational approach (preferring the Brotherhood's interest in each country to Egypt's, as defined by the state and public opinion) and to lower the intensity of confrontation on the Egyptian internal scene: in each alliance you can find occasional or structural tensions. But this is the broad picture, and it is clear Egypt was the main battle ground. Billions of dollars were spent to fund political actors and to win the battle.

How to Read the Brotherhood?

For two years and a half, the Brotherhood, the oldest Islamist group on Earth, was the main political actor on Egypt's scene. For a year and a half (December 2011—June 2013), it controlled the legislative branch. For a year (July 2012—June 2013) it controlled also the executive and wielded power. Certainly, the fact of knowing (but did they know?) that the army, the security organs, and large parts of the bureaucracy were very suspicious from the start and increasingly hostile thereafter perhaps slowed them down in their options (or perhaps not), but it did not fundamentally change the situation.[2]

The constitution that they had promulgated was Islamist-inspired: little does it matter to know that it went further than they wanted, in order to appease the Salafis, or not as far in paying heed to the middle classes of the large Egyptian cities and the Western capitals as they may have wished—the text is there, in eloquent response to all those who bet on a conversion of this group to democracy.[3]

Everything becomes "up for grabs" when studying this group. It is secretive, clandestine. Even in power, it has failed to regularize its still illegal status. Even inside it, very little information circulates, and there are various degrees of[4] initiation.[5] The most visible representatives of the Brotherhood are not those who wield the real power.[6] For better or worse, they do not partake in the same options as those at the top. The oral discourses that this force produces are insanely contradictory. The Brother cadres do not say the same thing—each with his own version that changes from one sentence to the next, from one contact to the next.[7] The promises the Brotherhood makes to its contacts are just as irreconcilable and the political actors that have dealt with them, from Saudi Arabia to various Communist groups, and on to the

Egyptian presidents, the Salafis, the liberals, the nationalists, the jihadist all claim that the Brotherhood consistently lies and, worse yet, never honors its commitments. There is room to believe that relating this way to the truth, to the lie, and to other protagonists is deliberate, assumed *by the top and the executive authorities*. I am personally firmly convinced of it.

All our sources of knowledge are more or less tenuous.

A) First, available to us are statements, confidential talks, explanations by the cadres, leading or not, of the Brotherhood. But it is impossible to do anything whatsoever starting from this corpus. Or, rather, it makes possible all sorts of contradictory explanations, none of which are capable of taking into account or putting in order the totality of what has been said (and this even if taking into account the context in which they were made).

B) Next, we can study the programs it has proposed to the voters at various points. But, as Leslie Piquemal suggested in her thesis,[8] their propositions are too vague, ambivalent, and contradictory, which opens them to various interpretations: it may be, as he asserts, that the principal actors use concepts borrowed from other "enclosures" and from other discursive systems whose meaning they fail to truly understand. They could just be lying. It could be they target so many different audiences that everything clashes, that the message no longer makes any sense, if one excepts this very simple one that says: when the society and the state become Islamized, all problems will be solved.

C) We can focus on their doctrinal texts, on the material they make their militants read, and their cadres during different stages of their initiation. Most of my colleagues[9] think that the "great narrative" has unraveled and that no one on the inside really believes in it any more. They base this contention on the great pragmatism that (according to them) the leadership exhibits, based on the fact that the Brotherhood for ages has not put out elaborate or constructed ideologies; that the Qutbism,[10] which is at the core of the Brothers' teaching is too revolutionary for the conservative provincial middle classes that are their recruiting focus in which we find those in command of the Brotherhood; or within the great plurality of the militants that are very different from one another; or in the fact that the discourse produced by the cadres and the executives are "potpourris," mixtures of little consistency, borrowed from different schools, postures, and Islamic paradigms.[11] None of these arguments seem decisive to me, but I am alone on that point. For me, pragmatism and adaptive capacity are not incompatible with dogmatism. The Brotherhood knows how to appear gradualist and patient, but it has never made a compromise that entailed a definite renunciation of (a significant part of) its "grand design." The blinders and ideological biases that organize its readings of what is real are there. One can even wonder if it will show itself capable of alternating the cycles of confrontation/détente (Islamism of war/New Economic Policy))[12]. Its first passage in power pleads for a negative response. But then, we only destroy what we replace. This is not because the Brotherhood understands that the moment is not propitious for reestablishing the jizya over the non-Muslims, that it is not necessarily led to discover virtues in the idea of citizenship. Another argument advanced by supporters is that no one in the Guidance Office is well acquainted with the thought of Qutb or produces texts that are clearly Qutbian. Admittedly, this is still not proven when it comes to the current Supreme Guide.[13] But was Brezhnev well informed on Marx? Unique to an ideology that structures the identity of an organization, that furnishes it the elements of its language, is that it is reducible to some simple, even simplistic, maxims, that explain reality, describe the totality, determine who are the friends and enemies (or, rather, in this case, the enemies and the useful idiots). Beyond their real divergences, all the Brothers we know more or less believe that a society or a power that does not mete out penalties of corporal punishment, does not prohibit alcohol and adultery, and in which women are liberated is not a "truly, completely" Islamic society or state.[14] They all think that it is enough for a power and society to be Islamic for all problems to be solved or to be ready to be solved. They all think that the Califate must be reestablished and that it is the route toward reestablishing Islam's political superiority and its global magistery. All, in addition, believe that, at minimum, all sorts of evil forces will collude to abort this grand design. Finally, I do not believe it necessary that everyone believes in all the credos of Qutbism, either in its simple or complex versions. It suffices that they recognize themselves "globally" in them and they accept them as a guide for action. In the end, I do not believe that the very great diversity to be observed among the cadres is reflected at the top. I do not underestimate the extent of the divergences, whether they oppose the cadres with identical or opposed sensitivities.[15] But the perspective of achieving the great design, the certainty (well-founded, seeing the Brotherhood's actions since Mursī assumed the presidency) of ending up in prison if power is lost assure of a certain cohesion.[16]

D) We can fall back on affirmations, discourse, and testimony by their adversaries, dissidents, security services, competing or even hostile political forces, whether Islamist or not, businesspeople, and so forth. Not all the accusations that they make are justified, but some diagnoses formulated before they took power and shared by all their Egyptian competitors, adversaries, and enemies seem to have been validated by observation[17]: a Brotherhood that almost never respects its commitments, whose members are past masters in the art of talking to lie, of saying nothing. It is a Brotherhood that does not count among its numbers many well-qualified ulemas and even fewer intellectuals. It practices a sectarian socialization, relates to its environment with suspicion and even hostility, enforces a highly constraining iron discipline that obscures somewhat the diversity of opinions and postures,[18] and, finally, it maintains a relationship to violence that does not shrink from it; far from it—during the two years it was in power it could be established with certainty that the Brothers had formed militias and did not hesitate to use them.[19] Their coming to power and the policy they tried to implement confirmed the worst suspicions. In order to discredit them, the Brotherhood exploited the similarity of accusations launched against it by these diverse sources and the excesses of some, claiming that they were all the work of the same hidden and hostile power (the security services, international Zionism, seculars, and who knows what else) or stemmed from a thinly disguised racist passion: Islamophobia.

E) Observing it in action—but clearly, all sorts of questions pose themselves about how representative the level considered is and about the respective importance of this or that aspect, and so forth. It especially poses the question about the "structural" part and that of contingency or of "agency": there is indeed something troubling in the following, dual observation: i) many huge errors seem due to chance and the observer cannot keep from thinking that they could have been avoided; and ii) on the other hand, the Brotherhood always makes decisions that are conducive to the most hostile interpretations of its behavior, as if it is organizationally structured for the worst.[20]

In view of the importance of ideological bias on the part of some or the other, and that all the facts are challenged by one actor or another, and given the extreme rarity of information about certain dossiers, or its profusion in excess about others, researchers have to fall back on formulating hypothetical-deductive theories and on accepting tested prediction and experience. But the problems are numerous: When, for example, I maintain that those who bet on the Brotherhood blowing up have, until now, been consistently wrong, I have to qualify it by saying that it should not be assumed that I will always be right. When I assert that the Brotherhood has never truly converted to democracy, and that many obstacles seem insurmountable, I cannot be sure that the exercise of power or wandering in the desert will not motivate it to nuance its views in the near term—even if I do not really believe it. The facts have sometimes gone against me—for example, when the Brotherhood gave the necessary guarantees to Israel.[21] The impact of "context," of "the past," or yet ideology on how the great orientations are determined can be debated ad infinitum. I nevertheless think that, for now, my own hypothetical-deductive model is rather confirmed by recent developments: Here we have a dual organization, at once mass movement and apparatus patterned on Leninism, conveying an ideology that must be classified as extreme right and not center, that is still effective even if it is somewhat diminished, that functions on a sectarian socialization model, maintains a hostile relationship with the environment and arouses equally intense hostile reactions, and that selects and appoints leaders based on criteria that favor the most extreme.

Bets Made by the American Government and Some Researchers

From Cairo it is quite difficult to know what is going on in Washington. Nevertheless, it can be told that the Obama administration had—very quickly—opened channels with the Muslim Brothers. A lot of "noises" were heard in 2009 and 2010. Muslim Brothers and members of Hamas started behaving as if they had American insurances. Sure, this should not be considered as a plot. The American administration's message, conveyed through emissaries, was: "we have nothing against you, we are not your enemy, and we do not have objections against your seizure of power if you give us the proper insurances." An American official told an Egyptian diplomat "the Muslim Brothers will surely govern Egypt at some point and we engaged them; they guaranteed us they would abide by the Peace Treaty Agreement." Almost all Egyptian actors interpreted this as a "green light" and maybe more. In light of actual evidence, this seems to be be a strong exaggeration.

After Mubarak's fall, and after some hesitations, it seems the Obama administration decided the Muslim Brothers were the most powerful and the most reliable Egyptian partner. They won elections, they gave the proper guarantees. Moreover, Ambassador Patterson did not hide her dislike of secular actors; she considered them to be lightweight and not serious. The American administration, while divided on the soundness of this assessment, decided that it should give the Brothers a chance and support them.

This strategic decision (fitting into a broader perspective of disengagement from the region) relies on analyses that, at best, are based on some risky bets. Some do not directly concern me here while others do.

The first bets were on the Brotherhood's converting to democracy and that it represents the strongest moderate Islamic force. Both assertions are wrong—moderate, democratic, quietiest or non-violent Islamisms do exist, but the Brotherhood is not one of them, as all of its actions since July 2012 show. At most, it recognizes (or pretends to recognize) that the holder of executive power should be elected by universal suffrage. This recognition cannot obscure the fact that the Brothers, together with Mubarak's former party, are the side that commits the most election fraud. Legislative and judiciary power must be rigorously limited, surveilled, and intimidated. The acts of the former must be subject to control by a body of ulemas. Civil liberties also are tightly restricted, the medias harassed in all kinds of ways, and extra-governmental violence frequently resorted to. The government of laws was destroyed by a cascade of decisions made by President Morsi, culminating in the constitutional decree of November 21, 2012 and by some deeply disturbing articles in the new constitution. But all this is of no concern here.

When optimists are forced to admit that such subscribtion to the rules of democracy is not genuine, they wager on historical necessity, on cunning reason. As far as they are concerned, whether the Brotherhood wants to or not, it will end up admitting that it cannot succeed in its passage in power unless it draws its inspiration from the Turkish AKP. Cooperation between the two forces was closer and closer. Various militant Brothers go through stages of training in Turkey and familiarize themselves with techniques of political communications, management, elections monitoring, exchanging views with their Turkish counterparts, and so forth. A strategic partnership between the two countries has been contemplated and at a point seemed promising. But claims of cooperation or even alliance do not equate necessarily to similarity of paths. No need to recall here that the AKP's recent evolution is troubling in several respects. Today nobody thinks President Erdogan is a committed democrat. Let us rather underline that the Turkish and Egyptian contexts are far from being the same—recall the importance and historic depth of Atatürk's legacy, the relationships maintained by the AKP with Sufism (which contrast with those entirely more strained ones of the Brothers with Egyptian Sufisms), the religious makeup, or yet again the relationship to the respective nationalisms of the two countries. This last point is crucial—but before elaborating on it, let us remember that the Brothers, when they study a nearby experience for cues, favor that of the Sudanese Islamists.

A particularly dangerous commonplace holds the Muslim Brotherhood to be "nationalists" like the others, distinguished from them by a stronger attachment to cultural authenticity, to the defense of "identity." It is true that this platitude describes a number of elected Brothers and several militants. It is equally true that in certain, religiously more homogeneous countries the Brothers' ideology could be in the service of constructing a nation state. Finally, it is true that the definitions of nationalism vary greatly and that some would probably allow, provided they are relaxed, considering the Brothers as nationalists. But it behooves us to remind the irenics of an unpleasant reality: The Brotherhood's ideology carries within it a religious conflict as threatening as a storm cloud. Let an occupier not of the same religion dominate a homogeneous population and it is, or can be, a powerful vector of nationalism or of mobilization in a fight for national liberation, but in multi-confessional countries or even nations it instead endangers civil peace or nation building even if it takes part in the struggle for liberation. Of course, determining if the propagation of this ideology is a symptom or a cause can be debated, but this does not qualify the diagnosis. Precisely in Egypt's case, the Brothers have always maintained a very hostile relationship to the whole enterprise, all the processes of building/modernizing the state begun under Mehemet Ali, which they often describe as de-Islamizing the country, imposed by evil forces and their allies.

Anyhow, al Banna had harsh words for nationalism, which amounted to the worship of dust. More recently, Supreme Guide Mahdi Akif caused an uproar in an interview in which he said that he did not mind seeing Egypt governed by a Malaysian Muslim. During the Morsi presidency, many militants said they did not see why Egyptians considered the frontiers to be so sacred: Ceding some territories to other Muslims was no big deal. President Morsi may or may not have had such designs, as claimed by their opponents; the militants' discourse gave credential to this accusation.

In the same vein, invoking an eternal and prescriptive "identity" mainly functions to delegitimize Egypt's "great culture," a product of the 1920s and 1930s; it is perfunctorily dismissed as imported and corrupting. The quasi-automatic habit of the Brothers in describing their competitors or adversaries as enemies of Islam and their attitude toward the Copt community are also factors weakening the national cohesion (even if the Mūrsi Government during the first months managed some thorny issues rather well,[CH3N23][22] before a string of missteps or worse in 2013). In other words, betting on the Brothers to "stabilize" the countries in the region is to ask something of them that they cannot deliver—at the very least, their discourse inflames polarization.

Along these lines, several colleagues think that the Brotherhood has given up on utopia or on the great plan of reestablishing the Caliphate. This assertion seems to be a fantasy—as is the one, perhaps more nuanced, which says that, in fact, its conception of the Caliphate is closer to a league of Arab states or a European Union than the caliphate model that prevailed historically. The Supreme Guide's declarations prove the opposite—he has frequently asserted that the hour of reestablishing the Caliphate was nigh.[23] During Mūrsi's presidential campaign, a preacher close to the Brotherhood proclaimed the imminent reestablishment of the Califate with Jerusalem as its capital.[24] To dismiss these comments (and a multitude of others) by declaring that they were "designed for internal consumption" seems to me to be a bad move.

For one thing, demagoguery is not without consequences; for another, Cairo press circles had it that the worried Gulf capitals demanded clarifications and were not pleased with the response ("We are all one tribe")—with said Gulf capitals ending up asserting, proof in hand (in the case of the Emirates), that the Brotherhood decided to stir up trouble in Kuwait and the Emirates, either because it was trying to run a blackmail of "peace in return for aid" or because it wanted to take over an oil state so as to finance the grand design of a Caliphate. To put it another way, it was a remake, fifty years later, of the Arab cold war between Egypt and Saudi Arabia, revived under the Mūrsi presidency. The unprecedented scale of aid furnished by the Gulf countries in support of the uprising and the coalition that overthrew Mūrsi (in excess of 25 million dollars in seven months) illustrates the hate and loathing that the Brotherhood aroused in the oil states whose state- and/or nation-building is still fragile. Finally, while it is impossible to have a look at the whole of the Brotherhood's book production, never have I laid eyes on a text that would permit thinking that the restoration of a Caliphate on the historic model has stopped being an ultimate goal (however remote). That said, this grand design probably would not have been met with so much rejection by a highly Islamized opinion had it not been accompanied by what looked very much like an absolute contempt for borders as drawn. I do not know if the version by Egyptian intelligence asserting that the Brothers intended to sell off a part of the Sinai to benefit the Gaza emirate and render it viable can be believed. Let us say that Egyptian opinion believed it, that the reactions of many militant Brothers ("What's the problem?") were worrisome, and especially that it is likely that the Brotherhood Government proposes to return to Sudan the disputed Halayeb and Shalātīn ... which brought a swift reaction from the army.[25]

But the Brotherhood's regional agenda did not only have drawbacks for the Western capitals. The "Brothers" regime had an objective interest in keeping the peace with Israel. It was not immaterial to have seen an Islamist regime forced to reaffirm the Camp David accords, to deal with Israel, to present guarantees to it (such as during the crisis of November 2012), and especially to keep Hamas "on the leash." The latter, interested in weakening the successive Egyptian regimes, saw itself compelled to manage the (Muslim) "big Brother" and take into account its hopes and wishes. It did not want trouble on its Eastern flank. Of course, this acknowledgment did not mean that the Brotherhood's views on Israel or Palestine were subject to revision or updating. In the longer term, the goals always remained the same. The same applies to the risk inherent in any pan-Arab or pan-Islamist program: the "tawrīt" strategy—incite a conflict in the hope that its own protector would be forced to intervene—is a temptation felt by all of the region's small actors, state or non-state, and it is not certain that Hamas would have accepted bending to the counsels, hopes, and diktat of the Brothers *ad aeternam*.

Another very dangerous wager wants the Brotherhood, decreed as moderate, to be the natural, strategic ally of the West, desirous and capable of facing off against, neutralize or even be victorious against the decreed, most obscurantist version of political Islam, to wit Salafism, and against the "fundamentalist" Salafist, jihadist, takfiri, or other terrorism. Plenty of arguments are advanced, but the principal one relies on the following description of reality: a) here is a fraternal ideology that is *radically* different from Salafism and opposes it. Variation: the first one is draped in nothing but good qualities; the other had nothing but faults; b) the Brothers are capable of forcing the various Salafist movements to recenter themselves, for competition will force anyone toward the center; and c) when the time comes, the Brothers naturally will choose the liberal, nationalist, leftist "seculars" or the Western countries over the forces of darkness and the various terror threats. All this is inaccurate if not fantastical. To begin with, to avoid any misunderstanding, I will assert that the Brothers are radically different from al-Qaeda, and I do not confuse the two entities. This is not only a question of the degree of moderation or extremism. The Brothers are engaged in building a new order (which a destructive phase may precede) while al-Qaeda in my view seems to be profoundly nihilist. The following expositions mainly focus on other Islamist or Salafist groups.

While it is generally correct that the Brothers are more flexible and moderate than the Salafis, there are enough exceptions to resist the temptation of devising universal rules for this problem.[26] But that is not what is of the essence here. What is considerably underestimated is the Salafization of the Brothers. There are many Salafis in the Brothers' ranks, especially in the provinces (and it is in the countryside that the Brotherhood scored its best election returns). Frequently, the religious education of militant Brothers or militant candidates is "outsourced," that is, entrusted to the Salafis. Qutbism and Salafism are very different, but they are not incompatible. The former is a teleological view of history; the latter, a theology, is a reading of the Holy Text and the hadiths. It is possible to be Qutbist and Salafist at the same time (even if Qutb's commentary on the Koran contains numerous assertions that all amount to serious errors as far as the average Salafi is concerned). In other words, the Brotherhood is deeply shot through internally by Salafism and happens not to separate itself from it as sharply as researchers who advise the Obama administration like to think. In addition, to think that electoral competition necessarily and invariably propels everyone toward the center is contradicted by the facts. Among the Brothers exists a powerful current that explains the size of the Salafist result in the legislative election of November/January 2011 by a too considerable recentering by the Brothers and that thinks the Brotherhood must revise its policies, practices, discourse, and practices to define them as more to the right. The Brotherhood base is much more inclined to accept an alliance with the Salafis than with non-Islamists, perpetually described by the hierarchy, the preachers, and the Brotherhood press as satanic, impure, and immoral enemies of God. Along the same lines, their teaching centers on the obligation to jihad—even if the latter is defined in a manner that allows not just reducing it to armed struggle (defensive or not). A consequence of this expansion is an abusive use of warlike metaphors. Defining politics or elections as war has deeply corrupting, even destructive, effects. It is at times very difficult to distinguish some Brothers from jihadists and many a young Brother has gone to fight in Syria. Lastly, even conceding—which I do not—that the description of reality effected by said researchers is right (that the Brothers are quite distant from the Salafis and are the ideal "antidote" to this very real threat) this reasoning remains highly vulnerable to criticism: When the Brothers are in power, they are the ones who discredit themselves and not the Salafis. The failure of the Brotherhood in power risks attracting even more recruits to the Salafis or to the jihadists—not the reverse. But it gets worse. Would the Brothers really *want to* attack the Salafis or the jihadists? The question posed itself well before President Mūrsi opposed the French intervention in Mali (which surprised no one in Egypt). Indeed, one of the president's advisers had asserted in an interview with *al-Shorouk* that those among the jihadists who happened to be in Egypt preparing for jihad in Palestine or Syria were "irreproachable" (lā ghubār 'alayhum).[27] Worse, the chief of state freed several jihadist Salafis, some of which immediately rejoined the armed groups proliferating in the Sinai. It is not known if this was naiveté on the part of the Brotherhood, or if this decision was the fruit of Salafist or Jihadist pressures or a Machiavellian calculation by the Brothers. But the result speaks for itself.

The answer is complicated. For one thing, the effective plurality of these monistic, indeed exclusivist groups, contradicts the claim of one or the other to be the true representative of Islam and its unique banner bearer. They are thus considerable embarrassments to each other and serious competitors. On the other hand, this plurality can provide diverse resources when it comes to the division of labor or positioning relative to the non-Islamists. There are cogent reasons for thinking that there is coordination and a division of roles between the different Islamist actors and that the Brothers, who themselves sent their troops and militias against the non-Islamist demonstrators, or against certain opponents or the judiciary apparatus, were not upset to see the Salafis of M. Abū Ismā'il do the same "dirty work," even if it means half-heartedly condemning them (all the while supporting them; here, too, the double-talk is prodigious). It is nonetheless troubling to realize that *not a single attack has been carried out* against the natural gas pipelines since President Mūrsi assumed full command. Moreover, when some jihadists groups kidnapped Egyptian soldiers in Sinaï, in May 2013, President Mursi gave instructions to "protect the lives of the kidnappers and the kidnapped."[28].

Along the same lines, all observers of the Egyptian scene are in agreement in thinking that the presence of Salafis, whether they are organized or simply free electrons, lets the Brothers pass as "moderate" in the eyes of non-Islamists and Western capitals without having to make much of an effort. In any case, the leniency of the Brotherhood regime for those who literally incited to murder or who lit small or large fires, is difficult to explain any other way. In the same vein, the Brothers seem to have, at least with respect to the "battle for promulgating the constitution," opted for putting together a large

Islamist coalition gathering with a maximum number of actors. Although since then the al-Nour Salafist party has chosen to stand out by distancing itself from the Brotherhood, the Brothers are still very close to other Salafist groups, certain of which cannot pretend to be legalist or non-violent. In any case, we can say that past experience shows that the way that the Brothers managed groups situated to their right has always produced disasters despite their best efforts. Or, furthermore, that the Brothers give more attention and weight to local and regional Islamist actors than to Egyptian non-Islamist political forces.

So it happens that an Egyptian journalist who knows the Brotherhood very well told the author that it is not content to merely aid or coordinate with jihadist groups: It recruited specific militants in order to strengthen its own paramilitary arm.[29]

For a long time, I have been astonished by the indifference of the American administrations of the past dozen years to the collusions and connections between the Brothers and jihadists. But I believe I have hit upon an explanation, which, admittedly, is based on a bundle of assumptions. Recently, a Sudanese Islamist reminded me that the Sudanese intelligence services had offered to turn over Bin Laden to Washington or Riyad during the late 1990s. However, the Sudanese services (and the Sudanese *deep state*) are Brothers. This same Sudanese Islamist asserted that 9/11 could have been averted had the two capitals accepted the proposed transaction. This led me to ask myself if 9/11 had fostered the development of cooperation between the USA and the Brothers involving the exchange of information on jihadists and al-Qaeda, indeed more—all the experts are convinced by the fact that Brothers infiltrated all the political actors with which they dealt or that challenged their pretense of representing or embodying Islam. Did they transmit specific information to the United States? The question appears legitimate given American indulgence of the Mūrsi regime and the Islamist group.

It should be noted that the connections between jihadists and Brothers and the ongoing intensification of the former's presence in Egypt are the principal reasons for the reproaches formulated by the Egyptian security forces against the Brothers. It is not our task here to evaluate the various accusations and diverse episodes cited to buttress them. Some facts cited seem very plausible (but are not necessarily accurate), some comport with verifiable data, while others are more farfetched (but are not necessarily false). We are on ground where it pays to mistrust the plausible and not shut ourselves off to what seems beyond belief—in short, in a very different universe. I simply wish to add that at present we can ask ourselves in which direction the balance of power between the Brothers and their more radical allies will evolve: While the former have greater financial resources, they have fewer carrots than several months ago and more need of their partners.

Postface: With the benefit of hindsight, we can say this: The Muslim Brotherhood tried to build an internal coalition including the whole spectrum of Islamists, from the moderate ones (al wasat) to the more extremes, including the jihadists. This was both a preventive strategy (to neutralize jihadists and give them a stake to not cause harm) and an offensive one (use the other forces as a scarecrow, entrusting them for the dirty work; fix the army in Sinai). Even if President Mursi spoke to Ayman al Zawahiri as if the other was a superior, it is clear that the Brotherhood saw itself as the unquestionable leader of this coalition. It viewed its Islamists, Salafists, and jihadists partners as being a resource and a threat. Their approach was a mixture of policies aiming at using them, placating them, neutralizing them, and weakening them in the long run. The picture is further complicated by their ambivalence toward Egyptian Salafists: They considered them to be a tool in the hands of their opponents in the Deep State and in Saudi Arabia:[30] a dangerous one as it targeted the same public, and a useful one as the Salafists frightened everybody. Co-opting them to choke them seems to have been the motto.

It remains to briefly examine the hope, cherished by some in 2012 and 2013, of seeing the Egypt of the Brothers become part of the Sunni bloc destined to oppose Iran's hegemonic aspirations. This hope is nourished by the interest the Egyptian Muslim Brothers have in seeing the regime of Bashar al-Assad, the principal ally of Iran and Hezbollah, fall. And it is true that on this question, the Brotherhood's views and those of Teheran are irreconcilable. But keep in mind the extreme animosity that pits the Muslim Brothers against the Wahabite monarchy—the latter and its allies (the Emirates and Kuwait) are, at present, their principal enemies. We cannot be certain if the various conciliatory maneuvers with Iran that could be observed during the *first* months of the Mūrsi presidency[31] were a normalization for the purpose merely of reestablishing contact, a simple exchange of views and know-how, a sort of clumsy—and highly counterproductive—blackmail designed for the petro-monarchies, *including Qatar*,[32] or if it would translate into a major upheaval in Cairo's foreign policy orientation, given that the Brothers figured that there was nothing more to expect from the countries on the peninsula (Qatar excepted). The various interpretations all have their supporters. But the Salafis, including those in the Brotherhood, are deeply opposed to this rapprochement, and it is not certain that they would not have had the means of checking it by fulminating against a supposed Shiite threat or by organizing pogroms of some Egyptian Shiites. I tend to believe the Brothers tried to have it both ways: to collaborate with Iran or to confront it according to the needs and priorities. For instance, the Brothers needed Iranian tourists. Regarding the Syrian question, in August 2012 President Morsi angered al Riyad by inviting Teheran to participate in the discussions for a settlement. This initiative was explained by my colleague Omar Ashour: "can you figure a solution without Teheran, a very plausible answer". But later on the Brotherhood concluded that Assad had to be toppled by force, and this famous "Syria speech" (june 2013) is one of the factors that convinced many in the "Deep State" to topple him.[33] This shift, from the search of a "peaceful solution" to the military confrontation, was explained by the growing implication of Hizbollah and Iran in Syria, and by a gesture to the other Islamist Egyptian forces at the eve of a decisive confrontation with the secular forces in Egypt.

I conclude this section by a brief allusion to a "grand design" explained by Brother Isam al Aryan to a colleague—even if he denied saying such things later. The Brotherhood wanted to slowly disconnect Egypt from the West, by building a huge Islamic economic partnership with the most successful Islamic countries: Malaysia, Turkey, and Indonesia.

Deciders, Constraints and Options of Egyptian Foreign Policy

During the last decade of Mubarak's very long reign, the president made the big decisions and set the foreign policy directions. The head of the IGS (the mukhābarāts ʿama or Islamic Guidance Society) General Omar Soliman was his principal adviser and aide, and the "center" managed the principal foreign policy dossiers, those of the bordering countries (Sudan, Libya, Palestine, and Israel), the Nile riparian states, the United States, and important or problematic countries (Saudi Arabia, Iran, and Afghanistan). The head of the diplomatic service and the Minister of Foreign Affairs, of course, gave advice and took care of the remainder. Under the Mūrsi presidency, things were different. The consensus is that he was nothing but the representative of the Brotherhood in the presidency and that the key decisions were prepared and made "elsewhere." If there was any kind of revolution, it is that the chief of state's maneuvering room had shrunk considerably. But it still is worth knowing where to situate that "elsewhere." Researchers who were able to interview members of the Office of Guidance (here I am thinking especially of Patrick Haenni) learned the following: 80 percent to 90 percent of decisions were taken within it. But an insider I had a chance to talk with said something else: The "decider" is Khayrat al-Shātir, the Brotherhood's strongman, assisted by his own men and cadres from the Brotherhood's international organization working in the presidency. The "real entourage," the "real team" (as distinct from the advisers and aides who were appointed for cosmetic purposes in the communications operation) that surrounds (stifles) the president is composed of those men. The president's adviser for external affairs, Isām al-Haddād, an Egypto-British doctor, is one of them. He is the man for delicate missions, the Father Joseph, the real head of presidential diplomacy who reports to Khayrat al-Shātir. A former diplomat, in a fit of temper during a colloquium, went so far as to assert that the Minister of Foreign Affairs was useless and was no longer informed. This was probably an exaggeration—for example, in Teheran, the chief of state was surrounded by professional diplomats—but it seems *probable* that the role of the minister today was more secondary than ever.[34]

This brings us to the question of what role is played by the Muslim Brotherhood's international organization. Husam Tammam (eight years ago), maintained that the organization had been considerably weakened by the regional crisis that Iraq's invasion of Kuwait precipitated and by the divisions pitting various national Muslim Brotherhood offshoots against one another at that time in deciding what attitude to adopt. The Kuwaiti Brothers had never forgiven the support that certain Brothers furnished to Sadam Hussein. The ruling principle since then among Brotherhood branches has been the following: The people living in Mecca know their allies best—put another way, each branch would decide which route to take. Still, there were frictions. Personally, I'm inclined to go along with reality in saying that the Brotherhood Internationale was "much less than the Komintern, but more than the Socialist Internationale." To give an example, the Supreme Guide of that era, Mahdi 'Akif, had affirmed that he would arbitrate between two rival factions within the same national branch if the two brought an appeal to him.[35] Today it looks as if the cadres of the international organization may have played a major role in the decision-making process and Egypt's foreign policy, so that it often adopted views that were different from those of the head office's members (with al Shatir as an exception), and that the different regional branches shrank a bit. But anyone who talked concerted action, interactions, and indeed even coordination on certain dossiers no longer does so. An exception must be made for Hamas: It is clear that, for the moment, the ties between the Cairo Brothers and those in Gaza are very tightly drawn. Recently published articles asserted that Qatar had advanced important sums of money to Hamas so that it could send hundreds if not thousands of men to provide protection for the presidential palace.[36] This information has not been denied and observers of the way the security forces acted during the big demonstration in November 2012 (refusing to open fire to protect the palace) do not consider this farfetched. It may very well be completely unfounded but the fact that political actors believe it is not inconsequential.

It is equally difficult to determine the role of the IGS, the security organs, and the army in the development of the Brotherhood's foreign policy. It seems some, in the Deep State, were very angry against many GIS members, believing, rightly or wrongly, they helped the Brotherhood, but nobody was really associated with the "Brotherhood" decision-making process. A prominent journalist wrote many articles to defend former IGS chief Ra'fat Shihata, saying in substance he never compromised himself with the Brotherhood—this implied that some people thought otherwise.[37] Some press articles give to understand that the service carefully filtered, too much so, the information that it passed on to the office of the presidency and that the Deep State had no confidence in the chief of state.[38]

As for the army, it seemed to conduct a parallel diplomacy, privileging its traditional allies in the Gulf. The most striking example is the chief of staff's visit to the Emirates, involved in a serious conflict with the Brotherhood after dismantling a Brotherhood organization accused of preparing a coup against the state.

It is, however, on the linked dossiers of the Sinai and Gaza that the differences over foreign policy are most pronounced. It is nearly certain that the decision in February 2013 to flood the Gaza tunnels was not made by the civilian powers that be, whether those of the presidency or the al-Shātir team. It was the Minister of Defense who issued a decree in December 2012 that prohibited land sales to foreign interests in the eastern part of the peninsula. The "sovereign organisms" of army and security services announced themselves as very hostile to Qatar's growing role in the Egyptian economy and in projects in the Canal zone and on the peninsula. Rightly or wrongly, these organs thought the Muslim Brotherhood was indifferent to their own sovereigntist preoccupations and that they were much more tied to Hamas and the jihadists. Added to that was that the former's political options, and regional agendas were dangerous to Egypt's national security as it was conceived by the army and security services.

Egyptian foreign policy must take a major economic factor into account: Over several years, perhaps a decade, the Egyptian economy must create from 800,000 to 1 million new jobs annually to absorb those entering the job market. However, the Egyptian budget and savings are clearly incapable of doing so. The country needs foreign investors, who will not come unless the budget is "in order" (and that needs a working tourism sector and a steady flow of diaspora's remittances). So support is also required from foreign donors, the International Monetary Fund (IMF), Western governments, and from the Gulf. During the first half of 2013, tourists and investors fled the country—the former because of the insecurity, the latter because of governmental incompetence or for political reasons.

The key problem for the Muslim Brotherhood has been the visceral hostility of the majority of the Saudi royal family and the other Gulf emirs and kings. Even Qatar's aid has been problematical: It comes with strings and it is not certain that the Egyptian army would not exercise its veto over Qatar's demands. The aid provided by Turkey, the Brotherhood's other great ally,[39] proved easier to obtain but is also much more limited (in material terms). In other words, the Brothers depend greatly, for the first time, on aid by non-state Islamic actors and the good will of international and Western authorities, be it the IMF, Washington, or European capitals. However, several among these actors have belatedly taken notice of the very brutal character of Brotherhood practices and of their authoritarianism, their disdain for the law, and anyone who questions them. Add to this that they are reputed to be highly incompetent when it comes to governance and managing the state apparatus. These "international" actors have (vainly) put certain pressures on the Brotherhood to get them to … become more moderate. The latter's response has been to pick up the pace, intensify the repression in order to "lock up" and create the maximum of irreversible facts on the ground, thus betting that if they win, they will at all events be indispensable and that Egypt's key position, its importance to Israel's security arrangements and the consequences of an eventual breakdown would keep the Brotherhood's detractors from being too exacting. Stressing that this was a very risky strategy is moot; we know how it turned out: the Brotherhood managed the feat of reconciling young revolutionaries and the military.

Conclusion

In absolute terms, all other things being equal, the Brotherhood's grand plan in foreign policy more or less had these features:

A) Reassure Israel and the United States, in order to gain their support or at least their neutrality; all the while, they were slowly "detaching" Egypt from the American protector by increments to render them less dependent on the latter. As we have seen, the Brothers went quite far in the guarantees offered to the Hebrew state and in the pressures they put on Hamas.

B) Work at having the largest possible number of countries in the region come under the Brotherhood's thumb—as a necessary prelude to reestablishing the Caliphate.

C) Conclude a strategic partnership with Turkey—and, if possible, a rapprochement by both countries with Iran, even if Iran's strategies and actions and their own tend to be irreconcilable, most notably on the Syrian question. More precisely, Iran has an interest in destabilizing certain of the Gulf countries. The Brotherhood in power tried the same thing, despite (or because of?) its great weakness by reason of the Egyptian economy's sorry state. A move toward Iran was a threat enabling Cairo to extract money from the Gulf States. In doing so, it forgot that the region's Egyptian expatriates are a vital source of currency earnings for the country and that their living abroad eases the pressure on its job market. Any destabilization of the Gulf would have highly prejudicial consequences for the Egyptian economy and treasury. We do not know how things would have turned out, the arm-wrestling between the Brotherhood and Riyad having been settled with a victory for the Saudi monarchy, traditionally allied with the Egyptian army;

D) Adjust the system of Cairo's alliances, if possible while safeguarding the relations and networks of the former regime (United States, Europe, Libya, Qatar substituting for Saudi Arabia). But the favored partners, besides Turkey, would become Qatar, Malaysia, China,[40] and Singapore. All this seemed to be a good idea (even if some Brothers, and not the least among them, asserted that they hoped to see Turkey and Qatar substituted for Europe and the United States, a project whose absurdity should not surprise), but we must be careful not to forget about Africa. The continent's capitals, exasperated by Mubarak's arrogance and authoritarianism, had very warmly welcomed Mūrsī's accession to power.

E) In the long term, the three main problems that a Brotherhood regime would have had to confront seem to be these: A) how to avoid the traps of the tawrit: don't get pulled into bad adventures by allies (Salafis) or protegés (Hamas) at the wrong time; B) how to manage or what attitude to adopt toward the Salafi jihadists, the Brotherhood brigades engaged in third countries (Syria, for example), and toward the war on terror; and C) how to pursue an activist policy in the region, especially in working toward the restoration of the Caliphate without jeopardizing the foreign-aid flows that the economy needs.

F) We do not know how they would have proceeded and if they might have succeeded where Nasser had failed, despite being much subtler and competent than they, given the permanent gulf between ambitions, great projects, and constraints, with a constant manipulation by double talk. Instead of marrying up the national security doctrines of the state bureaucracy and Egyptian security organs, or trying to find a modus vivendi with them, or getting busy with seriously managing the Egyptian economy, they would try to consolidate their grip on the Egyptian state in the face of the enormous resistance of two-thirds if not four-fifths of the population. They would ignore the preoccupations and conceptions of other Egyptian actors, would opt for brutality and resort to force. More and more numerous became those inside the state apparatus, the security organs, the political, media, and very influential middle classes in Cairo and the big delta towns who thought President Mūrsi and his crowd posed an immense danger to civil peace and Egyptian national security. These forces would seek and find support among the Gulf monarchies—which, after July 30, 2013 contributed more than 25 million dollars in support of the new regime and to guard against a return to power by the Brothers. The petro emirates may be the Holy Alliance, but the Brothers were no democrats.

Notes

1. Leslie Piquemal, "La montée révolutionnaire des mouvements islamistes par la voie électorale: le cas des Frères musulmans égyptiens," *Les Cahiers de l'Orient*, 2012/13, Vol. 107, 41–9.
2. The Brothers certainly knew that the great majority of the personnel in the interior and justice ministries considered them as enemies, in the strongest sense of the word. I do not know what they thought of the rest of the civil bureaucracy, but I am under the impression that they built their reading of the latter's actions on the theme, legitimate but simplistic and erroneous, of the defense of ill-gotten privileges——and with a strong tendency to think that ill-gotten gains, whether things or privileges, belong to the conqueror. The Brotherhood's strongman Khayrat al-Shatir told several contacts that the Brothers were going to set up parallel institutions, but it is not known with certainty what that meant, even if one may suspect the worst. What was most likely is that he had in mind first the ministries of the interior and of justice. As for the army, the Brothers' views are more difficult to fathom: It could be argued that they were always wary of it, but on the other hand also maintain that they did not see anything coming, with evidence to support both scenarios, and with less irreconcilability than may be thought. I am inclined to think that they believed the military to be so corrupt

that reassuring them of their privilege would suffice to buy their neutrality, all the while thinking that al-Sissi was too bigoted, tooo religious, and too good a Muslim to be their enemy. They failed to see that a sincerely believing Muslim often has excellent reason to detest them. The problem of the bureaucracy's hostility toward the fraternal project is crucial, if only because the Brothers attributed to it their failure and some of their mistakes and even going so far as to assert that they fell victim to a systematic sabotage. This Brotherly plea to me seems to be out of order. It ignores the enthusiasm, the euphoria, and the good will capital that initially accompanied the first "democratically elected" president. It forgets that the Egyptian bureaucracy has served some very different masters and to make an enemy of it takes quite a talent. As far as justice is concerned, it is the Brothers who were looking for a fight, from the first week of the Mursī presidency. And if a crushing majority of the country is hostile to them beginning in late November 2012, it is their fault (with the constitutional declaration and the repression that followed it). A group that has against it a near-totality of the security organs, the army, justice, the media, intellectuals, artists, the high public function, the Sufi societies, the population of Cairo, and a large part of the provinces, and the Salafis is a group that cannot pretend to represent "a happy medium." *Postface: the discussions I had with insiders tend to confirm this analysis. First, many intelligence officials, including prominent ones, were, at first, willing to collaborate with the Brothers. Second, al Sissi was the army's choice for Tantawi's succession, because his profile was deemed to be a clever trap for the Brotherhood: a very devout person, but a devout person considering them to be dangerous for religion?*

3. An important text on the constitution is that by Ellis Goldberg, who is more measured than me. http://www.jadaliyya.com/pages/index/8172/reflections-on-egypts-draft- constitution. See also the more restrained article by Joe Stork at http://www.hrw.org/news/2012/11/29/egypt-new-constitution-mixed-support- rights

4. The Brotherhood in its current configuration cannot be considered a political party, since its activities are not purely political and because nothing is known of its finances (or its international networks). It does not wish to normalize its status neither as an "association" nor as an NGO, because prevailing law calls for financial transparency, strict supervision by the Ministry of Social Affairs, and so forth. In other words, since it does not want to restructure, it has to change the existing legislation. However, it refrains from this, arguing the fact that there is no parliament yet. But this is a spurious pretext, since the presidency or the Consultative Assembly legislates on all kinds of subjects.

5. The Brotherhood recruits, selects, and inducts its members after a long period of observing them, surrounded, after having structured their environment. See my article Samir Amghar (ed.), *Les islamistes au défi du pouvoir: évolutions d'une idéologie* [The Islamists Challenge Power: Evolutions of an Ideology], Paris, Michalon, 2012.
6. Those most often seen are 'Isām al-'Iryān and Muhammad al-Biltājī. The real strongman of the Brotherhood is Khayrat al-Shātir, who is the strategist and controls the finances, the membership files, external contacts, and internal discipline. Five or six "strongmen" assist him, and none of them really talk with the press.
7. I put the question to several journalists who "covered the Brotherhood." If that does not seem enough, it suffices to consult the whole of the Cairo press, on any given day, particularly after a decision or taking of an important position by the Brotherhood. The same Brother cadre will have said two contradictory things to two different journalists; the Brother cadres will have contradictory versions of explanations; and so forth.
8. Leslie Piquemal, "Les Frères musulmans égyptiens à la fin de l'ère Moubarak (2005–2010). Identité et projet politique" [The Egyptian Muslim Brotherhood of the late Mubarak era (2005–2010)], PhD thesis, IEP Paris, 2012.
9. I take the opportunity to reiterate my being indebted to the late Husām Tammām, Patrick Haenni … and the late Ahmad Rā'if, who, in the course of long, stimulating conversations always imparted a great deal to me. The first two for a long time thought that the great narrative was no longer operative.
10. The thought of Sayyid Qutb, such as he had developed during the late 1950s and early 1960s, offers many points in common with Leninism. A) History has a meaning: the Creator, knowing His creature, He deprived it of the right to legislate, for He alone is capable of furnishing the Perfect Law. Men take credit for this law, in the guise of numerous ideologies and by doing so assault the Sovereignty of the Most High, and perpetuate relationships of oppression and domination for the greatest misfortune of all and society's perdition, returning it to states that came before the Revelation, eras of ignorance and error. B) A genius intellectual has discovered this meaning. C) A vanguard must prepare itself to achieve Utopia, to accelerate the movement. It is interesting to note that those who, inside the movement, do not adhere to this schema do not dare to say that Qutb has to be renounced. They assert that he did not say this, that he instead said other things and that he was misunderstood.
11. The doctrinal inconsistency of Brotherhood texts is deplored by Shaykh

Qaradāwī (who contented himself with describing it), for example, in an interview in *al-Dustūr* dated October 5, 2008.

12. I am thinking, of course, of the great texts by Alain Besançon, who explained that the Communist Party
in the Soviet Union alternated alternated "Communism of war/NEP" and that it must not be thought that the second cycle brought durable doctrinal revisions or irreversible compromises.
13. Muhammad Badī', before becoming Supreme Guide, was in charge of "educational" or "pedagogical" programs of the Brotherhood. He had been arrested in 1965 for being a member of the organization reconstituted by Qutb.
14. This passage owes much to long discussions I held with Mustapha al-Ahnaf. The central idea is his, but I reworked it slightly.
15. There are numerous differing susceptibilities/postures among the Brothers, but it is important to avoid reductive dichotomies, opposing an "enlightened" youth to a villainous old generation of obscurantist theocrats, or that such and such generation would have such and such a posture or susceptibility. I see the problem differently: a Brotherhood that relies on the principle of blind obedience, which collects 8 percent of its members' income, which is mostly not transparent, and can expect some members to claim the right of asking questions or receiving explanations on how funds are spent. Some lawyers are exasperated by the Brotherhood's disrespect for the law and the judicial system. Some provincial cadres are aware of the Brotherhood's loss of popularity and the deterioration in people's quality of life. Many palpable tensions concern nominations in the state or the Brotherhood party. One member of the Brotherhood's police contingent maintains that he left the Brotherhood because he was asked to torture some militants. Many observers noticed a battle for influence between President Morsi and strongman al Shatir, a battle lost by Morsi. And so on and so forth ...
16. It is supremely curious to "jump ship" on board one that has endured many trials at the moment when the goal is in sight and the reward for sacrifices made is imminent. More generally, it is very difficult to leave the Brothers: it would be to completely change worlds, in the radical sense of the term.
17. To mention only the testimonies of Brotherhood veterans: al Khirbāwī, Tharwat: *qalb al ikhwān, mahākim taftīsh al jamā'a,* Cairo, Dār al Hilāl, 2010, 250 pages. Al Khirbāwī, Tharwat: *sirr al ma'bad, al asrār al khafiyya li jamā'at al ikhwāān al muslimīn,* 3rd édition, Cairo, D ār Nahdat Misr, 2012, 359 pages. Durra, Usāma: *mon dākhil al ikhwān atakallam,* Cairo, al 'asr al jadīd, 2010, 128 pages. Durra, Usāma: *min al ikhwān ilā maydān al Tahrīr,* 1st edition, Cairo, Dār al

miṣrī li-l nashr, 2011, 102 pages. Al Milījī, al Sayyid ʿAbd al Sattār: *tajrubati ma' al ikhwān,* Cairo, al Zahrāâ' li-l i'lām al ʿarabī, 2009. Fāyiz, Sāmih: *jannat al ikhwān,rihlat al khurūj min al jamāʿa,* Cairo, Dār al tanwîr, 2013, 199 pages. Abûû Khalīl, Haytham: *ikhwāân islāhiyyūn, dâār dūn,* Cairo, dâār dūn, 2012, 265 pages.

18. The stifling character of the discipline is refuted by some cadres who assert that the Brotherhood is more homogeneous than those who wager on its diversity (subtext: discipline is freely consented to, no one feels compelled) and that discussions are much more frequent than is believed. Both objections do not strike me as decisive. On the other hand, it is true that it has been possible to observe on one or two occasions (post-2011) "refusals to obey" or very stormy dissents from the official line after its adoption.

19. The list of intimidating moves, beating opponents, and attacks on peaceful demonstrations is imposing. Now must be added abductions of activists followed by torture—and assassinations.

20. An example will illustrate the point: the candidacy of a Brother in the 2012 presidential elections, contrary to solemn commitments given, reiterated, and reconfirmed. All of our Brotherhood contacts say that the Brotherhood sincerely believed that it would abide by this commitment, but it had to change its mind when the Islamist democrat Abū-l-Futūh announced that he was running for the supreme court. As for the Brotherhood's adversaries, they never believed the Brothers' promise and thus saw their worst suspicions confirmed. I believe we can say what came next: even if the Brothers' sincerity was believed, it is clear— and it was clear from the first moment—that they lacked the "means" for keeping this promise, it being evident that there would be candidates and serious clients who could win without their support and who represented a threat to them. We are thus confronted with a dilemma: The Brotherhood leadership must be Leninist, Machiavellian, or completely stupid. The two propositions pose all sorts of problems: The explanation of stupidity is too short, for two reasons: For one, the Muslim Brotherhood have held power in one country—Sudan—for the last twenty-four yearsand no one explains that "balance sheet" by the stupidity or the leadership and the local Brother cadres. The Sudanese Brothers have a different status from the Egyptian Brothers and still the bottom line is a disaster. Lastly, it would be necessary to explain why the Brotherhood leadership is always made up of people making disastrous decisions. The explanation by way of "ideological-discursive closedness" to me seems more promising but does not resolve all the problems.

21. Of course, this does not necessarily refute my framework. Members of the

Muslim Brotherhood believe that "International Jewry" rules the world; it is therefore necessary to placate it as long as possible. That said, and this illustrates the problems many had with the Brothers, it should be added the Brotherhood went at lengths saying it never accepted the peace treaty and did not renege on it. Morsi, when he talked to the Israelis, acted as a president and not as a Muslim Brother. Of course, nobody believed this.

22. I think especially of the affair of the blasphemous film that a diaspora Copt produced. Brothers and Salafis succeeded in avoiding a new round of sectarian incidents by seeming to believe that the American administration was the "real" guilty party, thus diverting the vindictiveness of their militants and of the mob.
23. For example, late December 2011. See http://www.youm7.com/News.asp?NewsID=565958
24. http://www.youtube.com/watch?v=cUztA230IiQ, or also http://new.elfagr.org/Detail.aspx?nwsId=224064&secid=1&vid=2
25. http://www.elwatannews.com/news/details/173754
26. I still like the Salafist formulation: "Let us distinguish ends and means. The Brothers are prepared to make concessions on ends but not the means, while we do so for the means, not the ends." It may be invidious, but it is elegant.
27. http://www.shorouknews.com/news/view.aspx?id=b85a41bd-d442-4e59-b01fd-8ee3df8f7f04 http://digital.ahram.org.eg/articles.aspx?Serial=1096628&eid=1504
28. http://www.almasryalyoum.com/news/details/317252
29. It is a proven fact that the Brothers had militias, since many Egyptian demonstrators saw them. It is also an established fact that these were armed militias. On the other hand, their operational value is unknown and may be overestimated by both adversaries and allies. Najwān ʿAbd al Latīf, in a recent communication, confirmed that the veteran jihadist ʿAbbūd al-Zummur told him that the Brothers had the weapons but few men who really knew how to fight. The jihadists have both. It remains to be seen if this assertion indirectly corroborated the journalist's version or demolished it.
30. You can explain the Salafist al Nur decision to support the coup against the Brothers in three different ways: You say that this was a Saudi decision and they had to comply. You say Salafists were terribly afraid, as the Brothers tried to seize control of the Salafist Mosques and kept on harassing the Salafist leaders. The last one is that you say that the Salafists were smart enough to understand that the Brothers endangered by their mistakes the whole Islamist project and tried to distance themselves from this experience. I heard in Cairo the three

explanations: The Brothers and some Deep State journalists prefer the first one, the Salafist the third, and many journalists the second.
31. President Mursi went to Teheran and the chief of Iranian intelligence paid many visits to Egypt.
32. http://www.youm7.com/story/2016/4/2/%D8%A3%D8%B3%D8%B1%D8%A7%D8%B1-%D8%AC%D8%AF%D9%8A%D8%AF%D8%A9-%D8%B9%D9%86-%D8%B9%D9%84%D8%A7%D9%82%D8%A9-%D9%85%D8%B1%D8%B3%D9%89-%D9%85%D8%B9-%D8%B7%D9%87%D8%B1%D8%A7%D9%86-%D9%88%D8%B2%D9%8A%D8%B1-%D8%AE%D8%A7%D8%B1%D8%AC%D9%8A%D8%A9-%D8%A5%D9%8A%D8%B1%D8%A7%D9%86/2656367
33. http://www.aljazeera.net/news/reportsandinterviews/2013/6/16/%D9%85%D9%88%D9%82%D9%81-%D9%85%D8%B1%D8%B3%D9%8A-%D9%85%D9%86-%D8%B3%D9%88%D8%B1%D9%8A%D8%A7-%D8%B1%D8%B3%D8%A7%D8%A6%D9%84-%D9%84%D9%84%D8%AF%D8%A7%D8%AE%D9%84-%D9%88%D8%A7%D9%84%D8%AE%D8%A7%D8%B1%D8%AC
34. I replaced "certain," used in the French version, and preferred "probable." I conducted many discussions with Egyptian diplomats: All agreed to say that President Mursi sidelined the ministry, but some said that Mubarak did the same thing, a claim denied by others.
35. Read his interview in *al-Dustūr* dated December 20 2006. There is also an interesting article on the international organization in *al-Sharq al-Aawsat*, dated August 29, 2008. Or yet gain the article by 'Abdal Mun'im Mahmūd in *al-Dustūr* of January 28, 2009 that discussed the relations between Hamas, the Egyptian Brotherhood, and the international organization.
36. *Al-Fagr*, February 7, 2013.
37. Ra'fat Shihata was fired soon after Mursi's fall. I was unable to find this article on the web, but I am sure I saw it during the 2013 summer in an issue of the weekly *Al-Fagr*.
38. The services assert that it was impossible for their chiefs to see Mūrsi face to face to discuss the confidential defense dossier. He was always "flanked" by two people, one being a member of the international organization. After his fall, articles inspired by the services confirmed that the office of the president of the Republic systematically transmitted all confidential defense dossiers submitted by the services to the Hamas leadership in Gaza and that they had to take this into account in their policy of (not) sharing information.

39. I personally did not become aware of the importance of Turkey's role in the Brotherhood's network of alliances until after Mūrsi's fall (well after having written the first version of this article). The Brotherhood and Egypt were a dossier receiving high-level attention; several economic treaties had been signed that were criticized by the opposition as too favorable to Turkey (I am not equipped to evaluate this assertion, which has it that these treaties amounted to exempting Turkish firms from the tolls due to the Suez Canal Company). Many are the members of the Brotherhood international organization that left London, Brussels, and Berlin to settle in Turkey. It was in Turkey that the Brothers, then still in the opposition, met with Central Intelligence Agency (CIA) representatives in 2010, and so forth. After Mūrsi fell, the Ankara government systematically exerted daily pressure on its Western interlocutors to impose sanctions on the new Egyptian authorities.
40. President Mūrsi made a state visit to China in late August 2012. See: http://online.wsj.com/article/SB10000872396390444230504577761727155030 4082.html

5

"Islam and Resistance": The Uses of Ideology in the Foreign Policy of Hamas

Leila Seurat

To this day, the classic definition of foreign policy as the instrument by which the state tries to shape and interact with its international environment remains a widely accepted framework for international relations theory. Applied to the Palestinian landscape, this definition does not fail to raise important questions. Do the actors of the national liberation movement have the means for carrying out real foreign policy in the absence of true state institutions? If there is one, what specific practices of external action does Hamas put forward?[1] Can the transnational component that defines Islamist ideology be reconciled with the defense of interests that are more specifically national?

This chapter enlists against the realist theories of international relations, whose analyses remain focused on states.[2] In it, I try to show that, despite being a non-state actor operating in a territory over which it does not exercise classic sovereignty, Hamas does in fact pursue a foreign policy whenever it deals with actors located outside Palestine as well as formulate discourses and implement actions that address non-Palestinian actors. This observation remains relevant for the period following the take-over of Gaza in June 2007. Even if Hamas seems to fit all the criteria of a state entity[3] as classically defined, it must continue to be regarded as a "non-state," particularly because its control over the Gaza strip by no means implies any attribution of traditional sovereign resources.[4]

The transnational ideology advocated by Hamas is not really limited to this actor alone, because there are many examples of state actors who stood for ideological positions that were transnational in one way or another.[5] The Soviet Union, for example, comes to mind, for how it sought to advocate the Communist model even outside its borders, or yet again Syria and Iraq whose nationalisms not only addressed their own citizens but all Arabs. Nor does the religious aspect of Hamas transnationalism make it fundamentally different from these other actors, since even Russia's transnational ideological positions can be said to have been permeated by a religious dimension in the way it considered itself the protector of the Greek Orthodoxes.

Thus, even though Hamas remains a non-state actor tapping into the register of political Islam, the sources of its international practice are fundamentally the same ones organizing the foreign policies of states: defending its interests as perceived by the movement's leaders and advocating the values and constitutive norms of this politico-religious player's ideology. This dual observation remains valid even when its foreign policy defines itself both in relation to the occupying power and by interactions with other actors.

The principal element distinguishing Hamas foreign policy from "classical" foreign policy is the situation of the occupation and encirclement of the Gaza Strip both of which significantly impact its decision making.[6] Indeed, the main foreign policy authority, the Political Section[7] (maktab siyassi), is split up between the Gaza Strip, the West Bank, the Israeli prisons that hold some of its members,[8] and finally, the exterior, which, until recently, fell within the purview of the movement's Damascus offices. This dispersal leads to adoption of different, more or less inclusive decision-making processes that most often reflect the unilateral action of members settled outside the Occupied Territories. At the same time, these disparities provoke a heightened competition between the leaders in Gaza and those in the exterior with regard to the conduct of diplomacy. While a foreign policy only rarely responds to the exigencies of a supposed national interest and is not always just the result of various inputs reflecting the coalition of forces in power, this pluralistic game takes a specific form in the case of Hamas and thus obliges us to acknowledge its specificity. Moreover, the exterior leadership's recent departure from Syria prompted a fracturing of this authority, whose members henceforth are themselves dispersed over several Arab capitals, notably in Qatar.

A historical analysis will let us show that, since the early 1990s, the use of ideology in the foreign policy of Hama evolved to respond to the realization of the movement's interests. In what follows, we will try to present the principal ideological redefinitions that ensued after it carried the legislative elections in January 2006 and the events following its victory, starting with the taking of power in Gaza in June 2007. Finally, the start of the "Arab Spring" opens a period of uncertainty during which interests are no longer easily identifiable.

These developments are not without their consequences for the resort to ideology.

A Foreign Policy in Gestation

Relying on Ideology with Regard to Israel Raises Hamas' Status Vis-à-vis the PLO

Formulated in conformity with what the movement's leaders regard as the "Islamic norm,"[9] the Intifada lets Hamas boost its status in Palestine by differentiating it from the PLO's political program.

The Muslim Brotherhood participating in the first Intifada in December 1987 is concomitant with the birth of Hamas. The movement thus took shape through a foreign policy action defined as an instrument of rebellion against the occupying power. For an organization that until then had kept its distance from various armed conflicts,[10] this choice proceeded from an internal interest: Protect the group's structures in order to avoid findings itself marginalized on the national political scene. In this enterprise, Hamas largely defended its action as conforming to a specific "Islamic norm" principally by exploiting religiously significant dates or by mobilizing primarily during sermons or days of fasting. Recourse to religion hence derived here from a desire of differentiating itself from the Unified National Command, the body called into being by the PLO for waging the Intifada after 1991. Hamas has always oscillated between its attachment to the "historic solution," which envisions the liberation of all of Palestine and its capacity for living with the "interim solution" of advocating the creation of a state with the 1967 boundaries. As Khaled Khroub commented during the post-Oslo period,[11] the movement's leaders resorted to the first option: The "historic solution" is clearly ideological since it is based on the idea that Palestine constitutes a *waqf*.[12] During the same period, the leaders also seek to sign on to the recommendations of the second perspective, "the interim solution," but when it is put forward, it still turns out to be coupled with "Islamic conditions" that require it to remain faithful to the *sharia*, the leaders by then largely turning to concepts from the Koran such as *sabr* (patience) to bolster a solution that may appear to be deviant.

These different examples illustrate the fact that, when it comes to Israel, the use of ideology can serve the movement's interests including wanting to compete with the PLO's prestige on the national scene. Like any actor in contention with other groups in the same political system, Hamas must assert its identity and distinguish itself from its competitors if it is to positively influence public opinion or important players. Besides the affirmation of righteousness and defense of the population's interests, the resort to ideology helps Hamas distinguish itself from other political forces, especially Fatah. As a matter of fact, all Islamist movements appropriate this strategy of counter-legitimacy against opponents.

Relations with the Other States: A Non-ideological Approach lets Hamas Avoid Isolation

While the movement falls back on an Islamic discourse in criticizing Oslo, its opposition to the accords signed between the occupier and Arab countries is seldom formulated in an ideological idiom. Indeed, on the signing of the peace treaty between Israel and Jordan in October 1994, Hamas contented itself with deploring "a new crack in the Arab wall of solidarity."[13] This is mostly explained as an attempt by the movement to garner support in a regional environment in favor of normalization with the Jewish state while still remaining a fervent proponent of the military option.[14] Sidelining the constricting ideological discourse in its charter—which denounces the existence of a dual "imperialist–Zionist" conspiracy and makes the problematic failure of Arab policy toward Palestine the center of its rhetoric—in practice makes room for pragmatic declarations.[15]

In this context, the movement's silence at a time of successive Islamist victories in Jordan in November 1989 and Algeria in 1990 is particularly revealing.

The diplomatic road that Hamas embarked on when Iraq invaded Kuwait also illustrates this setting aside of ideology. The movement succeeds in finding a position of equilibrium allowing it to maintain good relations with the Gulf countries while it avoids alienating a largely pro-Iraq Palestinian public opinion. Its various communiques[16] thus witness to a subtle interweaving of multiple positions, which, despite their seeming contradictions, end up in a pragmatic posture that assures it of continued financing by the petro monarchies and simultaneously reinforces its regional status relative to the PLO. In addition, preserving friendly relations with the petro monarchies has the effect of not excluding the movement from the community of Arab states just when it is being accused by the PLO of serving Iranian interests in Palestine.[17]

Adoption of this new parlance will allow the movement's leadership to make numerous visits throughout the region.[18] In 1991, the delegation to Iran, Iraq, Jordan, and Saudi Arabia led by Ibrahim Ghosheh[19] provides the opportunity for the leaders to gain real visibility and to appear for the first time as diplomats from then on. Sheikh Yassine, upon his release from prison in 1997, toured Kuwait, Qatar, Sudan, the United Arab Emirates (UAE), Yemen, Saudi Arabia, Syria, and Iran from February to June 1998.[20] With its spiritual and charismatic leader officially received by numerous states despite heavy pressure from certain actors, especially the PLO, this was a seminal episode in the movement's foreign policy.

Finally, adopting a pragmatic foreign policy will also free the movement to start talks with Western countries including the United States.[21] When the incident at Marj al-Zouhour[22] happened, leading Israel to expel 415 Islamists to South Lebanon, Hamas contacted the five members of the UN Security Council through their embassies in Amman, lobbying them to take a position on Resolution 799 that demanded the immediate return of the expellees. The movement's representatives at the time delivered letters written personally by its leaders explaining their position and making the focus of their remarks the legitimacy of resistance to the occupation in conformity with international norms, in this way trying to deter the United States from putting their group on the list of terrorist organizations.[23]

The uses of ideology depend primarily on the degree of the movement's integration on the national and regional scenes. In contrast to the actions against Israel registering in an "Islamic doxa" and in the wish to assert itself against the PLO, action by Hamas toward the other states lacks this dimension. The reluctance of a number among the latter to develop relations with an Islamist movement largely explains Hamas's ambition to appear as an actor capable of understanding diplomatic issues and of respecting the principle of non-interference in the internal affairs of these countries.[24]

A Specific Hamas Aspect Justifies the "Exceptional" Dimension of its Diplomacy

The dispersal of the maktab siyassi, the central authority for foreign policy matters, caused a similar fragmentation of decision making as the Hamas leaders found themselves geographically dispersed and with limited means of communication. Moreover, this scattering caused an imbalance between the interior and the exterior because the members of the external leadership had an edge in terms of "day-to-day" management of diplomatic affairs.[25]

It is the cadres living outside the Territories who constitute the decision makers rather than the actual Political Section institutionally. This phenomenon would be linked to the aptitude of members living abroad in reaping financial resources for the movement.[26]

This preeminence goes back to the arrest of Sheikh Yassine along with many other Gaza leaders in 1989. Faced with the urgent reorganization of the organization's structures, the diaspora then and there took control of Hamas under the leadership of Musa Abu Marzouq,[27] followed by Khaled Mechaal.[28] This foreign policy decision-making monopoly would have been fostered by the Muslim Brotherhood's wish to see power mainly in the hands of a diaspora Palestinian.[29] Even with the interior regaining part of its influence when Yassine is released in 1997, the exterior retains its hegemony thanks in large part to foreign donations that entailed control of the movement's financial but also its military apparatus. This phenomenon of competition between the two leaderships is reflected in foreign policy strategies: unlike the leadership in the Territories, the diaspora had a longstanding hostility toward collaborating with the Palestinian Authority.[30] In fact, at the time of the Taba accords in September 1995, the interior leadership that sought to protect its members against arrest by finding common ground with the new Palestinian administration decided to suspend its attacks on Israel. It was then that several Fatah leaders met members of the interior in the summer of 1995 in Cairo and then in Khartoum. Opposition by the decision-making pole in

Amman to stopping the violence and to the entente with the Authority partly explains the failure of these meetings and the resumption of attacks in 1996. Fearing it would be marginalized politically, the exterior cadres then tried to undermine the chances of dialogue between the interior and the Authority.[31] The extent of these fractures in part explains the movement's foreign policy during the second Intifada: Sheikh Yassine is alleged to have accepted the possibility of a ceasefire proposed by Yasser Arafat while Khaled Mechaal opposed it and is said to have issued an order to the al-Qassam brigade to organize an armed operation at Rafah.[32]

Governance and Foreign Policy

Limited Uses of Ideological Discourse against Israel

The Hamas victory in the legislative elections of January 2006 and the movement's integration with the Palestinian institutions induced a distinct change in the deployment of Islamic values against the occupier. An abandonment of the religious-type arguments is perceptible in the numerous accords signed between Fatah and Hamas, which involve new demarches with Israel and encourage the Islamist movement to limit its armed interventions in the territories occupied since 1967. While the "Document of National Accord"[33] signed in June 2006 called on all Palestinian political groups to come together under the PLO aegis and to clearly express their will of seeing a state constituted within the 1967 borders, it implied that Hamas acquiesced in transferring the dossier of negotiations with Israel to the PLO and to let the president of the Palestinian Authority conduct direct negotiations with the Jewish state. By the same token, the "Mecca Accord" signed in February 2007 that put a temporary stop to the armed conflict between the two factions while opening a path to a national unity government, implies that the Movement of the Islamic Resistance recognizes the validity of the accords concluded previously between the PLO and Israel under American patronage. These pragmatic steps primarily signaled a will to consolidate its popular base, to strengthen its cohesion and to garner new support.[34] The reconciliation agreements most often are devoid of any reference to the fundamental ideology, even while they entail measures directed at the occupying power.

That said, ideological arguments would not be taken leave of entirely.

They are, for example, mobilized on the occasion of indirect negotiations with the occupying power, such as when signing truces. While signing the *hudna* of June 2008 under Egyptian auspices, Islam and the resistance thus appear to be instrumental in justifying what some regarded then as a doctrinal drift.

This truce entails the bilateral cessation of all military operations, the partial reopening of checkpoints, as well as the progressive lifting of the blockade by Israel. It is explained as easily by external factors as by internal motives, since it also offered a means for appearing like a responsible player in the eyes of the international community: The truce ought to permit lifting of the blockade, an objective linked to internal legitimacy, but also offer the benefit of a period of respite for organizing the interior scene. This lull nevertheless also entailed the risk of having the compromise be seen as compromising with the enemy. Therefore, phrased in conformity with the "Islamic norm," the *hudna* lets the movement continue to advertise its difference with the PLO that, for its part, explicitly recognized Israel. This legalistic invocation moreover is coupled with a historical legitimization. By referring to the distant past and fitting this process into the long term, the Hamas leadership was able to give an Islamic justification for the reconciliation: "In the history of Islam, during the era of the Prophet and the ensuing centuries—during the time of Salahuddin (Saladin), for example—negotiations were held with the enemy, but within a clear framework and specific philosophy, within the context of a vision, of rules and of regulations governing this negotiation."[35]

On the other hand, in order to deflect the charge of compromising with the enemy, the truce is characterized as just one more stage in the armed conflict and thus could be presented as a kind of "resistance."[36]

After Many Attempts at Pragmatic Overtures, a Hamas Isolated Regionally and Internationally Again Resorts to Normative Elements

After scoring its victory in the legislative elections of January 2006 and forming the tenth Palestinian Government in March, the movement flaunted pragmatic positions far removed from the original ideology, especially with regard to the Western powers.[37] But the continuing refusal by the Quartet[38] to open any kind of dialogue with the movement, combined with the continuing blockade imposed by Egypt and supported by the "moderate" Arab countries, led the movement to restart a specific religious or normative discourse designed to advance certain specific interests.

Thus, the strategic alliance that has Hamas side with Iran is the one most often analyzed in terms of values held in common. Kahled Mechaal's various declarations during his Teheran visits indeed move in this direction by accentuating a religious referent advanced as a common denominator: "We wish to unite the Arab and Islamic nation on the Palestine question."[39] This same formula allows Hamas to legitimize its diplomatic visits to the Arab countries. In 2006, a delegation sent by the movement thus made the rounds of many states in the region.[40] The movement leadership then insisted strongly on the ideological unity that, according to them, gathered up the Islamic actors in the struggle against Israel. These foreign policy declarations compatible with their values thus responded to several imperatives.

As contacts with the different Arab countries dwindled, the assertion of a "united Arab front" to fight Israel assumed all the more importance, with Iran constituting a main source of material, political, and military support. The resort to ideology also made it possible to minimize an alliance that was not approved unanimously, given that it included a Shiite actor. Hamas thus favored the common denominator among Sunni and Shiites compared with the doctrinal specificities that might put them at loggerheads.

When this alliance is not described in Islamic terms, it is formulated starting with a mobilization of the concept of "united resistance front," which made aggregating more countries, including non-Muslim ones, around the Hamas vision possible. This partly explains the official meeting between Khaled Mechaal and Russian president Dimitri Medvedev in May of 2010 in Damascus.[41] The "resistance front" uniting actors such as Russia, Turkey, or Qatar around Hamas let the movement assert that attempts to isolate it had failed and that, going forward, there were many who would treat it as a legitimate and indispensable player. In the same vein, the resort to the ideology of "resistance," in giving the impression that an "axis" existed, can equally serve to stigmatize a purported alliance between Israel, Cairo, and Abbas. Erasing the lines dividing internal and foreign policy let Hamas delegitimize its Palestinian competitors, starting with Fatah.

If some external actions are presented as deriving from a religious matrix or are defined in normative terms or suprastate ones, this does not stop the movement from pursuing an agenda resembling "classic" foreign policies. The use of ideology depends on the place it occupies inside Palestinian institutions, on its capacities for governance, but also its integration with the regional field. The effects of the economic and diplomatic isolation of Hamas explain in part the doctrinal renewal that reinforces the rapprochement with allies such as Iran, Syria, or Hezbollah and permits integrating new actors in a common front. However, the hypothesis of "normality" once more encounters limits due to the geographical dispersion of the movement's members and the scattering of its decision makers.

New Tensions Born of Winning the January 2006 Legislative Elections

The splintering of decision authorities continues to exert a key influence on the elaboration of foreign policy. The signing of the "Document of National Accord" in June 2006, involving recognition of the 1967 boundaries as well as the transfer of the dossier of negotiations with Israel to the PLO, from then on constrains Hamas to heeding the weighty voice of the prisoners within its leadership authorities. The latter find it difficult to disregard or suppress such a stance, which, clearly, represents what the prisoners want.[42]

The problem of the center of gravity (*markaz al-qiwa*) between the two leaderships is at the core of the antagonisms between the interior and exterior, the more so since Gaza dominates the institutions of government as well as Gaza's economic, security, and military activities.[43] The tunnel economy, moreover, reduces the interior leadership's dependence by its taxing of imports from Israel and Egypt. In spite of the Gaza leadership's claims, the exterior considers that power should remain centered outside Palestine. Thus, while the government of Ismaël Haniyeh conducts its official foreign relations through the figure of its minister, Mahmoud al-Zahar, it is Khaled Mechaal and Oussama Hamdan,[44] operating out of the Syrian capital, who nevertheless enjoy much greater freedom in organizing the bulk of meetings and invitations of foreign heads of state to Damascus. The reconciliation dossier is once more at the heart of these cleavages, since in October 2009, while Mahmoud al-Zahar[45] approves and signs the Egyptian document, Khaled Mechaal opposes it and refuses to ratify the accord.[46]

The New Uses of Ideology Confronted with the Arab Spring

When the Efforts at Legitimization Conflict with Defending Interests

The arrival of the "Arab Spring" forced Hamas into adapting its external action to the new reality emerging in the region. Its foreign policy therefore continued to register a certain pragmatism toward Israel. In November 2011, when Fatah and Hamas met in Cairo, Khaled Mechaal recommitted to respecting the 1967 borders and endorsed a new form of resistance calling itself "popular" or "peaceful."[47] Choosing such an approach was all the easier because its implications corresponded with the critical line on armed struggle taken by the Egyptian Muslim Brotherhood.[48] It thus let the Movement of Islamic Resistance stress its ideological kinship with an organization that was on the verge of normalizing its relationship with the United States and the European Union.

With regard to the Arab states, Hamas adapts its discourse to the demands of the new environment by formulating it around the notion of "resistance." Considering that its action and popular uprisings are two aspects of a single phenomenon, it takes to the field of the Arab Spring by presenting itself as one of the agents of change. It reckons that the "heroic resistance" of Gazans has provided the Arab peoples with the example for rising up against despotic regimes whose oppression is compared to that of the Israeli occupiers: "We pride ourselves on having sparked this awakening; the Palestinian cause remains the focus of these peoples who rejected the injustice of the regimes in power."[49]

However, this new formula, calculated to show a direct link between the intransigence of the Gaza Strip toward Israel and the determination of the Arab peoples in the face of dictatorial regimes, runs up against the risk of seeing some Arab states succeed in stifling the nascent social and political contests. This means that we are witnessing the implementation of an extremely pragmatic policy by the Islamist movement where this new discourse evolves as a function of which Arab or Islamic actors it addresses. Once again, resorting to the ideological argument finds itself blunted by considerations that are exclusively political.

In the course of his numerous trips from late 2011 to early 2012, Ismaël

Haniyeh intended to restore to the Palestinian cause its religious depth in a context of regional upheaval that saw a growing number of countries emerge more disposed to welcoming a movement ideologically close to the Muslim Brotherhood. During his visits to Egypt and Tunisia, he attempts to congratulate these two peoples on the accomplishments of their revolutions all the while he is reframing the Palestinian cause in its largest sense as the same quest for dignity and justice that characterize these upheavals.[50] In Qatar, Haniyeh visits the head office of the *al-Jazeera* network to praise its objectivity and professionalism as well as its propensity for evidencing its support of the Muslim uprisings throughout the region.

Conversely, when he touched down in countries where there was no "spring," this type of normative reference vanished. While visiting Bahrain, Kuwait, and the United Arab Emirates (UAE), the connection between the popular uprisings and the Palestinian question disappeared in favor of other topics, such as that of blockade. In Jordan on January 29, Khaled Mechaal and his delegation were very careful to drop any references to the revolts visible in the region, Abdallah II himself being threatened by the beginnings of a Jordanian revolt.[51] Discourse that posits an unwavering link between Hamas and the "Arab Spring" therefore constitutes a form of ideologization of interests that is promoted or not depending on who is being addressed.

With the external leadership of the organization headquartered in Damascus until February 2012, the Movement of Islamic Resistance had everything to lose by pronouncing such an ideological discourse with regard to Syria. Preserving the Syrian support constituted an imperative for the movement by enabling it to retain the economic support of the Islamic Republic and then being threatened in numerous statements by Iranian dignitaries with a cutoff in financial support, military hardware deliveries, and provision of military training in Iran to the party's armed wing.[52] At the same time, given its pro-revolutionary stance this posture of distancing itself from the Syrian uprising puts Hamas in an awkward position. How then to reconcile efforts at ideological legitimization with defending its interests when the two are at odds?

The movement managed to find a compromise by engineering the departure of exterior leadership cadres while maintaining a symbolic presence ensured by the top leaders. This policy of "presence in absence" (*tawājud*)[53] let it minimize the costs of breaking with the Syrian regime while still appearing to be an actor opposed to Bashar al-Assad. The Syrian crisis once again illustrates the dilemma of diplomacy in which Hamas would henceforth find itself and testifies to how it managed to define a position that to this day allows it to reconcile its different interests and multiple constraints.[54]

The statements made by Ismaël Haniyeh during his visit to Iran on February 17, 2012 can also be read as an attempt to obscure this contradiction between efforts at legitimization and pursuit of specified interests. This recalls the cogency of the maximalist strategy of rejecting any normalization with Israel (*tasswiyya*) and reasserts the religious dimension of the Palestinian question. Despite the risk of seeing the return to the "rejection front" displease the new regional actors that Hamas hopes nevertheless to appeal to, the movement feels itself obliged to maintain this rhetoric of the Islamic resistance pole in order to assure continuity in its longtime sources of support.

The Splintering of the Decision-making Bodies: Ideology in the Service of the Group

The start of the Arab Spring, which allowed the Gazans to move around and be received abroad,[55] amplified the phenomenon of competition between the Gaza decision-making group and the one abroad that continued to exercise a monopoly on foreign policy decisions.[56] Still, since 2011, these unilateral decisions are being publicly challenged by different (groups of) actors with parochial causes and interests. We also note that unilateralism henceforth is criticized in a context of an external leadership weakened since its departure from Damascus: From now on, its members also find themselves dispersed among several Arab capitals, with Khaled Mechaal having returned to Qatar while Musa Abu Marzouq, vice president of the Political Section, settled in Cairo.

To cite an example, the topic of reconciliation was a frequent source of discord between the leaders. Signed by Khaled Mechaal in February 2012 at Doha, the agreement envisioned the formation of a provisional government in which Mahmoud Abbas, president of the Palestinian Authority, would also assume the post of prime minister, was something violently denounced by a part of the leadership in Gaza as well as by Mahmoud al-Zahar[57] who objected to Mahmoud Abbas becoming prime minister.[58]

This opposition then expressed itself in dogmatic terms, the objecting members of the movement giving ideological motives for their rejection: Why grant such concessions when the victories of the Islamists in Tunisia and in Egypt or elsewhere set the stage for a global Islamic project centered on Hamas in Gaza that would end in Israel's defeat? These justifications according to the Islamist norm, however, do not imply any correlation between geographic splintering and ideological opposition[59] and must not be construed as meaning that the Gaza leadership may be "tougher" than the external one.[60] The refusal to validate a foreign policy decision for not being coherent with the movement's doctrinal principles is a way of serving the positioning of its cadres. It is not directly opposed to the objectives pursued, but can serve the policies of one particular group.[61]

The sermon delivered by Youssef al-Qardawi in the al-Doha mosque on May 3, 2013 with Khaled Mechaal[62] present also provoked very sharp dissatisfaction among a part of the Gaza leadership.[63] Indeed, as he preached, Sheikh Youssef al-Qardawi said some insulting words about Hezbollah when he called out the Shiite movement as the "party of Satan,"[64] thus in the same breath not only insulting the Party of God's Secretary General Hassan Nasrallah but also the Islamic Republic by calling it an ally of Zionism.[65] Imad al-Alami and Mahmoud al-Zahar then had sent an urgent letter to Khaled Mechaal to have him clarify his position and distance himself explicitly from the sheikh's words.[66] Part of the Gaza leadership at that point spoke up about the report of the visit by Youssef al-Qaradawi to Gaza: Imad Al-Alami supposedly tried to convince Ismaël Haniyeh of the urgent need to cancel this visit given what had been said some days earlier at Doha.[67]

Conclusion

Although it doubly differentiates itself from the "classic" international actor able to mobilize the resources of a state entity and defining itself in national rather than supra-national terms, Hamas pursues a foreign policy that resembles those of most states in the international system. Any actor, be it a state or not, religious or secular, always favoring its interests, must take its values and norms into account when formulating foreign policy.

We have tried to demonstrate here that the latter most frequently are marshaled in defense of Hamas interests. In the early 1990s, with the movement marginalized on the national political scene, it invoked justifications of a religious nature in confronting Israel as a way of gaining popularity and credibility. On the other hand, its isolation on the regional scene involves a total break with using ideological references. Starting in the middle of the first 2000 decade, when it decided to stand for the legislative elections and take part in Palestine's political life by integrating with the Authority's institutions,[68] the movement's interests having evolved, the resort to ideology also went through a profound transformation: The policy toward Israel is most often presented in a pragmatic way, the religious references nevertheless serving to justify the reconciliation and to give credit to measures that may appear as deviant relative to the "Islamic norm." This is the case, for example, with the *hudna* concluded in June 2008. With regard to other actors, the movement falls back on an ideology that is sometimes Islamic, at other times focused on the notion of a "resistance front," to serve interests both external and internal, such as ensuring the continuation of economic support, expanding its network of alliances, and delegitimizing its political rivals in Palestine. With the outbreak of the Arab Spring, the movement performs an ideological redefinition and actuates a new formula that lets it position itself in the heart of the revolutionary process under way.

Yet, the Hamas foreign policy remains different from that of a state in that its authorities in charge of foreign policy are geographically dispersed, an element that exacerbates the tensions and inconsistencies inherent in any decision-making structure. This splintering itself is fractured a second time in connection with the "daily" management of decisions relating to the international since it is the external leadership that wields a quasi-monopoly over these decisions. Starting from 2011, the exterior's unilateralism is challenged and can express itself in normative terms to favor the interests of a group or a specific leader. Still, this plurality of actors with diverging interests does not preclude the existence of a base of shared interests within Hamas. Also, the capacity for transcending the split in the movement between the interior and exterior even if apparently structural proves the existence of shared interests.

It is too early to know the precise impact of the "Arab Spring" on Hamas foreign policy. Even though the divorce between Hamas and Syria appears to be final, the movement's regional realignment has not taken place as yet. It remains dependent on Iran's financial aid and the Syrian "revolution" is far from an outcome that would cause a radical realignment in the regional configuration.⁶⁹ On the Egypt side, Hamas, which appeared to be the prime target of a vast campaign waged by numerous Egyptian media against their president, had anticipated the risks of associating with the Muslim Brotherhood. Mohamed Morsi's overthrow on July 3, 2013 seems in fact to have prolonged the isolation of the Palestinian movement. Thus, more than ever, it appears that the policy of Hamas will still have to depend for some time yet on a regional context that is in uproar. The question remains, therefore: Just what contortions of an ideological order should we expect for justifying the movement's evolving interests?

Notes

1. The word *Hamas*, which means zeal or enthusiasm, is also the acronym for *Harakat al-Mouqawama al-Islamiyya*, the "Movement of Islamic Resistance." Although the presence of the Muslim Brotherhood in Palestine dates from 1935 and because, from the late 1960s on, the *ikhwan* had cast a wide social and welfare network around the figure of Sheikh Ahmed Yassine and under the patronage of the *moujama' islami*, the birth of Hamas as a political movement is dated December 8, 1987, at the time the first Intifada broke out. The Israeli government at first adopted a relative benign policy toward the spread of Palestinian Islamists, thinking that they could constitute an alternative to the nationalist claims of the Palestine Liberation Organization (PLO). The repression of the movement only dates from 1988. For a detailed study of the origins of Hamas, see especially Khaled Khroub, *Hamas, Political Thought and Practice*, Washington, DC, Institute for Palestine Studies, 2000.
2. Frédéric Charillon (dir.), *Politique étrangère: Nouveaux regards* [Foreign Policy: New Looks], Paris, Presses de Sciences Po, 2002.
3. The Montevideo Convention (1933) assigns the quality of a state to political entities combining the following four criteria: a) a permanent population, b) a defined territory, c) a sovereign political entity, and d) the capacity to enter into relationships with other states.
4. This is explained by the Israelo-Egyptian encirclement of this terrain although at times the blockade is eased, as, for example, in May 2010, following the incident of the Turkish *Mavi Marmara* flotilla, or also in the spring of 2011 after Hosni Mubarak fell.
5. The foreign policy of a state partly expresses a society's values and norms on the

international stage. See O.R. Holsti, "Foreign Policy Decision Makers Viewed Psychologically: Cognitive Process Approaches," in G. Matthew Bonham and J. Michael Shapiro, *Thought and Action in Foreign Policy*, Basel, Birkhäuser, 1977.

6. This trait should not lead to grasping Hamas as a unique case, since other movements that present themselves as national liberation movements have had significant geographic distributions, such as the PLO operating for a long time outside Palestine's borders or, more recently, the Syrian National Coalition.
7. The Political Section or maktab siyassi is the Hamas executive authority in charge of foreign policy. It is composed of fifteen members divided into four leaderships: West Bank, Gaza, the exterior, and prisons. This department makes decisions in conformity with prior directions issued by the majlis al-shura, a body similar to a legislative assembly. Local Hamas members elect their representatives to this Consultative Council (of from 70 to 90 members). The West Bank would be divided into seven districts, Gaza into five, with each district divided into units. Once elected, these members sitting in council in turn elect the members of the Political Section.
8. The Hamas leadership dealing with the Israeli prisons comprises twenty-three members. According to Badura Fares, director of the *Palestinian Prisoners Society*, Hamas militants account for approximately 2,000 of a total 5,000 prisoners. Yahia al-Sinouar headed the prisons leadership unit until his release at the time of the prisoner exchange accord between Israel and Hamas. He is the only high-ranking personality among the 1,027 released prisoners.
9. It is not possible to give a definition of what is meant by "Islamic norm" since, as Badouin Dupret points out, Islam is what Muslims make it. For Hamas, this norm is whatever it chooses to define it at a given time. See Baudouin Dupret, *La charia aujourd'hui: usages de la référence au droit islamique* [*Sharia* Today: Uses of the Islamic Law Reference], Paris, La Découverte, 2012.
10. Except for the 1948 war that saw the Palestinian Muslim Brotherhood rally to the ranks of nationalist factions to wage war against Israel, the *ikhwan* ceased to take part in the armed struggle until the triggering of the first Intifada in 1987. But from 1980 on, they stationed a military arm in Gaza commanded by Ahmed Yassine.
11. Khaled Khroub, *Hamas, Political Thought and Practice*, op. cit.
12. Palestine is regarded by the Islamists as a *waqf*, in other words, a sacred legacy, hence an inalienable territory in conformity with Islamic law.
13. See the text of the October 27, 1994 communiqué in Khaled Kroub, *Hamas, Political Thought and Practice*, op. cit., p.158.

14. Hamas was criticized directly and indirectly by a number of Arab states for the abduction and subsequent assassination of the Israeli sergeant major Nissim Toledano in December 1992 and then for a series of attacks on buses in Israel in 1994 and during February and March 1996.
15. Article 14 of the Charter in the appendices of the book by Khaled Khroub, *Hamas, Political Thought and Practice, op. cit.*
16. For an analysis of Hamas communiqués during the Gulf War, see Jean-François Legrain, "A Defining Moment, Palestinian Islamic Fundamentalism," in James Piscatori, *Islamic Fundamentalism and the Gulf Crisis*, Chicago, American Academy of Arts and Sciences, 1991, p. 70.
17. With the outbreak of the Iran–Iraq War and the PLO's backing of Saddam Hussein, the privileged relationship that Khomeini maintained with it deteriorated rapidly, until the holding of the Madrid conference on October 22, 1991, which marked the debut of Iranian support for all the resistance movements and the opening of a Hamas office in Teheran in February 1992. Iran then was the only country to be officially recognized by the Movement of Islamic Resistance.
18. Until 1990, Hamas did not have any official representation in the Arab countries or a spokesman outside the Territories. According to Khaled Khroub, the birth of its foreign policy is primarily explained by the change of tone and adoption of a new idiom from 1987 to 1990, *Hamas, Political Thought and Practice, op. cit.*
19. Ibrahim Ghosheh was the Hamas spokesman in Amman during the 1990s and a member of the Political Section. Arrested by the Jordanian authorities in 1990, he was expelled from the country. Some years later, the kingdom authorized his return to its territory on the condition that he would cease his political activities.
20. On April 28, 1998, he went to Iran and met the Supreme Guide of the Revolution Ali Khamenei, President Mohamed Khatami as well as Minister of Foreign Affairs Kamal Kharazi who accorded him substantial political and financial support. Since the winter of 1992 and the expulsion to South Lebanon, the great majority of what Hamas obtained in the way of financial aid and military support came from Teheran.
21. The United States had made contact with Hamas during January and February 1993 through the American Embassy in Amman at a time when it had no official relationship with the PLO. See Khaled Khroub, *Hamas, Political Thought and Practice, op. cit.*
22. In December 1992, following the assassination of Sergeant Nissim Toledano on the thirteenth of that month after he had been abducted by the al-Qassam

brigades, Israel expelled 400 Palestinian Islamists to Marj-al-Zouhour in South Lebanon.

23. In an interview that appeared in the *al-Hayat* newspaper on January 23, 1994, Mohammed Nazzal affirmed that the American position was momentarily up in the air because they were thinking that it would be important to maintain contact with Hamas once the PLO was established. According to him, the issue was still being debated in May 1993.

24. The movement's leaders referred repeatedly to respect for the principle of non-interference and never mobilized the popular indigenous base to achieve their objectives outside Palestine. The failure of the Political Section experiment in Amman in addition is explained by the non-respect for this commitment, since a kind of mobilization existed in Jordan and it pointed to the Jordanian Section of the Brotherhood in this country.

25. This preeminence of the external leaders in the definition and elaboration of foreign policy is claimed by them as much as by the analysts. According to Usama Hamdan, whom the author met in Damascus on January 25, 2011, the Damascus section is in charge of the problems of "day-to-day management" in keeping with the aims set by the *majlis al-shura*. In an interview with the journalist Mohammed Daraghmeh in Ramallah on February 25 2011 it was revealed: "In Hamas, foreign policy is the prerogative of the Political Section which comprises the West Bank, Gaza, the prisons, and Damascus. The Section members debate, then they decide. Nonetheless, it is the Damascus group which takes care of daily implementation of diplomacy, including questions of sensitive foreign matters."

26. Mishal Shaul and Sela Avraham, *The Palestinian Hamas: Vision, Violence and Coexistence*, New York, Columbia University Press, 2000.

27. Musa Abu Marzouq directed the Political Section of Hamas from 1991 to 1995 when he was arrested by the CIA at John F. Kennedy International Airport in New York and jailed in the United States until May 1997 when Israel dropped its request for extradition. In Damascus, he held the post of vice-president of the Political Section and took part in numerous negotiations including those that led to the truce of June 2008.

28. Khaled Mechaal is the founder of the Palestinian Islamist networks in Kuwait. In 1990, he went to Jordan where he worked with Musa Abu Marzouq. When the latter was arrested in the United States, Mechaal took over as Political Section chief. In 1997, he survived a Mossad assassination attempt in Amman. In 1999, he returned to Syria to direct the organization from Damascus. Since early 2012 he has been living in Doha, Qatar.

29. Hamas was conceived as the armed wing of the Muslim Brotherhood in Palestine for launching a dynamic of resistance against the occupation. Relations between the two organizations developed ad hoc and whether Hamas wanted to appear as one of the branches of the Muslim Brotherhood or, on the contrary, to advertise its independence. For a more precise description of the relationship between the Brothers and Hamas, see the analyses by Abd al Mu'min Mahmoud in *al-Dustūr* dated January 28, 2009.
30. These elements recall the differences in positioning in the PLO between the leaders in exile and those in the Occupied Territories; the former remained attached to the concept of Palestine as a whole while the latter preferred the option of a "mini state" contiguous with Israel. See Allon Groth, *The PLO's Road to Peace: Processes of Decision Making*, London, Royal Services Institute for Defense Studies, 1995.
31. Aude Signoles, *Le Hamas au pouvoir et après?* [Hamas in Power and After?], Toulouse, Milan, collection Milan actu, 2006.
32. The exterior leadership's financial management would have granted them heightened control over the brigades. However, the relationship between the military wing and the political apparatus did not always work that way; the brigade members were able to carry out armed operations without prior notice to the leaders resident outside the Occupied Territories.
33. Drafted by fighters imprisoned in Israel in the hope that their common effort and legitimacy imparted by being imprisoned would lend more weight to these proposals, the document was signed by the different factions three months after the formation of the first Palestinian Government dominated by Hamas. The document in Arabic can be viewed online here: http://www.aljazeera.net/news/pages/5583e506-50a3-4368-8a08- 4f995c783141, and a French version is available here: http://www.france-palestine.org/Le-document-des-prisonniers
34. Some authors, such as Jeroen Gunning, have tried to demonstrate that the explanatory factors for political actions by Hamas, including armed ones, are explicated by the wish to preserve the connection with its militant base and in a wider sense with Palestinian public opinion. See Hamas in Politics: Democracy, Religion, Violence, London, Hurst and Company, 2007.
35. "Mechaal Spells Out the Political Orientation of Hamas," an interview conducted by the journalist Silvia Catori, *Al-Sabeel*, July 2010, translated to English by the Centre Afro-Moyen Orient (Afro-Middle East Centre – AMEC).
36. Bilal al-Shobaki, "*Hamas et la dialectique de la résistance et du gouvernement*" [Hamas and the Dialectic of Resistance and Government], *Falistin al-Muslima*,

Vol. 27, no. 1, January 2009, cited by Yezid Sayigh, *We Serve the People: Hamas Policing in Gaza*, Crown Center for Middle East Studies, April 2011.
37. *Al-Joumhouriyya al-Masriyya*, January 3, 2006.
38. The Quartet brought together the United States, the European Union (EU), the United Nations (UN), and Russia. On this topic, see the article by Caroline Goerzig, *Transforming the Quartet Principles*, European Union Institute for Security Studies, September 2010.
39. On January 27, 2008 on http://www.youtube.com/watch?v=ooEr5WbPdh8, repeated on September 29, 2010.
40. To Egypt, Saudi Arabia, Syria, Oman, Libya, Qatar, Sudan, Bahrain, Kuwait, Yemen as well as Turkey and Iran.
41. *Al-Sharq*, May 2, 2009.
42. Paola Caridi shows how the external leadership first tried to minimize the importance of this document before insisting on a change in its content prior to approving it. See *Hamas, from Resistance to Government*, New York, Seven Stories Press, 2012.
43. Jonathan D. Halevi, *Power Dynamics Inside Hamas*, Jerusalem Center for Public Affairs, 2012.
44. Assistant initially to Imad al-Alami, the Hamas representative in Teheran, Oussama Hamdan took over the post himself in 1994. From 1998 on, he represented the organization in Lebanon. In 2009, he joined À Khaled Mechaal in Damascus and took over the movement's external affairs section.
45. Mahmoud al-Zahar is one of the founders of the Islamic University of Gaza and also one of the first members of Hamas. In 1992, he was among the 415 deportees to South Lebanon's Marj al-Zouhour camp. Since the assassination of Sheikh Yassine, he is one of the principal leaders in the Gaza strip. In March 2006, he was designated Minister of Foreign Affairs of the first government formed by the "Change and Reform" bloc that represented Hamas in the Palestinian Legislative Council.
46. According to the interview with Mohammed Dahlan on Palvoice dated April 3, 2010: "It is Khaled Mechaal who is sabotaging the Shalit deal, despite Mahmoud al Zahar's support for its completion. Unfortunately, Mash'al wants to get the deal that is considered to be ideal, but it so happens that this is impossible."
47. Recall nevertheless that to minimize the cost to the organization of such a measure that risked appearing as a strategic turnabout to its base, the leaders denied its novel characters by assuring that "popular resistance" would never take the

place of armed resistance. See Izzat al-Richq, Centre Palestinien d'Information, November 27, 2011.
48. On February 24, 2012, the Party of Liberty and Justice (hizb al-huriyya wa al- 'adala), an Egyptian political organization issued out of the Muslim Brotherhood, testified to the fact of its liking for the Camp David accords. See especially the article by Kifah Zaboun in *Sharq al Awsat*, dated February 24, 2012.
49. Statement made by Salah Bardawil on the occasion of the twenty-fourth anniversary of the founding of Hamas, Centre Palestinien d'Information, December 14, 2011.
50. "Ismaël Haniyeh Congratulates the Tunisians on the Victory of their Revolution," Centre Palestinien d'Information, November 26, 2011.
51. With the external sections of Hamas having their seats in Amman from the early 1990s until 2000, for there to be a normalization of relations with Jordan without arousing suspicion or worries is a priority for the movement. Interview with Izzat al-Rishq, *al-Hayat*, January 22, 2012.
52. "There was at a certain point a misunderstanding between Hamas and Iran over the Hamas position on Syria: We advised the Syrian regime to choose the political position but it was the security solution demanded by the party of Maher al-Assad that was chosen. Because of that, Iran cut off our funding." Interview with Sayyid Abu Musameh, Geneva, on January 15, 2012.
53. Derived from the verb *wajada*, which means "being present," this well-thought-out form implies the recognition of a presence without, however, indicating an intention to pay it any heed. The noun is used to evoke, for example, the manner in which Lebanon's religious minorities live side by side.
54. This recalls the dexterity with which Hamas faced the Gulf War in 1990. See Jean-François Legrain, "A Defining Moment, Palestinian Islamic Fundamentalism," *op. cit.*
55. After the fall of Hosni Mubarak, the relative relaxation at the Rafah checkpoint allowed the Gaza Strip leaders to move around and fundraise more easily, thus reducing the exterior's monopoly on diplomacy. Larbi Sadiki, *Tests and Contests: Hamas without Syria, Al-Jazeera*, March 12, 2012.
56. This recalls the monopoly on decisions by the PLO's external general staff based in Tunis and this despite the eruption of the first Intifada, which, however, had restored the equilibrium between the two locations by giving more of a role to the internal leaders. See Nadine Picaudou, *Retours en Palestine: trajectoires, rôles et expériences des "returnees" dans la société palestinienne après Oslo* [Returns to

Palestine: Trajectories, Roles, and Experiences of "Returnees" in Palestinian Society after Oslo], Paris, Karthala, 2006.
57. Mahmoud al-Zahar is the Gaza personality publicly displaying the strongest opposition to Doha. He thinks this accord is a "mistake." *Le Point*, February 12, 2012.
58. In some instances, the competition can cross the interior/exterior divide, as when Musa Abu Marzouq aligns himself with the rejectionist position of Mahmoud al-Zahar specifically in order to compete with Mechaal during the Hamas internal elections.
59. Based on the article by Mohammed Hijazi, which appeared in June 2011 in the *Revue d'études palestiniennes* (volume 22, number 87), the conflict over the Doha accord illustrates the reality of the opposition between the interior and exterior Hamas, each side representing a perspective on what ought to happen and the decision-making process.
60. Some members of the external leadership like Musa Abu Marzouq or Mustafa Leddawi opposed it. See Mustafa Leddawi, "Que Dieu maudisse l'accord de Doha" [May God Curse the Doha Accord], *Falistin al-Youm*, April 6, 2012.
61. "Zahar looked tougher in the media but in reality he is no tougher than Mechaal. In 2006, he wanted to head the government but Mechaal said no. It is mostly because of that that he blocked Mechaal's move. He tries to block Mechaal because it was Mechaal who blocked Zahar." Interview with Hassan Balwawi, Ramallah, February 2011. See also *al-Hayat* of February 6, 2008.
62. http://www.alquds.co.uk/?p=50471
63. http://www.alarab.co.uk/?p=41817
64. http://www.echoroukonline.com/ara/articles/163674.html
65. http://elbadil.com/political-research/2013/06/16/159241
66. http://www.alquds.co.uk/?p=50471
67. http://elbadil.com/political-research/2013/06/16/159241
68. Hamas had opted not to participate in the first Palestinian legislative elections of January 1996 because, according to its leaders, they legitimized the Oslo accords.
69. In early October, when Khaled Mechaal stated during a visit to Beirut that "the people have the right to rebel to defend their rights but they must do it in a peaceful manner. And the organizations that fight in Syria ought to turn their weapons in the direction of Palestine," this was interpreted as the first sign of seeking a reconciliation with the Syrian regime: http://www.raialyoum.com/?p=11410

6

A Fighting Shiism Faces the World: The Foreign Policy of Hezbollah*

Aurélie Daher

Studying the foreign policy of Lebanon's Hezbollah is no easy task. From a methodological standpoint, it is an exercise that first of all entails untangling a very tightly woven mix of internal and external strategies: More than any other Lebanese party, Hezbollah is a political apparatus whose reason for being, universe of meaning, and propensity for action are largely determined by a specific relationship with the external, in this case regional, world. Next, on the analytical level, the challenge consists of clearly grasping the multiple and multiform character of this foreign policy: Hezbollah's leadership does not just have one but diverse foreign policies; depending on the context, it does not hesitate to change its relationship with the world in an explicitly pragmatic logic, but it also projects its relations with the outside through different organizational and institutional supports. The red lines defined a priori by its ideological paradigms are not perfectly inflexible, and its relations with the national political system—of which Hezbollah, like other of the country's groups, is simultaneously a component and a competitor—lets it develop foreign policies from differing platforms that appear at times contradictory but are functionally quite complementary.

Difficult to dissect it may be, but the subject keeps its hold on the interest. Close to thirty years after Hezbollah's birth, the study of its foreign policy has in the main constituted a subordinate subject to the study of Western foreign policies, which has been content to view it as subcontracting on behalf of more important regional actors. Hezbollah's interaction with the world, thus limited to a series of anti-Western and anti-Israeli terrorist initiatives carried out on the orders of the Syrian and/or Iranian regimes, becomes a favored way for getting at the real nature of the organization, so that Hezbollah sees itself summed up as an essentially violent organization whose field of action is by nature extra-national. Indisputably, Hezbollah's foreign policy reflects a series of elements that reveal the organization's true identity; however, it is really nothing more than an evolving strategy hinging on other means of action, in the service of an order of priorities that are definitely Lebanese-centered: For Hezbollah, as for quite a few other political actors, its foreign policy is above all a *domestic* policy. In order to understand the latter's relationship to the world and its strategic choices in that regard, it is necessary first of all to discard certain received ideas, and then to return to the reasons that brought the party into being and refocus on the principal goals it makes its own.

Hezbollah, Passive Instrument of Syro-Iranian Policy?

The ties that rule relations between Hezbollah and Teheran on the one hand and the party and Damascus on the other are not only of a dissimilar nature, but each of them of a substance that has been modulated multiple times in line with the contexts.

Revolutionary Iran is habitually regarded as Hezbollah's matrix as much on the organizational as ideological plane. The argument essentially rests on the party's declared allegiance to the principle of *wilāyat al-Faqīh*, or the "rule of the jurisprudent," the hierarchizing doctrine of authorities within the politico-religious Shiite world, which, in practice, installs the Guide of the Iranian Revolution at the top of the pyramid. If this means that Hezbollah has to take into account the general strategic orientations laid down by the Guide, the connection between the party and the Iranian president still is not officially one of subordination.[1] Moreover, and contrary to the widely held idea that the principle of *wilāyat al-Faqīh* acts as a constraining tie to the point of making Hezbollah a tractable satellite remotely controlled from Teheran, the modalities of this relationship are well-defined and only function in certain situations. The authority of the *Faqīh* in fact translates itself as (i) "good by consent," by which the Guide *a posteriori* blesses certain decisions made by the party's leadership, and (ii) a power of arbitration that only intervenes if solicited by Hezbollah's leadership. That leaves the latter all kinds of room for maneuver in the decision-making process, management, and execution, since the two men who have held the office of *waliy*—Khomeini, and then Khamenei—have been and remain relatively unintrusive mentors in the party's day-to-day affairs.[2]

During the 1980s, abductions of a number of Western nationals and attacks directed against the Multinational Forces in Lebanon and the American Embassy were attributed to Hezbollah, which thus is supposed to have been responsible for delivering mission-messages addressed by the Iranian revolutionaries to its Western rivals.

Teheran, the prime beneficiary of the "affair of the hostages," in having facilitated their liberation by interceding with the various abductors and simultaneously settling its differences with Paris over the Eurodif matter, denied having instigated the abductions.[3] The party likewise always firmly denied its involvement; in point of fact, while some familial and friendship ties could be established between some kidnappers and party members, to this day there does not appear to exist any proof of a definite responsibility of its leadership.[4] Whatever real links that may have attached Hezbollah and Iran to the abductors, the 1990s saw this bridle, which allegedly made the party subject to Teheran's whim, relax significantly. During the terms in office of Rafsandjani (1989–97) and Khatami (1997–2005), Hezbollah lost the support of the presidential link, incarnated during Khomeini's time by Khamenei. In fact, a just-elected Rafsandjani warned that the Lebanese protégé party must become "like any other party." The first new translation of this distancing, a drastic reduction in the financial support the party had enjoyed previously, encouraged it to choose an intensive policy of self-financing. Khatami, intent on an opening to other Lebanese political tendencies, set in motion an even sharper weakening of Hezbollah's privileged status by insisting on making the Lebanese state Teheran's premier partner in the Land of Cedars. Hezbollah would have to wait until the election of Mahmoud Ahmadinejad in 2005 to once again become the protégé organization and principal interlocutor in Lebanon.

If the relationship between Hezbollah and Teheran however vertical still remained relatively supple, the relationship with the Syrian regime was less so, horizontal as it may have been in this case. Damascus, during the years of its tutelage over Lebanon (1990–2005), regularly intervened, directly and in detail, it its neighbor's political affairs. Desiring to maintain a certain equilibrium between the local forces, on occasion it imposed limiting edicts on Hezbollah as it did on other Lebanese groups. But the party, while continuing to depend on the good will of the Syrian regime to sustain resistance against the Israeli occupation of South Lebanon and weapons shipments from Iran, progressively became a key asset for the Syrian mentor in return. By virtue of its support for Hezbollah's cause, the Assad dynasty managed to wrap itself for many years in the mantle of a "resisting Arab" regime,[5] helping it to sustain legitimacy in its own country at very little cost. There was only a more-or-less well-balanced bilateral contract between the party and the Syrian regime, whereas between Hezbollah and the Iranian Guide there existed an affinity and ideological engagement.

As it has in its relations with the Lebanese state, since the late 1980s Hezbollah has opted for prudence in its relations with Damascus, by advocating non-confrontation in the hope of not compromising the interests of fighters engaged in South Lebanon. That said, whenever possible, the Syrian desiderata have been ignored when it benefited the party's key interests. This was the case, for example, during the municipal elections in 1998 and in 2004, when Afwāj al-Muqāwamah al-Lubnāniyyah (the Brigades of the Lebanese Resistance) (AMAL), the second Lebanese Shiite grouping, insisted on putting up combined slates with the more popular Hezbollah in hopes of riding its coat-tails. The party leadership, sure of its victory, was opposed and even the pugnacious interventions by the Syrian authorities on AMAL's behalf failed to change its mind. Likewise, in the spring of 2000, the Syrian regime was worried about Israel's being resigned to making a unilateral withdrawal from Lebanon, which, some weeks later, would indeed mark an end to twenty-two years of occupation of the Country of Cedars. Damascus tried hard to temper the aggressiveness of the Lebanese fighters in hopes of preventing the retreat, but Hezbollah, determined to achieve a quick, clear victory over Tel Aviv's troops, disregarded the Syrian wishes by intensifying the pace of the attacks against the occupier to keep the Israeli general staff and government from backtracking on their decision to pull its military back unconditionally.

If the grand outlines of Hezbollah's policies, among them its foreign policy, are not completely determined by its regional godfathers, and if the party ventures to bypass the latter's aspirations when it thinks its own interests demand it, what then are its own priorities?

Objectives, Institutions and Reinterpretation of Hezbollah's Foreign Policy

Three Decades of Service to the Islamic Resistance

When Israel invaded Lebanon for the second time in June 1982, a resistance effort immediately welded together large parts of the country's Shiite militant groups. In the Bekaa, the north-eastern Lebanese hinterland, a first network of clerics, who, for several years, had advocated anti-imperialist paradigms, simultaneously used their backing within the revolutionary world of Iran and their popularity with the local young people to set up a new paramilitary organization dedicated to repelling the occupier: al-Muqāwama al-islāmîyya fī Lubnān, the "Islamic Resistance in Lebanon" (IRL). Then its general staff joined to it a network of civil institutions responsible for mobilizing in its name and developing within the society and then among the political class a certain number of support levers. This network, soon to diversify and professionalize itself, took its permanent name in May 1984: Hezbollah, or *Party of God*. Relations between the IRL and Hezbollah are defined by a logic of complementarity: The former takes on the military combat role, harrying the occupation forces in the hope of convincing them to withdraw completely and permanently; the latter furnishes a discourse of justification and mobilization, social action of compensation and participation in the national political life with the objective of defusing any challenges arising in the population and any threat that may emerge from the leadership spheres of the Lebanese state. Hezbollah's foreign policy (as distinct from IRL external, para-military action) does not evade this task distribution: Like the party's other types of activities, the primary function of its foreign policy remains the defense of IRL's interests.

With this postulate in mind, it becomes possible to discern the logic that underpins Hezbollah's external preferences and to grasp how the context may suggest friendships or enmities. Logically, Israel remains irrevocably enemy number one. On this level, Hezbollah makes sure to clearly differentiate Zionism and Judaism, stating officially that it has no quarrel with the latter.[6] Washington, Tel Aviv's quasi-organic ally, cannot expect to be regarded better than its protégé. The other actors in this world are alternately elevated to the rank of respectable interlocutors, if not favored allies, or else condemned publicly for their policy or that of their governments. To cite France's image as an example, it has clearly improved over the past three decades. A member of the Multinational Forces stationed in Beirut in the days following the 1982 invasion by Israel, Paris was criticized for the support it rendered at the time to the pro-Israeli Lebanese Christian militias despite its obligation to remain neutral.[7] But, the end of the international armed presence in 1984 then allowed France to become a "reasonable Western partner." The presidency of Jacques Chirac (1995–2007), in particular, is approved of for the most part, essentially for its multiple condemnations of the Israeli attacks on Lebanon during the second half of the 1990s. The vote for UN Security Resolution 1559 in September 2004, which provided for the disarmament of "all militias" in Lebanon—the IRL included—was a disappointment. But France actually did not lose its status as favored interlocutor, even during the great crisis moments like the summer of 2006, during the 33-Day War, when Paris would represent the sole Western firewall against Israel's destructive capability.[8]

Internal Production Sources

From an internal, institutional perspective, the production of Hezbollah's foreign policy is distributed on several levels. Contrary to what certain media have liked to assert, there is no "Foreign Affairs Ministry" in the party. It does indeed have a "Foreign Relations Unit" (Wahdat al-'Ilāqāt al-khārijiyya), which, without being a decision-making organ, looks after a part of public relations and in particular provides advice and assistance to the authorities actually responsible for foreign-policy planning. Hence, the unit's president takes care of general contacts with international organizations or foreign embassies, while his assistants comb through the foreign press and write memos that are sent to higher decision-making authorities. Depending on the nature of the delegations visiting Hezbollah, the meetings are organized in a fashion best suited to the visitors' profile and they may be redirected to other units: Emissaries from embassies or international organizations may be received by the president of the foreign relations unit in a framework of routine communications meetings, but foreign professors, journalists, and other professionals are most often received by party cadres belonging to specialized entities (the unit for student mobilization, information unit, and so forth).

The substance and methods of foreign policy are decided at higher levels. Hezbollah's secretary general, supported by the Consultative Council, has the final say on what positions to adopt. The Political Council, one of five central councils supervised by the Consultative Council, is subdivided in turn into working groups responsible for individual "dossiers." Among these are the external relations dossier, the dossier of relations with Arab countries, that of relations with the Palestinian factions, and one for relations with Islamic groups. More systematic contacts for mutual cooperation are established on this level. There are numerous exceptions when the exchanges are delegated to higher instances if the content is judged to be sensitive. The secretary general himself or his deputy handle strategic political cooperation as well as certain contacts that need to remain secret or are intended for passing along unofficial messages. Finally, military and security cooperations fall within the competence of the IRL general staff and the individuals who run the security apparatus.

Logically, this splitting of contact levels from those making the decision may augur a fragmented foreign policy for the party. However, for several years already, it appears to have been well-managed and with a remarkable coherence of the positions of the different levels, producing a uniform discourse of justification and action lastingly aligned with the stipulated choices. In this regard, solid internal discipline and a vertical organizational structure that effectively forestall differences definitely are of great help. The fit is that much more successful because it also incorporates Hezbollah's external action via the state apparatus.

The State Platform

In practice, Hezbollah's efforts in the foreign policy realm translate mainly into a permanent attempt to defuse through exchanges with foreign actors to the best of their ability any threats that may impede the Resistance continuing in action. In particular, its foreign relations platform acts as an extension in communications terms of the battle field where the IRL and Israel habitually confront each other: Numerous indeed are the occasions when Hezbollah resorts to diplomatic channels to counter campaigns instigated by Israeli Foreign Affairs aiming to have Western governments punish the party and the IRL. But the main thrust of Hezbollah's efforts in reality is foreign communications by proxy, embodied in a policy of lobbying the Lebanese state authorities.

Research into Hezbollah's recourse in foreign-policy matters to institutions of the Lebanese state is relevant really only since the start of the 1990s, when the party decides for the first time to enter the national institutional arena. It was in fact in 1992 that the first post-war (1975–90) parliamentary elections took place and Hezbollah opted to take part. Its goal? *isāl sawt al-Muqāwama lal-Barlamén*, or "Make the voice of the Resistance heard in Parliament."[9] In other words, it wanted to expand the array of levers already at its disposal for defending the IRL's interests. Seeing that the Lebanese state, with the application of the Taëf accords that had just ended the civil war, was about to regain a certain authority, Hezbollah thought it prudent to acquire the means of countering the state's potential nuisance power from the inside. Far from working to obtain subsidies for its institutions as is the wont generally of the region's politico-religious groups and refraining from any debate on the opportunity for regime change in favor of an Islamic Government, Hezbollah's parliamentary deputies remained faithful to their original mission. They did so by demanding that the IRL's actions in South Lebanon be recognized officially and legitimized by the state, by calling for aid to the victims of the Israeli bombardments and for initiatives to free Lebanese prisoners held in Israeli jails; in addition, they tried to weigh in on Beirut's foreign policy. This they did explicitly for every military crisis with Tel Aviv: for the Israeli army's expanded offensives in July 1993 and April 1996 and the various, more or less significant, skirmishes punctuating the relative calm that reigned on the border in the days immediately following the Liberation of 2000. The government, at Hezbollah's urging, not only had to officially support the Resistance cause but also do its utmost to counter any international attempts to bring the resistance to heel. This expectation by the party was not simply one request among others: Its implementation was nothing less than a sine qua non for maintaining a good understanding between Hezbollah and the government. From when it entered politics, the party, in fact, quite explicitly established the rules of the game: As long as the state did not challenge the IRL's interests, it had no reason to fear a destabilizing action by the party. Deferring its aspirations for an Islamization of government into a hypothetical future, Hezbollah therefore conceived of the state above all as an instrument of its policy for defusing any foreign threats.

As long as the Syrian regime remained the supreme arbiter of Lebanese politics (1990–2005), Hezbollah had no complaints about the service rendered by the Beirut authorities: Prime Minister Rafic Hariri himself more than once went out of his way to defend the IRL's cause against his Western allies. Hezbollah's awareness of the state's potential role in foreign influence continued after the Syrian troops pulled out in 2005 and the victory of the March 14 coalition, which was hostile toward Damascus, in the parliamentary elections that same year. Despite marked ideological differences, relations between the party and the new Lebanese regime thus started off under acceptable auspices, thanks to a more or less explicit commitment by the new government not to damage the IRL.

The strategic importance to Hezbollah's foreign policy of the state lever was illustrated with unprecedented clarity during the crisis in the summer of 2006, when Israel bombarded Lebanon non-stop for thirty-three days and thirty-three nights following the abduction of two Israeli soldiers at the border by the IRL in the early morning of July 12. For the first time in Hezbollah's history, the government broke ranks with the IRL and part of the political class hostile to Hezbollah collaborated with the attacker. The political escalation led by Hezbollah after the war in large part originated with this disappearance of the state go-between, just as it explains its insistence on getting a firmer grip on the reins of power. From 2006 on, more than ever, the president of the Republic, the prime minister, the head of the army, and the high officials of the forces of order and security would not be appointed without Hezbollah's stamp of approval—on the first and last condition that the candidates were committed to defending the IRL. In this, the party's task was aided by the fall of the Hariri Government in January 2011 and the reversal of the trends in Parliament that followed. The March 8 coalition gained the majority of seats in the Parliament and the privilege of forming a new government. However, the outbreak of the Syrian crisis at the same time forced Hezbollah to revise its modus operandi in foreign-policy matters in spite of itself.

Anti-Assad Revolution: The Irl's Exceptional Deterritorialization

In the spring of 2011, Hassan Nasrallah, the secretary general of Hezbollah, did not temporize. Faced with the rising political unrest in Syria, he publicly declared a preference for keeping the regime in power while calling for a dialogue between it and the opposition. This caused a serious setback to Hezbollah's popularity among a large part of the Syrian public. It was logical for the relations between the party and the forces actively protesting to be tainted by animosity: disagreeable accusations erupted between the Syrian National Council (Snc) of Burhan Ghalioun and the party leadership: Ammar al-Wawi, spokesman for the Free Syrian Army, warned Nasrallah that he would be judged by "the Syrian revolutionary tribunals once the Revolution had achieved victory."[10] Tension arose especially around the presumed intervention by the IRL on the side of Bashar al-Assad's regime. Report after report came from the Syrian opposition claiming that hundreds if not thousands of fighters were deployed on the side of Damascus, with several accounts asserting that dozens of IRL men had been killed in combat. Videos were posted on YouTube that showed armed militants purported to be IRL members in action in Syria. However, until the spring of 2013, it appeared upon checking that the Syrian accusations remained largely unsupported, the IRL by all appearances not having rendered any manpower support to Assad's army.

Nevertheless, this does not mean it had no presence on the ground. Its field of action is a well-defined part of the border, the Syrian region bordering on northeast Lebanon: Some IRL members living in the sector joined up with local militias that were defending several villages in the zone mainly inhabited by Lebanese Shiites and regularly targeted by the radical Sunni opposition groups.[11] The Hezbollah leadership therefore justified the IRL's action by claiming that these were not troops dispatched there from Lebanon but instead were Lebanese residents in Syrian territory acting in self-defense.

A participation by the IRL in combat between the regime and the opposition in Syria that proved to be true and was acknowledged by the party took place in late May 2013. Syrian rebels battled IRL fighters backed by regular Syrian forces for three weeks at Qusayr, which the opposition had taken several months earlier. It was a ferocious face-off, with the two sides reporting casualties in the hundreds.[12] The number of fighters who took part is difficult to establish: Media reports had from 3,000 and 6,000 rebels fighting the Syrian army, reinforced by an IRL contingent of 3,000 to 4,000 men according to French authorities, of 1,500 men according to Hezbollah, of a few hundred according to other Lebanese sources.[13,14]

The Syrian army and IRL won a decisive victory in early June: The latter's intervention especially is credited by observers of all persuasions as the decisive factor enabling the regime to prevail. The Syrian army previously had been mired for weeks in low-intensity fighting with the rebels without achieving a positive outcome.

The justification put forward by the Hezbollah leadership for this first intervention of its kind on Syrian territory alludes to a concern at the progress by radical jihadists in the border zone of a key region for Hezbollah—the region of Baalbeck al-Hermel in the North Bekaa—and the growing frequency of their attacks on Shiites both on Lebanese and Syrian territory.[15] Fearing to see them advance deeply into the (Shiite) Lebanese zone, the IRL had no choice but to launch a blitz designed to push them back far enough to restore calm and security on both sides of this sensitive part of the border.[16] Thus, Hezbollah portrays the IRL intervention not as an offensive but as a defensive move. This argument seems to comport with the fact that if the IRL intervened in Qusayr and Homs, both very close to the Shiite Bekaa, it did not penetrate deeply to Aleppo, a city located far from the border.[17] Fear of a massive presence of anti-Shiite radical fighters at the gates of northeast Lebanon justifying the need to make the Homs area a secure zone emerges genuinely enough from the accounts by IRL fighters to withstand scrutiny and offer a reasonable explanation for the choice made by the IRL's leadership to go into battle, for the first time in its history, on national territory other than its own. But evidently it is not the only explanation.

The most plausible interpretation of the IRL involvement in Syria therefore remains one of two converging interests. The Syrian regime, by retaking the Qusayr and Homs region, "unblocks" the two great transport and traffic routes linking Damascus to the country's northwest, including the coast; at the same time, it renders access to the Sunni part of the Lebanese Bekaa more difficult for the rebels that, since 2011, have established a rear area resupply and rearming base there. The IRL's participation in the fighting in Syria appears above all to reflect its own interests; it is less about an attempt at saving the Syrian regime than anticipating the eventual adverse repercussion on these same interests from Bashar al-Assad's fall. Let it be recalled that the modalities of the strategic alliance that govern Hezbollah's relationship with Damascus since the early 1990s consist mainly of facilitating the logistics of transporting IRL weapons coming from Iran across Syrian territory. In all probability, these arrangements would not be sustained in case the Syrian regime falls, as the opposition groups, while unquestionably divided, are united in their aversion toward the Iran–Hezbollah tandem. Thus, the party cannot expect the fruitful cooperation with the Assad regime that it still benefits from today to continue forever. It is highly likely that the IRL and its Iranian mentor will have to resign themselves to getting their fingers burned in the rearrangement of relationships of Syria's internal powers, but, a well-thought-out finessing of the new order may allow them to preserve their main assets in spite of it. Thus, they will not have to be welcome on all of Syrian territory; a stable and secure sanctuary will suffice, provided that it possesses certain logistics facilities. Already the sectarian Syrian geography seems to present in the northwest—mainly Alawite and Christian, hence doubly favorable to Baath regional preferences—a natural prime territory where the IRL and Teheran can reestablish a presence and functioning organization: precisely the space that stretches between the Syrian coast and a line drawn through Damascus–(Qusayr)Homs–Aleppo. The IRL's armed intervention in the region therefore seems to respond as much to a preventive self-defense reaction as a securing ahead of time of part of a zone where the IRL may be obliged, for a more or less long term, to confine its logistical maneuvers on Syrian territory.

In foreign policy terms, this engagement by the IRL on the ground does not prevent Hezbollah from supporting the Lebanese Government's policy of dealing with the Syrian crisis by officially distancing itself from it. Split like this, the party's foreign policy may seem contradictory, but the two positions are nonetheless complementary. On the one hand, the IRL tries to save a part of the regime of a strategic ally out of fear of a new power, secular or religious, that is equally intent on cutting off the support that Assad provided to the

IRL, perhaps even to entertain good relations with Israel. On the other hand, as it always has, Hezbollah tries to prevent domestically an explosion, both ideological and confessional, the party having always categorized the civil war as a framework conducive to weakening the IRL. To prevent this, keeping the government in a more or less neutral position appears necessary for maintaining calm on the domestic scene—and so, by extension, not exposing the IRL even more than it already is.

Judging by the Syrian conflict, Hezbollah does not therefore appear to have rearranged its priorities, utilizing all the leverage available to it in defense of the IRL. After having resorted for years to a discourse of justification focused on the necessity of not detracting from its primordial and necessary role in protecting the national territory against all attacks from the south, Hezbollah in its argumentation on the Syrian crisis quite logically connected the fall of Assad and the Israeli threat. Rhetoric and real strategic option naturally are not to be confused, but one constant emerges: If the IRL for the first time in its history attacks a non-Israeli, extra-Lebanese enemy, and for the first time outside its national territory at that, Hezbollah, for its part, does not change. The IRL's interests come before all else, and the dividends that it may collect by detaching itself and redefining itself as a mere political party, would seem small change compared with doing right by the original mission.

Notes

* The publication of this article was made possible thanks to support by The Institute for the Transregional Study of the Contemporary Middle East, North Africa and Central Asia (TRI), Princeton University, USA.
1. Practically speaking, Hezbollah's dependence on the Iranian Government for weapons hardly lets the party be insensitive to "suggestions" addressed to it by the former.
2. The first because of disinterest in a possible Lebanese option and the second because of what appears to be a definite confidence in the party leadership. For more detail, see Aurélie Daher, *Hezbollah, Mobilisation et pouvoir* [Hezbollah, Mobilization and Power], Paris, PUF, Proche-Orient, 2014, Chapter 3.
3. For a more detailed report on the hostage affair, see Hala JABER, *Hezbollah, Born with a Vengeance*, New York, Columbia University Press, 1997.
4. In the summer of 2013, the European Union decided to list Hezbollah's "military wing" as a terrorist organization. Although France would already have decided

to do so following the participation by the Islamic Resistance in Lebanon (IRL) in the battle of Qusayr in Syria (see below), the official reason advanced for the condemnation is the terrorist attack perpetrated in Bulgaria in July 2012 against an Israeli tourist bus. However, in the summer of 2013, the inquiry was not yet closed, and the trails seemed to lead nowhere. For more information on the international political stakes in the so-called "Bourgas" affair, see Aurélie DAHER, *Le Hezbollah, mobilisation et pouvoir, op. cit.*, chapter 10.

5. The Syrian army no longer wars against the Israeli army in Syria since the Yom Kippur war of 1973, even though Tel Aviv's troops occupy the Golan since 1967.
6. Going as far as supporting the renovation of Jewish places of worship in the very center of Beirut and to receive with honors non-Zionist personalities, intellectuals, or Jewish clerics. Among them were Noam Chomsky, received by Hezbollah's leadership with honors in 2006 and 2010, Norman Finkelstein in 2008, and several rabbis from the *Neturei HaKarta* movement in 2005 and 2012.
7. Elizabeth Picard, *Liban, État de discorde* [Lebanon, State of Discord], Paris, Flammarion, 1988, pp. 198–9.
8. From the start of the fighting between Israel and the IRL in July and August 2006, the French government tried to obtain a cease-fire. *A contrario*, the American, British, and German Governments for more than a month opposed a cessation of hostilities for fear it would cause the Israeli offensive to fail.
9. To repeat the phrase used by a Hezbollah parliamentary deputy. (Interview, 2007.)
10. "Nasrallah sera tenu responsable de ses actes 'devant les tribunaux révolutionnaires' syrien, avertit l'ASL," *L'Orient-Le Jour*, February 1, 2012.
11. This region is an atypical case. The borders between Lebanon and Syrian never having been officially and accurately traced left some paradoxical pockets between the two, such as that of Qusayr with close to thirty villages (about 30,000 people) that, despite being populated by Lebanese citizens, is situated in Syrian territory. In the absence of any sovereign protection, Lebanese as well as Syrian, the inhabitants organized self-defense militias to face attacks by certain Sunni opposition groups.
12. "Ma'rakat al-Qusayr: Nuqtat al-tahawwul," *Al-Akhbâr*, May 20, 2013; Barluet, Alain, "Syrie: des cargaisons d'armes russes arrivent 'tous les deux jours,'" *Le Figaro*, June 22, 2013; El-Hassan, Jana, "4,000 Hezbollah Fighters Reach Rebel-Held Aleppo: FSA," *The Daily Star*, June 4, 2013; Cohen, Gili, "Thousands

of Hezbollah Troops Fighting, Hundreds Killed in Syria, Study Confirms," *Haaretz*, June 5, 2013.
13. Interview of Hezbollah cadres, May 2015.
14. "La situation est 'désespérée' à Qousseir," *L'Orient-Le Jour*, June 3, 2013.
15. Since 2011, numerous incidents and attacks ascribed to the Syrian opposition Free Syrian Army or jihadist groups are regularly reported from the Lebanese Bekaa (Shiite) bordering the Syrian frontier.
16. Paradoxically, it would thus have favored the same strategy as the Israeli army in 1978 when it set up a buffer zone in South Lebanon that it "cleansed" of all armed Palestinian presence in the hope of stopping the launching of rockets on northern Galilee and preventing incursions into Israel by Palestinian fighters from Lebanese territory.
17. Reports from on the ground seem to show that the IRL fighters in the main were content in Aleppo to take on an advisory and training role for regime troops; only a few among them would have sporadically supported the regular forces.

7

Identity of the State, National Interest, and Foreign Policy: Diplomatic Actions and Practices of Turkey's AKP since 2002

Jean-Baptiste Le Moulec and Aude Signoles

The commonly held view of Turkish foreign-policy action in both European and American political and media circles is that it changed radically with the coming to power in 2002 of a government they label as "Islamist." Specifically, it is the foreign policy of the Justice and Development Party (AKP)[1] Government that they depict as breaking with the ideological Atlanticism that successive (republican) governments had adopted since the end of the Second World War. The "break" would have proceeded equally from the fact that Turkish diplomatic actions would henceforth look to "the East," including the Middle East,[2] in being guided by an Islamic thread would present as a right-thinking "paternalism" a strategy of Empire that dare not say its name (the famous "neo-Ottomanism"[3])—which to some meant that the Turkish foreign policy action was "Orientalizing," even "Islamizing" at the same time that prospects for a rapid entry into the European Union were receding.

These Western representations can also be found in the academic literature that, in recent years, regularly made the study of AKP foreign policy toward the Arab world its subject.[4] By themselves, such perceptions say more about the actors who contribute to spreading them than the action frameworks and contexts that play a role in crafting Ankara's diplomatic positions. They seek to discredit the AKP Government's external action by reading them through the sole prism of the religious and cultural variable.

What is more, they have the effect in Europe of producing a diffuse fear of Turkish activism abroad that reinforces the rejectionist positions on, and reactions to, this country's candidacy for entry into the European Union. This highly politicized reading is also shared by the Turkish elites who were in place before R. T. Erdogan took power. The former, mostly belonging to the so-called "secular" current, accuse the AKP—and hence the "Islamo–liberal–conservative" current[5]—of interring, in the name of a pan-Islamic Brotherhood and ties of a common legacy culture, the state's modernity and secular identity that they are attached to.[6] For their part, the AKP leaders present their foreign-policy actions as acting to "repair" connections with the regional, especially Arab, environment that ruptured when the Ottoman Empire crumbled.[7] Therefore, they consider their directions as "innovative" and as "breaking" with what came before.

All these points of view on Turkish foreign-policy actions since 2002 ultimately say little about the protagonists at work, the representations of the national interest that they bring to their self-perception, or about the aspirations and strategic goals pursued. This article, therefore, aims to conduct an in-depth analysis of the foreign-policy agendas that Ankara brings to the international scene since the turn of the twenty-first century, particularly in the Arab world. The deliberate emphasis put on the relationships Turkey weaves with its Arab neighbors should not ignore the global vision advanced by the Turkish state in international precincts by multiple diplomatic means. Nor should it obscure the fact that it carries on an active policy of influencing the Turkish-speaking populations of Central Asia in the now independent former Soviet Republics (Kyrgyzstan, Uzbekistan and so forth) as well as in the Balkans.

However, the focus of Turkish diplomacy on the "Arab" agenda is justified as simply a matter of circumstance in that it specifically translates the ambition of a state whose position as geographical pivot where Europe borders on Asia has lost its strategic relevance in the post-Cold War context. Approaching it in this way also permits examining the evolution of Turkey's partnerships with the United States and the Atlantic Pact on the one hand and the European Union on the other. Starting from there will require stating how the government of R. T. Erdoğan has attempted to restore Turkey's geopolitical role. What are the domestic and international policy stakes at the heart of his "reformist" undertaking? On what theoretical foundations has it rested and in what respect can its major lines provoke acts of "rupture"? What actor-types are invested in it and in what manner, considering that traditionally the army and the executive power have monopolized this domain. Finally, how have Turkish foreign-policy actions been reshaped in light of the Arab revolutions and, especially, of the Syrian crisis? Conversely, how will the political uncertainties that weigh on the fate of the Arab regimes in transition lead the AKP Government to reconsider its role and eventual leadership in the region?

The theoretical approach opted for here is that of the constructivist current in international relations theory, which pushes the study of the connections between a state's identity (changing over time), national interest (multiple and variable according to the actors), and the foreign-policy orientations (not fixed and sometimes competing). To accomplish this, we studied what is—or becomes—the object of security for the AKP leadership since their taking power, but also against what they must guard against as they see it. Next, we turned our attention to the actors of Turkey's "Arab" policy, as well as the interdependencies woven between the areas of political, economic, and cultural power. One of the aspects that strikes us as the most determinative is the relationship between the producers of knowledge about the Middle East (within the framework of a true institutionalized community of experts) and foreign-policy decisions. Lastly, we addressed the means of intervention and diplomatic tools deployed by the actors of the Turkish-Arab rapprochement, by way of also describing specific cases of cooperation empirically. The methodological approach blends sociological interviews, direct observations, public discourses, and grey literature.

Understanding the "Arab" Agenda of the "New" Turkish Diplomacy. Between State Voluntarism, Strategic Contingencies, and Transformations of Relations with the Alterity

Putting Turco-Arab relations into a historical context shows that the attention paid by the Turkish state to its near abroad has been systematically nourished by public debates erupting over the question of the visibility of religion and the role of Islam in political life. Still, if a priori there are strong links between the orientation of successive governments and their diplomatic priorities, an ideological reading does not suffice to explain the active engagement by R. T. Erdoğan's government with the Arab world. In point of fact, the international system in which the states operate places constraints on the autonomy of the actors. It is therefore necessary to resituate foreign-policy action measured against the international and regional balance of power existing at the moment the AKP took overy the government in 2002. Moreover, the structure of the international system also influences the identity of states, namely how they portray themselves and others. Yet, starting from 2003, the AKP Government has wished to distinguish itself from its predecessors by formulating its own foreign-polic doctrine whose specifics it forges on the discursive level while on the level of actions per se its initiatives reprise some that were conducted during the time of the Özal Government. For this reason, we also take into account the perceptions that contemporary Turkish society develops with regard to its neighbors—especially bordering ones.

"Restoring" Turco-Arab Relations: The Uses of History as Instrument of Foreign Policy

Since taking office in 2002, and once again with their second term beginning in 2007, the AKP leadership promotes links based on geographical solidarity in order to justify and legitimize the idea of a necessary rapprochement with the Arab neighbors. This utilization of history, which leads them to refer to a heritage in order to justify a foreign-policy position, is constantly very "present in the public discourses on foreign policy and the official discourse legitimizing them."[8] It is true that "any government upon installing itself inherits previous decisions which constrain its own action."[9] In Turkey, however, the Ottoman heritage is not invoked traditionally as a reference in justifying an international position. The imperial period for a long time even seemed to be treated more as a "foil"—particularly from the perspective of political and military forces that contributed to fashioning the national identity and establishing Turkey's political legitimacy as a nation-state that is recognized and stable within its borders. The "new thing" here thus comes from choosing to reference a past that for a long time has been troubling in order to favor an—Islamic—identity that has been arbitrarily denied, distorted, even hidden and rejected.[10] However, it is not the first time that a political force has seized on the Ottoman past to burnish it and employ it as an instrument of international action in the "Arabo-Islamic" world, and certainly also not that Islam—as a system of religious referencing and civilizational space—has been brandished as a shared universe of meaning for orienting choices and diplomatic decisions on the ethical or ideological plane. In fact, Islam has already been given pride of place on four occasions since the founding of the Republic[11] by governments concerned with basing a national identity on it capable of influencing the course of foreign relations.

The first steps toward a Turco-Arab rapprochement were taken from 1950 to 1960 by the government of Adnan Menderes and his Democratic Party (DP).[12] It was Menderes and his party who, in these first days of the Cold War when Turkey occupied a strategic position due to its kilometers of shared border with the USSR, chose Atlanticism and drew closer to the United States, and worked toward the country's membership in the Atlantic Pact[13] (achieved in 1951), and then the Baghdad Pact[14] (signed in 1955). The military and strategic alliance woven between Turkey and Iraq thus allowed the Western bloc to check the territorial expansion of the Soviet "enemy" in the Middle East and Persian Gulf. This choice of alliance was informed by the tense diplomatic relations between Turkey and the USSR since Ankara had opted for neutrality during the Second World War.[15] But it is also explained by a strong anti-Communist feeling within the Democratic Party. Indeed, while the Soviet regime prohibited and combated any religious practice, the DP, in contrast, contributed to the introduction of an Islam-focused religious rhetoric in official political discourse and focused on Islam, seeing to it that religious practice would be increasingly tolerated in the public sphere. It was one of the very reasons why the Turkish armed forces overthrew the Menderes Government in 1960. After the military coup d'état, Turco-Arab diplomatic relations "chilled" again as military regimes carried by "leftist" national forces affiliated with the USSR took over in Syria and Iraq.[16]

The détente of the 1970s, coinciding with a series of decisive events,[17] offered the coalitions led by Prime Minister Bülent Ecevit, composed of members from the National Salvation Party (MSP) of Necmettin Erbakan (a group that insisted on the Islamic referent and extolled "disalignment" with the West),[18] the opportunity for a new rapprochement with the Arab countries. Détente between the two blocs let Turkey adopt a more conciliatory attitude with the Arab countries that, in part, are supported by the USSR but are no less majority Muslim. Therefore, under the MSP's leadership, the government openly threw its support behind Yasser Arafat's Palestine Liberation Organization (PLO) established in 1964[19] and reconnects with Egypt when Cairo adopts a more pro-American policy after Nasser's death. The MSP membership and the government of B. Ecevit also multiply their demarches toward the Gulf states (including Saudi Arabia) starting with the 1973 "oil shock," in order to secure the country's hydrocarbon imports whose financing put an increasing strain on the national budget.

The 1980 military putsch led to the fall of the B. Ecevit government, accused by the military high command of creeping "reIslamization" of society, then followed by the takeover of the government by the army's general staff (MGK) headed by General Kenan Evren. It also led to the promulgation of a new constitution that is a milestone in Turkey's political history by inspiring the promoters of the current called "Turco-Islamic synthesis,"[20] that would have put the Turks in charge of sustaining the Islamic civilization after the Arabs. This new constitution confers a religious legitimacy to the military regime, as the latter tries to rally the people to its side. Prime Minister Turgut Özal, elected president (1983–9/1989–93), is the first to operate within this new constitutional framework with the aim of (re)initiating a policy of rapprochement with the Arab sphere. This policy translates into the conclusion of commercial trade pacts with hydrocarbon producers. In parallel, T. Özal pursues the strategic line of his Kemalist predecessors that makes anchoring Turkey in the West a matter of national security. It is also by virtue of this well-understood alliance of interests with the United States that he chooses to enlist Turkey in the international coalition that, from Washington, declares war on Sadam Hussein's Iraq.

Finally, on the foreign-policy front, the years 1996 and 1997, during which N. Erbakan and his National Salvation Party (MSP) furtively reembark on the path to power in coalitions with the Democratic Party (DP), led to a burgeoning of cultural projects carried out by private foundations often linked to the Fetullaci movement[21] and targeting Muslim populations—notably Turkish-speaking ones in Central Asia[22] and, on the domestic side, for the adoption of measures seeking to "moralize" the public sphere. The "pro-Arab" bent of Turkish diplomatic actions, however, is abruptly stopped by the leaders of the "post-modern" coup d'état of 1997,[23] declaring openly "that the Turks don't need to be Arabized."

Studying these four historical experiences, during which the Turkish leaders gave impetus to diplomatic initiatives toward the Arab world, allows nuancing the AKP's "break" discourse while underlining how difficult it is to "disconnect" Turkey's "Arab" agenda from the domestic political issues—particularly those involving identity. It would not be necessary, however, to put these diplomatic experiments of the years from 1960 to 1990 on a parallel with those conducted during the years 2000 under the leadership of the AKP Government. Indeed, the intensity of exchanges, the kind of actors involved, but also the modes of action promoted, contribute to this agenda appearing as potentially "foundational" for a regional order in transformation—within which Turkey would have a major stabilizing role. We can therefore call it a difference of degree and of nature with the foreign policies initiated previously.

Turkish Diplomacy in a "World Turned Upside Down"[24]

The period inaugurated by the fall of the Berlin Wall is particularly propitious for the redefinition of national interests because the "bipolar" dimension of interstate relationships tended to lessen with the military and ideological "enemy" having vanished. The change in the international context in the late 1990s initially confronted Turkey with a situation of strategic insecurity.[25] Indeed, Ankara wondered which geostrategic role to continue playing within NATO when the Soviet enemy had ceased to be and Washington pondered the future of the Atlantic Pact. While it was very quickly reassured of the interest that its position took on in the American view,[26] rifts did open up between the two sides on how to read international relations and, more to the point, on the definition of "common threats." In spite of a genuine American interest in relaunching a strategic partnership with Turkey,[27] the post-9/11 bilateral relations resembled a "dialogue of the deaf." In fact, even while both the Turks and the Americans made "the fight against terrorism" a priority, differences arose in their strategic documents about the contours of the new "enemy." For the United States, it had changed radically—the strategic and ideological enemy represented by the Soviet Union had been replaced by an enemy both multifaceted and labile that knew how to battle the values of

"Western civilization" (including freedom American-style) by metapolitical means. In contrast, on the Turkish side, the disappearance of the Soviet foreign enemy did not lessen the power of the "domestic enemy"—namely, the PKK,[28] and all the Kurdish movements firmly established in South East Anatolia—not even that of their allies.

On the other hand, the end of the bipolar world led to a "displacement of the center of gravity in Turco-American relations from Eurasia to the Middle East"[29]—the attacks of September 11 only accelerated this process. The AKP assuming power took place in this context, which quite radically transformed the foreign policy of the United States in the Middle East. Indeed, while successive American governments until then had sought to maintain the territorial and political status quo to ensure that no single state in the region would emerge as a hegemonic power, G. W. Bush and his advisors henceforth made regime change one of the policy tools for fighting "Islamist terrorism." Because it draws direct causal connections between Arab regime authoritarianism, the (suspected) presence of terrorists or weapons of mass destruction, and political instability,[30] it buys into the idea that regional stability and international security can only be guaranteed by building a "greater democratic Middle East." In this context, several states, so-called "rogue", find themselves caught in the American administration's sights—with Iraq, Syria, and Iran, three countries bordering Turkey, at the head of the line. However, this new aggressive and "warmongering" American line puts the Turkey of R. T. Erdoğan in a bind. In fact, Turkey continues to have a vital stake in preserving Iraq's territorial integrity—putting in question this state's unity is perceived as risking (re) energizing Kurdish separatism strongly entrenched in the country's north[31] and resurgent since the mid-1990s.[32] This is the reason why, in 2003, when the United States under G. W. Bush called for a "preemptive" military intervention against Iraq, the government played the card of alliance with Syria, Iraq, and Iran (countries with large Kurdish minorities whose nationalist aspirations they are also trying to "tame") and tries to organize a regional consultation to prevent the Americans resorting to war—but in vain. The vote of the Turkish parliamentarians, who vote on March 1, 2003 against the deployment of American troops on the national territory must therefore be read as a sign of the autonomization of Turkish foreign policy vis-à-vis its American ally—even though the Turkish prime minister had previously acquiesced in principle to the United States on this very point.

Thus, the change in the structure of the international system (with a bipolar world transformed by an aggressive American unilateralism) limits the Turkish Government in redefining its American partnership as well as relations with its "near abroad." Even so, Turkey's autonomization with respect to the United States should not be thought of as a break in the alliance any more than an "Islamization" or a "(re)Orientalization," so much do the foreign-policy stakes remain unchanged for Ankara in the post-Cold War period—namely, preserving the political and territorial stability of the Middle East.

Paralleling this, another regional political factor helps explain the autonomization of Turkish foreign-policy action relative to the "Western bloc"—and that is the European dossier. While Turkey is officially a candidate for joining the EU since the Helsinki European conference in 1999, with many reform "packages" adopted by the Turkish Parliament to harmonize national legislation with European directives[33] by 2004 and with negotiations for admission having started in 2005, perspectives for an end to the process deteriorated as Brussels' reservations on integrating Turkey were asserted more and more openly and assumed to be such, notably on the part of the Franco-German "power" couple.[34] The 2008 global economic crisis that severely impacted Turkey also contributed to Turkish entrepreneurs looking for development potential and investment perspectives outside the EU's borders. This politico-economic context explains why, from 2010 to June 2013, neither the Europeans nor the Turks felt compelled to pursue the membership negotiations.[35] However, negotiations did resume in October 2013 with a focus on regional politics and this despite European criticism of the suppression of anti-government demonstrations that took place in Istanbul and many other Turkish metropoles starting in the spring of 2013.

All these factors led the Turkish AKP Government henceforth to follow a "multidimensional" policy aiming both for diversification of its strategic alliances on the regional level and for gaining influence and visibility on the international level.

State Identity and Relationship to Alterity at Issue

Turkish diplomatic dynamism with regard to the Arab world in the first decade of the 2000s results from political voluntarism coupled with the necessity of (re)making sense of the country's geostrategic position in a world in flux. It is accompanied by a multiform discourse intended to promote the image and action of Turkey on the regional scene and by fielding a cultural diplomacy.[36] The "Turkish model" figure of speech contributed to modifying the state's social identity in the eyes of the elites and political society that carry it, just as it did the Arab rulers and actors who adhere to it. In fact, the state's identity is largely the result of a process of intersubjective construction.[37] In this case, as the upholders of the constructivist current stress, this identity ranges across "corporate, type, role, and collective identities."[38]

If the corporate identity relates to characteristics that make the state a full actor on the international scene (marking of borders, retaining a physical monopoly on legitimate violence, and so forth) and may thus antedate the interstate system, this is not the case with the other three kinds of identity that are constructed and are "negotiated" in the relationship to the Other.

In the Turkish case, the "type" identity—which relates to internal characteristics of the state but also to the manner in which these help determine how states are "labeled" on the international scene—is subject to particularly rapid and structural transformations starting from the end of the Cold War and, once again, from the first decade of the 2000s on. These transformations are largely attributable to the waves of economic reform starting in the early 1980s given impetus by the S. Demirel Government (with T. Özal working the levers), later deepened by the government of T. Erdoğan in the sense of liberalizing trade and opening the national markets to foreign investments.[39] These changes are equally linked to the adoption of new political measures that contribute to the development of state of laws and guarantee freedoms of expression in Turkey. But, beyond the content of the reforms, what matters is the way in which the surrounding Arab governments and populations portray as "positive" the capacity of Turkey to transform itself. Public statements that make Turkey into a "model" thus dwell on its seventeenth place in the world economic rankings or again its admission to the exclusive club of G20 members. The 6 percent growth rate that the country resumes shortly after the

2008 international financial crisis also contributes to the social fabrication of the Turkish economic "miracle" in Middle Eastern perceptions. At the same time, the regime's democratic character (testified to by holding regular elections and the progressive separation of the army from Turkish political power) coupled with successive electoral victories by the AKP cause a number of those living in the region not only to think of Islam and democracy as compatible but as equally virtuous. It must be said that the government of R. T. Erdoğan, which identifies itself as "conservative democrat" and rejects the "Islamist" label, is eager to appear as a party with respect for the rules of pluralism—and therefore as resolutely "modern" and "European"—in a context where, on the contrary, his opponents accuse him of "Islamizing" the state identity and taking the country (back) down the road of "archaism" and "tradition." Finally, the depiction of Turkey as both Muslim *and* democratic imposes itself as constitutive of the state identity, as much with the national populations (although this is a debatable definition) as with Arab popular opinion.

As for the "role" identity of the Turkish state, which relates to the "priorities that characterize a state in the perceptions of others and which causes the other states to expect it to behave in a certain way relative to them [and] that it takes on a certain role internationally"[40] also experiences a notable reconstitution starting in the early 1990s and, yet again, with the AKP's assumed power. Indeed, during the Cold War, the Arab states—including the "progressive" camp aligned with the Soviet Union—quickly classified Turkey as a regional ally of their American "enemy" (as they did the state of Israel).

What they have primarily remembered about Turkey, therefore, is the role if played as strategic "pivot" for the Western bloc and its hegemon, the United States. However, this image of a "NATO's forward pawn in the region" is challenged starting in 2002 by a whole series of diplomatic positions advocated by the government of R. T. Erdoğan—which are seen from outside the country and especially the Arab world as "breaking" with the past.

In the academic sphere, but also in the affected "civilian societies," the seminal "gesture" attaches to the refusal of the Turkish Parliament to involve the country in the military attack against Iraq that the Americans were preparing in March 2003. During the second AKP term (2002–7), it is the positions it takes favoring Palestine and being hostile toward the state of Israel that accentuate the idea that Turkey from now on is a country "no longer aligned with the West." Appeals to political reconciliation and for exchanges with the partisan, economic, and cultural actors of the Arab countries advocated by the Turkish prime minister's team, as well as diverse actions taken within this framework, give substance to the hypothesized change of diplomatic direction. They also substantiate the thesis of co-construction of a new identity "of type" around partnership and Turco-Arab mediation.

Finally, also developing from when the AKP takes power is the "collective" identity, "which relates to a state identifying with the interests of another to the point where it integrates them in the definition of its own national interest."[41] Indeed, the Middle East region experiences rapid adjustments in the existing equilibrium balance of power, starting with the September 11, 2001 attacks and, once again, with the American invasion of Iraq in 2003. In this kind of environment, Turkey's ambitions turn regional, to the extent that the country's security is endangered by changes in the domestic order affecting the leaderships, regimes, and neighboring states—starting with S. Hussein's Iraq. From then on, for the ruling elites in place, assuring the country's security no longer means just seeing to the national defense; it also consists of reducing the risks to the surrounding, especially the bordering, states, from compromising the nation-state's own fate. These twin concerns of security and stability, both economic and political, implies that the leadership of the Turkish state takes "an interest [in] the reduction of conflicts *with* and *within* other states."[42] From this flowed new foreign-policy tools that turned Turkey into a power that portrays and imposes itself as a "mediator" of regional conflicts by the use of "preventive diplomacy."

Does the AKP Promote a Strictly Islamic World View? State Identity, National Interests and Foreign-policy Goals

Posing questions about the Turkish state's identity is not trivial if we postulate that "identities are at the root of interests."[43] Thus, what are the key values that the AKP leadership wants to promote?

The answer presents itself first in the form of a defense white paper [Strategic Depth. Turkey's International Position].[44] Declassified in 2001, this programmatic text was authored by a university scholar, A. Davutoğlu, a well-known theorist in the international relations field, close to two of the movement's top leaders—Prime Minister R. T. Erdoğan and President (from 2007 on) A. Gül. Turned into a book and translated into many languages,[45] this text quickly became a best-seller in Turkey as well as in the Arab world where its author is often found promoting it (meanwhile, R. T. Erdoğan has become president of the Republic, while A. Davutoğlu took the prime minister's post in 2014). However, the intent here is not to reduce the AKP's diplomatic action toward the Arab world to the sole doctrinal views of its "mentor," as much as these are "molded" by the interpretation of actors who seize on it, diffuse it, and make it into a required reference. Thus, the government fleshes out its political voluntarism with leading actors who do not directly emerge from the diplomatic or military field to take an active part in its doctrinal corpus. In fact, a number of experts from the academic world, corporate chieftains, associated militants, or members of religious Brotherhoods participate in giving concrete form to the "new" Turkish foreign-policy action at the grass roots and, by so doing, make it simultaneously a unifying and catalyzing axis.

The Davutoğlu Doctrine of Foreign Policy or Expanding the Notion of National Security

The starting point for the book-opus by "Professor" A. Davutoğlu[46] is the idea that contemporary Turkey has the potential to assert itself and be considered a major power on the international scene—including in the region—but that this is not yet the case.

Among the power factors invoked, he cites: geography (explicitly referencing Turkey's position astride different continents and at the crossroads of several cultural zones); history (invoking the Ottoman past, even holding it up as a "golden age" to serve as a benchmark for the current era); the economy (pointing to his country's "takeoff" and repeat double-digit growth rates); political stability (a source of pride for the AKP after several decades marked by successive coups d'état); military strength (exemplified by an army with a solid reputation in the region as well as the external NATO "umbrella"); the collective identity (subject of multiform and competing definitions in the past that the AKP is trying to reconcile—with difficulty), as well as the political voluntarism and the capacity of elites to conceive of, project, and impose a foreign-policy strategy and actions. Taking off from there, two orders of explanation are advanced to rationalize Turkey's strategic weakness on the international scene of the 1990s: on the one hand, an underutilization of the country's power capacities by previous governments and, on the other, a self-perception coupled with a representation of the Other—notably, its Arab neighbors—not highly thought of and even negative (what A. Davutoğlu calls the "psychological background"[47]). This way, the "professor" in essence attacks the strategies of deterrence and threat minimization, but also the conception of the national interest as the secularist parties conceived it before. In fact, beyond the ideological rivalry between them, the Islamo–liberal–conservative strain and the secular strain are differentiated by their conception of the state identity and their definition of the national interest.[48]

Indeed, the secular current's strategic doctrine (born of the War of Independence of 1919–22 and progressively imposed on the political elites and on society as a whole by the military "establishment") perceives the national interest exclusively in security terms. The major aim is therefore the inviolability of borders, which is guaranteed by constituting (and maintaining) a deterrent capacity. Concern over the territorial status quo therefore guides Turkey during the Cold War. It is translated by a façade of neutrality until 1952, and then by Turkey's entry into NATO and leads to a kind of "isolationism," or, at least, of distrust of the attitudes and geostrategic choices of the neighboring states. This "obsession with security" resulting from what Mümtaz Soysal calls the "Sèvres syndrome"[49] is also translated by the imposition of an aggressive nationalist discourse that defines the contours of national identity in not very inclusive terms—especially when it comes to ethnic and religious minorities. It also harks back to manufacturing a menace described as capable potentially of emerging from the country's "interior"—nourished by the existence of competing social and political movements, of which some have secessionist claims that organize the national chessboard and, in particular, the political life in certain regions of Southeast Anatolia starting in the late 1950s.[50] Lastly, the Cold War alliance with the United States and Europe reflects the will to provide the populations a cultural model and—Western—ideological references for them to follow. Beyond this observation, the mentor of the "new" foreign policy doctrine proposes a palliative solution for the lack of heft and recognition for Turkey on the international scene. In concrete terms, A. Davutoğlu suggests that Turkey should gradually open to the external world, starting with the closest bordering neighbors, by weaving relations of mutual trust with them that would permit securing the Middle Eastern zone, assuring the state's survival with respect to its territorial integrity and helping to change its image for the better.[51] Therefore, the time for isolationism or neutralism is over. Building on this, A. Davutoğlu defines three "contiguous basins" in which to expand Turkey's influence and by so doing recapture the old imperial glory: the "contiguous land basin" (Balkans, "Middle East," and Caucasus), a "contiguous maritime basin" (Black Sea, Adriatic Sea, Western Mediterranean, Persian Gulf, and Caspian Sea), and the "contiguous continental basin" (Europe, North Africa, South Asia, and West-Central Asia). This "rediscovery" of former Ottoman spheres of influence should also allow complementarities of an economic order to emerge for the benefit of the region's national populations. Conceived in this way, national security is also enhanced by non-military aspects that put the accent on possessing the attributes of economic power (for example, trade volumes) or political power (for example, ability to influence regional geopolitics). In addition, even the term "national security" is progressively put aside and replaced by new official jargon, such as the famous expression "zero problems with the neighbors."

Does this means that the army is sidelined when it comes to foreign-policy decisions as the AKP consolidates its power at the head of the state? Certainly, the National Security Council led by high-ranking military men no longer has a monopoly on the decision-making process since 2002, so much do the presidency with A. Gül, the office of the prime minister with R. T. Erdoğan, and the Ministry of Foreign Affairs with A. Davutoğlu take a hand in directing diplomacy on questions linked to the Arab world, relying in the process on posted ambassadors, high functionaries, and select Parliamentary deputies.[52] However, the observed process reflects expanded contours of national security with new, non-military stakes carried by "new" players.

The Actors in the Turco-Arab Rapprochement of the 2000s

Compared to previous eras, the Turkish foreign policy under the AKP governments is devised and carried out by a multitude of players whose spheres of activity increasingly interlock. Economic entities, political parties, humanitarian organizations, research and teaching institutions, designated representatives of ethnic and confessional minorities, development NGOs, or also cultural actors all go international with projects requiring research, sojourns, communications, partnering, and networking of knowledge and competencies. Since 2002,[53] this plurality of actors finds itself taking part in official delegations that accompany regular visits by R. T. Erdoğan and A. Davutoğlu to the Arab world.

If the media and academic literature often puts the accent on the role of economic actors in the matter, little attention is paid, by contrast, to the actions of "knowledge producers" regarding the Arab world. However, this action turns out to be crucial. In fact, when *Stratejik Derinlik* came out in 2001, the Counselor for Foreign Affairs A. Davutoğlu had no inkling of its future success despite the fact that he already enjoyed some notoriety within the AKP and the academic milieu he came from.

In the beginning, he relies on academic colleagues to publicize his new diplomatic line and spread word of the new report to the world and to the alterity his book is about. The latter largely relay his thoughts by elevating his program-book to a "manual" of international relations.[54] Some go further by participating in the production through their research and teaching activity of "scholarly" knowledge about political societies in the Arab world. The public universities, beginning with Marmara University (in Istanbul) where A. Davutoğlu is tenured, but also Bosphorus University (Istanbul) or the Middle East Technical University (Ankara) beginning in the mid-2000s establish teaching and research tracks in the social sciences dealing with the Middle East.[55] The same goes on at some private universities, such as Bilkent University in Ankara, or, in Istanbul, Fatih or Şehir universities (the latter founded in 2008 by the same A. Davutoğlu) that see in this niche a means of gaining a comparative advantage in a sector where there is a plethora of offerings.

Involvement by universities in the "fabric" of foreign policy is practically unheard of in Turkey. In fact, it responds to a call by the minister who advocates the creation of "research centers, academic institutes capable of pursuing regional studies."[56] For A. Davutoğlu, the Turkish state owes it to itself to set up a panel of "autochthonous" knowledge of Middle Eastern political societies in order to better conduct his aimed-for policy of "restoring" Turco-Arab ties. This is his reason for obtaining financing for the first Turkish research on the Middle East (also, more marginally, the Persian world) by public authorities as well as private actors.[57] With this, the scholars—and, more specifically, the professors of international relations—became fully engaged actors in the "pro-Arab" direction of the government by acting as "advisors to the Prince." Taking an increasingly key role in elaborating the foreign policy,[58] they develop an expertise for the purpose of informing, orienting, and stimulating foreign-policy choices, as well as those of other players engaged in developing ties with the Arab world. Turkey's national interest thus no longer is to ignore the Other; rather, it consists of getting to know the latter by accumulating knowledge about it so as to better grasp its foreign-policy "habitus" and anticipate its behaviors with regard to Turkey and third-party states.[59]

Outside the university precincts, research on the Middle East also has grown for more than a decade in think tanks like TESEV, SETA, USAK, ORSAM or SDE.[60] These private institutes, with the status of foundations or associations, devote the major part of their activities to publishing studies on the Middle East.[61] In part, they operate by sub-contracting the analytical work to university faculty. Benefiting from public subsidies that sometimes amount to more than half of their respective budgets,[62] these institutes also finance their activities with advisory assignments to private entrepreneurs prospecting and investing in Arab lands.

Private entrepreneurs are actually most visible in the "new" AKP policy for the Arab world where they see a means of securing and diversifying sources for national economic growth at a time when the European economies are in crisis. They therefore especially commission expert reports that let them evaluate the "country risks" but also the level of available resources in the various neighboring states. Two employers' organizations in this regard appear to be the favored instruments for the Turkish policy of "conquering" the Middle Eastern markets: On the one hand, there is MÜSIAD[63] formed in 1990 by a network of Anatolian businessmen close to the "Islamic conservative" current and, on the other side, there is TÜSKON[64] founded in 2005 in the orbit of the Gülen movement.[65] In this territory, they eclipse TÜSIAD,[66] the other large employer association that started the network of close economic relationships woven with Europe by Turkish entrepreneurs identified with the secular current. Although involvement by these associations in the region is not new, since they were already on the ground during the Özal years (mainly in the Gulf countries and Northern Iraq), they nevertheless possess a novel character. In reality, the economic activities they engage in are directly "connected" with the government's "pro-Arab" diplomatic agenda and have simultaneous political aims as much as economic ones. Thus, depending on individual cases and negotiated partnership agreements, promoting freedom of trade and movement by the Turkish import–export companies must contribute to regional economic development, the fight against poverty, political stabilization, or the promotion of human rights and democracy. As a result, MÜSIAD and TÜSKON participate in numerous consultative meetings on the future of the Middle East that bring together business people and politicians close to the AKP. These two employers' associations are also very active in international economic associations, such as the Mediterranean Association of the Chambers of Commerce and Industry or the Islamic Chamber of Commerce and Industry, but also DEIK, the (national) Platform of Foreign Economic Relations that stand for the idea that strengthening the private sector and liberalizing trade contribute to regional political stability. For these associations, therefore, as for the government, promoting regional commerce is an important key to political peacemaking in the Middle East.

Thus, since the first decade of the twenty-first century, political and economic actors close to the AKP rally around the "Davutoğlu doctrine" to redefine the contours of the state's identity and the national interest and to make the Arab world the priority target for a "pluridimensional" foreign policy.[67] Beyond that, they agree on the tools likely to promote their worldview and regional ambitions and, in this regard, innovate by advocating the use of so-called levers of public diplomacy.[68]

Regional Ambition and New Action Instruments: Peace through Trade and Mediation

Since the AKP took power, the Turkish state has sought to project itself as a key state in the Middle East—meaning that it is able to exert influence on the regional environment—rather than as a pivotal state playing the part of forward outpost of the United States in the area. In the Arab people's perspective, the 2003 Iraq war, as we have seen, marked an evolution in Turkey's strategic positioning. The Turkish Government at the time under the leadership of the Minister of Foreign Affairs A. Davutoğlu actually put forward geographic and historical characteristics (which he called "strategic depth") to justify its new ambitions. "Ankara [then] 'distances itself' from the classic realist concepts of international relations such as 'power,' 'balance of power,' or 'zero-sum game' [and] tries to ... evolve its approach ... [by seeking to] move beyond the historical conflicts that for a long-time handicapped [its] relations with the Arab world."[69] The Turco-Syrian rapprochement as the twentieth turned to the twenty-first century is a good example of the AKP's new diplomatic line, designed to bring stability and security to the region through improved ties with the Arab countries, especially the border states. Beyond that, the quest for "zero problems with the neighbors" leads the leaders in office to work on transforming conflicts by establishing a relationship of interdependence with the close-by and the more remote environments. The conclusion of bilateral economic pacts and, in a wider sense, the development of sectoral partnerships, work toward this. The Turkish state's recurring involvements in conflict prevention abroad also testifies to a new—growing—ambition: aiming to appear as a builder of bridges and thereby a key actor for regional political stability.

Peace with the Neighbors: The Turco-Syrian Rapprochement of the First 2000 Decade

The Turkish commitment to the foreign policy of "zero problems with the neighbors" is illustrated almost emblematically by the Syrian case. The diplomatic rapprochement between the two countries, engineered during the late 1990s before the AKP came to power, revved up during the 2000s, legitimized by the Turkish elite largely by references to the past and shared culture. The recourse to Ottoman history, that the Turkish and international media made much of as an indicator of the "Islamization" of Turkey's foreign policy, must nevertheless not obliterate what is essential—namely, the use of tools of technical and economic cooperation for settling political differences. Ankara and Damascus drawing closer illustrated the new Turkish strategy of economic peace promoted by the AKP Government—at least until the "Arab revolutions" of 2011.

Until the end of the 1990s, many factors made for conflict between Syria and Turkey and were sources of a permanent state of tension. Historically, they stemmed from diverging readings of the Ottoman past (in the early twentieth century, with the emergence of Syrian and Turkish nationalism); from territorial disputes revolving around the province of Alexandrette (called Hatay in Turkish); from ideological differences linked to Cold War logics (Baathist Syria siding with the USSR and Turkey siding with the United States); from conflict over sharing the waters of the Tigris and Euphrates (which was heightened during the 1980s); or, finally, from misunderstandings about Turkey's policy toward Israel (especially after the signature of a bilateral military-related accord in 1996).[70] But it was especially the Kurdish question that cast a shadow over diplomatic relations between the two countries. In fact, "until the late 1990s, Turco-Syrian relationships were at their lowest … [on account of] the support rendered by the Syrians to the Kurdistan Workers' Party … a Kurdish nationalist organization in a state of rebellion against the Turkish state since the early 1980s."[71] Here, the Kurdish problem is more precisely correlated with the division of the Euphrates river's water that flows from Turkey into Syria. Starting in the mid-1970s, Turkey launched a huge development plan for Southeast Anatolia—an economically marginalized region largely peopled by Kurds—that entailed the building of numerous dams. However, a direct consequence of this project, designated by the acronym GAP (Güneydogu Anadolu Projesi), was that it diminished Syria's usable water resources downstream. The Damascus regime then decided to sanction Turkey by financing and sheltering the PKK on its territory—including its top leader, Abdullah Ocalan.[72] Throughout the 1990s, the Kurdish rebellion, with its rear bases in Syria, regularly took on the Turkish armed forces stationed along the border as well as in Southeast Anatolia. The number of dead and wounded soldiers but also civilians aroused widespread indignation in Turkey. Several attempts to resolve the conflict were made from 1987 to 1996 and several treaty protocols were signed providing for an end to Syrian support for the PKK in return for Turkish guarantees of water flow, but none of this had any concrete effect on the ground.

This context of "suspended crisis" explains why, on the Turkish side,[73] Syria would progressively be perceived as a major security threat. It is also behind the break in diplomatic relations between the two countries in 1996 and it led Ankara to threaten the military option in 1998. Damascus rapidly gave ground before the deployment of Turkish troops on the border. This showdown ended with the signing of the Adana protocol, in which Syria committed to no longer support the PKK and to stop sheltering A. Ocalan.[74] From then on, and even more so with the AKP taking power, relations between the two countries were on the upswing.[75]

The thaw between the two countries in the 2000s is in large part imputable to regional considerations and, particularly, to the Kurdish problem in Iraq. It so happened that the latter country's Kurdish population enjoyed growing political autonomy in the wake of the occupation by the American military in 2003 and the fall of the regime of S. Hussein.[76] However, these populations are primarily settled in the north in the border region with Syria and Turkey. Their autonomist demands (and, in particular, their advocacy for a decentralization law) revive fears in Ankara and Damascus of once again seeing demands arise for constituting an independent Kurdish state. The two states, quite to the contrary, plead for maintaining the territorial integrity of Iraq and share a common opposition to the integration of the city of Kirkuk in the territory of Iraq's northern region—while the latter, for its part, calls for an Iraqi regional Kurdistan Government.[77] The Kurdish problem, which had been the source of violent conflicts between the two countries in the past, thus was the origin of the post-2003 Turco-Syrian rapprochement. It took on the traits of a veritable partnership at a time when the stakes in post-Saddam Iraq's political reconstruction saw the views of the two former rivals converge. Bashar al-Assad's diplomatic visit to Turkey in January 2004, followed by the Turkish prime minister coming to Syria in December that same year, inaugurated a new era. First, the Syrian president accepted the idea that the Hatay region was an integral part of Turkish territory—which the state that he represented had refused to do since 1939. The two parties also agreed that the question of the water sharing had to be addressed in common and should not obstruct their diplomatic relations. To accomplish this, they opted to set up a tripartite technical committee (including Iraq, equally concerned as a downstream country) whose task would be preparing and implementing projects to help meet the three countries' immediate needs. The problem of one or another party's sovereign rights respecting the waters of the Tigris and Euphrates[78] thus is left unresolved, not even squarely faced; rather, it is sidestepped in the hopes that rectification would "dissociate" itself from the political questions to which it is linked until then, namely those of Hatay and the Kurds. Treating the contentious dossiers piecemeal rather than globally and emphasizing their technical rather than their political dimensions constitutes a new way for the two parties of handling conflict—one especially promoted by the AKP leadership. This strategy allows them to bypass the "heavy" conflicts and the resort to the balance of political power (or "hard power"), betting instead on the establishment of common and sectoral authorities for managing problems. Cooperation in economic matters has the same aim. In this domain, Syrians and Turks signed a free-trade agreement in 2004 (taking effect in 2007) with the goal of boosting bilateral exchanges by lifting visa requirements, followed by creation of a (joint) Strategic Partnership Council[79] (in 2009). The accelerating take-off of commercial and industrial exchanges between the two countries benefited Turkey in particular, making it "the number one [foreign] investor in Syria and an essential business partner for Damascus" in the years from 1998 to 2009.[80]

For Ankara, at stake in the rapprochement with Damascus is a better ability to "penetrate" the entire Arab Orient for selling its products (notably in Iraq) while shrinking its commercial dependence on the European Union. It is also specially designed "to boost its influence in the region, more particularly on dossiers relating to the Israeli–Palestinian conflict or the Lebanese issues."[81] For its part, Syria sees in the rapprochement with Ankara a way out from being "blacklisted" by the United States which, in the post 9/11 context, views the Bashar al-Assad regime as offering potential support to jihadist groups. However, the American threats of excluding it from the international sphere became more intense[82] after the assassination of Lebanese Prime Minister Rafic Hariri in 2005, which the Syrian regime was accused of instigating. Thanks to Turkey's intervention, Damascus appears to be an approachable and reliable regime. The diplomatic rapprochement of the two parties is, on balance, therefore more vital for Syria than for Turkey—explaining, no doubt, that the agreements arrived at (on Hatay and water, especially) on the whole answer more to Ankara's security concerns and demands.

This power disequilibrium in Turkey's favor on both political and economic levels is far from being a constant in the "new" relationships that Ankara knits with its Arab neighbors. On the contrary, quite frequently, the exchanges are to Turkey's detriment. This is particularly so in the case of the business partnerships that it negotiates with the large petro producers in the region. This touches on a key element in the AKP's policy of "economic peace."

The Energy Challenge at the Heart of the AKP's "Good Neighbor" Policy

Since the 1970s, geo-economics is a driving element of Turkish foreign policy toward the Middle East.[83] Indeed, the oil shock of 1973, manifested by a rapid increase in hydrocarbon prices, led the Turkish Government on a search for business partners in the region. In exchange for purchasing gas and oil, Turkey there and then negotiated special access to jobs in construction and public works as well as food processing. Iran and Iraq but also Saudi Arabia are its key targets. This exchange of processed goods allowed Turkey to reduce the bill for its hydrocarbon purchases, even if its overall trade balance remained deeply in deficit. During the 1980s, the modernization of the Turkish economy, linked to the opening of domestic markets to foreign investment and an industrialization policy linked to the production sector brought with it a significant increase in energy requirements. This situation pushed the Özal Government (1983–93) to upgrade the economic partnerships initiated earlier. Ankara's neutrality in the Iran–Iraq War (1980–8) let the leaders at the time supply themselves from both sides. If the political challenge is always to ensure that the hydrocarbon bill does not burden the national budget excessively, it is also—in a context of externalizing the national economy—to offer outlets to its own entrepreneurs, in particular those from cities in central Turkey (Kayseri, Konya), called the "Anatolian Tigers" that carried the "Islamic-Conservative" current to power.[84]

The AKP's economic policy after 2002 accentuates this direction for

Turkish economic exchanges. The free trade agreement with Syria in 2004, the forging of economic ties with the regional Kurdistan Government in Northern Iraq starting from 2008–9,[85] the dynamics of investment in Libya beginning in 2003, or yet again the organization of the first Turkish-Arab world economic forum in Ankara in 2005 testify to the growing will of Turkish entrepreneurs as well as of the political leadership that negotiates the association agreements and "entry" conditions for business people in foreign countries to offer themselves new export perspectives in a context of growing globalization and structural fragility of the domestic economy because of its strong energy[86] dependence and the then still lasting effects of the 2008 European economic crisis.[87]

Three major oil producers profit to the hilt from this new Turkish activism in the Middle East: Libya, Iraq, and Iran. The economic exchanges with Tripoli consist mainly of oil imports against the opening of the Libyan building and public works sector (BTP). Until Khadafi fell in 2011, Turkish entrepreneurs constituted the second overseas market for building and public works in Libya. For its part, the abolishment of visas is why there are approximately 25,000 Turks in Libya in 2010 (of which a good part were "exfiltrated" during the NATO intervention against the Khadafi regime).[88] In Iraq, Turkey's economic position asserted itself in growing fashion since 2003 and the end of the oil embargo in sectors such as public construction, the oil and steel industries, or yet again in the food-processing industry, especially in the country's north. Today, Turkey is the primary trade partner of the Kurdistan Regional Government (KRG) and the leading investor in the area. A total of 740 companies and approximately 20,000 Turkish expatriates are settled throughout the country. Energy takes center stage: Turkey ranks fifth among importers of Iraqi oil, after Germany, Great Britain, Italy, and France, buying 25 percent of total national production.[89] Finally, as concerns Iran, the economic exchanges are very asymmetric, since Teheran remains rather closed to foreign investors while Ankara buys some Iranian gas that covers 30 percent of its annual energy requirements.[90]

Turkey's "entry" into the Middle East must therefore be related to security needs covering oil supplies rather than a calling into question of ties woven earlier with the West. It addresses evident energy worries that the discourse of "Islamic solidarity between Brother people" does nothing to dispel. Two Turkish diplomatic strategies overlap from now on in the Arab world:[91] on the one hand, research into the economic interdependencies, which lets Ankara affirm peace by trade and to reduce its oil import bill by procuring new trade outlets for its entrepreneurs and, on the other, the deployment of a multilateral diplomacy, with ambitions of aiding the prevention, the transformation, or settling of regional conflicts. In both cases, the new strategies testify to an expansion of the security concept that, for the Turkish Government, no longer confines itself to just the national defense. Mediation notably implies the idea that it is necessary to assist in "settling foreign conflicts before they turn into destabilizing factors or military risk."[92]

"Good offices" Turkish diplomacy or laying claim to regional leadership

Does the interventionism of the R. T. Erdoğan Government in the political conflicts rending the Middle East states aim to protect Turkey's interests or buttress its seeming role as an indispensable player in stabilizing the region? Since 2002, Ankara strives to be promoted (and recognized) as a mediator in different conflictive regional dossiers, a tendency that was accentuated from 2007 on during the current prime minister's second term. There is no question that the American military invasion of Iraq in 2003 had destabilizing effects on the entire Middle East. In an environment of renewed political violence, numerous Turkish mediations aimed simultaneously to build trust between adversaries to get them to the negotiating table, facilitate the passing on of messages, or again create perspectives for emerging from crisis. They are especially conspicuous in four hot spots:: Lebanon (and its Syrian "patron"), Palestine (and Israel), Iran (and the nuclear problem), and Iraq (and its sectarian tensions).

Bilateral relations between Turkey and Lebanon for a long time have depended on Turco-Syrian relationships, because of the political and military clout wielded by Damascus in the Country of Cedars, including during the post-civil war 1990s. These relations, however, were separated from the Syrian tutelage starting in 2004, with the beginning of official visits to Ankara by the Lebanese foreign affairs minister (Jean Obeid) and prime minister (Rafik Hariri), followed by the Beirut visit of Abdullah Gül, then Turkey's minister of foreign affairs. It is true that the AKP Government played a decisive role in the Syrian decision to withdraw from Lebanon (accomplished in April 2005).

The assassination of Prime Minister Rafik Hariri (in February 2005), nevertheless opens a period of uncertainty that keeps the Turkish Government from openly siding with its new Syrian ally. Indeed, the Bashar al-Assad regime is suspected of having instigated the attack, which causes the United States and European Union to launch an embargo and an international commission of inquiry. The visit of Turkish president Sezer to Damascus, which he made despite criticism leveled by the American ambassador seconded to Ankara at the time, was thus made with the aim of clarifying the assassination's circumstances but, especially, to assure the Syrian authorities of Turkish support. This involvement, however, is not totally criticized by Brussels and Washington, because it lets the Western powers hope for a deradicalization of the Syrian regime (even for its "reform" in the sense of democratizing its institutions) as well as distancing itself from its Iranian ally. On the Syrian side, this support, which keeps the regime from being "expelled" from the international scene, is taken advantage of to open negotiations with the Israeli Government led by Ehud Olmert.[93] Turkey's mediation, started in 2007; it nevertheless stalls two years later (while the negotiations were progressing fairly well) as a consequence of the large-scale Israeli military attack against Hamas in the Gaza Strip.[94] R. T. Erdoğan was, in fact, rueful at having been left in the dark by Tel Aviv about its plans involving one of his regional allies, Hamas, affiliated with the Muslim Brotherhood for which certain currents within AKP had an affinity. However, in 2006, Turkey was already involved in Lebanon as intermediary with Tel Aviv following the war started by Israel against the politico-military Hezbollah faction.[95] The government of R. T. Erdoğan appeared to be both an agent for "pacification" (since it had sent an armed unit to reinforce UNIFIL, the United Nations peacekeeping force in place) and a favored go-between of the parties to the conflict (on the one hand, dissuading Syria from intervening in the conflict and, on the other, severely criticizing the Israeli bombardment).[96]

As for the Palestine dossier, R. T. Erdoğan's Turkey first threw itself into mediation between the Palestinian and Israeli sides. It did so by facilitating contacts, passing on messages, and getting secure meeting places when the United States to some extent pulled back, focused as they were on the Iraq War. Then, starting in 2007–8, the government tried to lend a hand in reconciling the two rival Palestinian factions of Fatah and Hamas.[97] At the time it had the ear of the Palestinian President M. Abbas and of Ismaïl Haniyeh, leader of the Islamists at a time when the latter resisted any mediation with provenance, either in the United States or the European Union, which were boycotting the government running the Gaza Strip. However, starting with the Israeli military operation "Plomb durci" (Hard Lead) of December 2008–January 2009, R. T. Erdoğan ended the policy of neutrality and his government's involvement in the Israeli–Palestinian negotiations (also the Israeli–Syrian ones mentioned earlier). He even regularly took overtly anti-Israel positions publicly that made him a hero in the eyes of the region's Arab populations. Such was the case, especially, at the Davos International Economic Forum in 2009, during which Erdoğan took Shimon Peres, the Israeli president at the time, thoroughly to task, exclaiming "just a minute" for not having been given a chance to excoriate the military occupation of the West Bank.

Following the Israeli assault on the *Mavi Marmara* (a ship under Turkish flag taking part in a humanitarian mission known as the "Gaza Flotilla"),[98] an operation that resulted in nine dead on the Turkish side—he called ceaselessly for Tel Aviv's apologies, sprinkling his appeals with clearly anti-Israel digressions.[99] In so doing, R. T. Erdoğan looked less and less neutral to the Fatah political faction and its chief, Mahmoud Abbas. Thus, Turkey's position as mediator that it had occupied until then in the Palestinian national reconciliation process was weakened by the support rendered to its Hamas ally by the R. T. Erdoğan Government.[100]

In parallel, the Turkish Government plays an intermediary's role in the nuclear affairs between Iran on the one side and the American and European chiefs of state on the other. It was called on to play a key mediating role in this matter because it maintains communications with all involved parties. Thus, in opposition to the official Washington and Brussels positions, it campaigned against the imposition of new economic sanctions that would further impoverish and radicalize Iran, all the while still seeking to slow the Iranian efforts to develop a nuclear potential. Playing off his privileged contacts with Teheran, the Turkish prime minister received the Iranian president Mahmoud Ahmadinejad in 2008 and went to Iran himself in 2009.[101] His efforts led to talks between Iran and the G5 in September 2009 in Switzerland (which, however, do not meet with success). They do demonstrate the Turkish Government's capacity, in this dossier as in others, to establish its autonomy with regard to the immediate policy interests of the United States without irritating its transatlantic ally or, above all, without rupturing the alliance. It is therefore on the occasion of a UN Security Council vote in June 2010 that Turkey opposes Washington's demand for tightening financial sanctions against Teheran.[102]

Finally, turning to Iraq, here Turkey is trying to pose as promoter of an even-handed policy toward the country's different politico-sectarian factions. The R. T. Erdoğan Government for starters involved itself in negotiations on forming a national government following the parliamentary elections of March 2010. Two electoral slates finished "neck and neck" that held diametrically opposed visions for the Iraqi state: that of Nouri Al-Maliki, heading up and backed by voters of the majority Shiites and advocating the political marginalization of the Sunnis, and that of Iyad Allaoui, coming in second and with more Sunni support, calling instead for their reintegration. As it were, this was also Ankara's position and so it successfully put pressure on Prime Minister Al-Maliki to integrate members of the opposition slate in his government. To the R. T. Erdoğan Government what matters is having the camp pushing for the idea of a unitary Iraqi state represented in the government and to raise its voice against the prime minister's party that favored installing a federal state.

This "obsession" of the Turks with the preservation of the political and territorial unity of the Iraqi state (to counter the autonomization of northern Iraq and control of the revenues from oil fields located there) also led the government of R. T. Erdoğan to support the party of Moqtada al-Sadr, despite its anti-Sunni rhetoric, so long as it also advocated maintaining the territorial integrity of Iraq.[103] By doing so, Turkey projects itself as a power capable of communicating with all the actors on Iraq's political scene, unlike Saudi Arabia, which is viewed as pursuing a "Sunni agenda" and from Iran, accused of having a "Shiite agenda."[104]

Conclusion

Given these elements, focusing on the blocking of Turkey's accession to the European Union as decreeing the redefinition of the Turkish national interest due to an "Islamist" agenda appears to be wrong. It no doubt does constitute a short-term setback for the government of R. T. Erdoğan, but it partakes of a complex causality arising from sociopolitical processes, internal debates, and economic realities in both parties so that reducing it to the "Islamist agenda" of the AKP is to render it unfairly.

What is more, confronted with the Arab "revolutions," the tone in Turkey is progressively one of concern and disappointment. Originally attempting to diffuse, not without ambiguity,[105] a discourse promoting dialogue and democratization, the R. T. Erdoğan Government progressively lets go of the lucrative friendship with Libya (in July 2011), and then "betrays" the preferential cooperation it maintained with the Syrian regime of B. al-Assad (from June 2011 on). Somewhat later, however, the victory of the Islamist an-Nahda party in Tunisia's constituent assembly elections in October 2011, that of the Egyptian Muslim Brotherhood with the accession of one of their key personalities, Mohamed Morsi, to president of the Republic in June 2012, (re)animated rhetoric of the "Turkish model." In fact, the United States under Barack Obama, but also certain Arab "leftist" leaders, made AKPist Turkey into the political ideal to be followed, as the only one able to offer a government of the "moderate Islam" type capable of staving off the risks of radicalization by Islamist forces henceforth competing in societies roiled by "revolution."[106] This context contributes to the government of R. T. Erdoğan assuming a kind of regional leadership that is increasingly viewed by the Iranian political leadership and the Shiite leaders in the Arab Near East as a mode of defending the Sunni world. But the prolongation of the Syrian conflict, the violent repression of its people, the number of civilian victims but also of refugees thronging makeshift camps on the Syro-Turkish border prompted the Turkish leaders—and especially A. Davutoğlu—to support the rebellion openly, to call for a regime change in Syria as well as to urge military intervention by the international community in the conflict. This "exit" from neutrality is read as a sign and admission of the failure of the AKP's vaunted "zero problems with neighbors" policy by the major Turkish opposition leaders (including the secular camp), the military High Command (even if it is divided on the question), and a growing fraction of public opinion.

The AKP's foreign policy thus is confronted by a fairly radical challenge, seeing that the Arab countries with which relations have developed the most since 2003 are also the ones whose regimes were overturned or are violently conflicted. At the same time, the "Gezi Park" protests that took place in the center of Istanbul in May 2013 that violently opposed diverse former opposition or ad hoc movements against AKP partisans (and the police) weakened the ruling government's legitimacy and that of the state.[107] The (multiform) protests all tended to question the model of the state being formed that, as we have seen, underwent profound changes in ten years and not without provoking major sociopolitical fractures. Thus, while throughout the Turkish Republic's history, interest in the Arab world went hand in hand with attempts at redefining the national identity as violently opposing Islamist and secularist currents, the Arab revolutions and Syrian crisis brought with it a change of internal fault lines. In fact, the Turks who rejected the AKP also rejected all aspects of its foreign policy and even though what happened at Gezi in June 2013 caused them to focus their critiques on the "failings" of democratization, many of these opponents seemed to view what they called "setbacks" in the Middle East as that much more proof of the futility of the Davutoğlu and Erdoğan policy.

What is more, the fact that the AKP Government should have developed intensive relations with now deposed regimes tells some opposition commentators[108] that this should enlighten the Turkish public on the real nature of the AKP's democratic ambitions. Moreover, even within this party, those favoring its non-involvement in the Arab world would be numerous starting in late 2012 and would today wish for A. Davutoğlu's departure if not that of R. T. Erdoğan. The close think tanks themselves seem to have recommended caution, but have not been heeded on this point.[109] On the contrary, we are witnessing an ebb in the cooperative links established ten years earlier—a retrograde surge orchestrated by the political power itself—or even an institutionalization of de facto highly conflicted situations. In other words, the secularist camp going forward opposes the AKP Government's interventionism in the Arab world, all the more openly as it is no longer either friendly or cooperative like it was from 2003 to 2011.

Notes

1. The Adalet ve Kalkınma Partisi, the Justice and Development Party, which was formed in 2001 by Recep Tayyip Erdoğan, then a member of the Refah partisi and lieutenant to Necmettin Erbakan, the dominant personality in Turkish

political Islam since the late 1960s. The AKP is one of two splinters of the Refah, along with Saadet Partisi—the Welfare Party. Its political program grew out of economic liberalism and social conservatism.

2. The term "Ortadoğu"—"Middle East" in Turkish—implicitly including the "Kurdish question" and Iran is probably one of the most frequently repeated geographic references as much in the media and discourse of Turkish politicians and diplomats as in the production emanating from the more specifically intellectual and academic "sphere." This term is often used to the detriment of more precise designations that also exist in Turkish—Arab world, North Africa, Bilād Ach-Chām, Near East, and so forth, perhaps reflecting the need to still and always talk about this "Ortadoğu" without always bothering to qualify it. It is that the zone designated in this vague sense concentrates everything that many Turks, starting with the elites, consider as foreign, exogenous, and undesirable. Additionally, without this being a definitive criterion, evidently the term "Ortadoğu" is often used by actors and institutions seeking media visibility. Conversely, among the most scrupulous observers, sometimes Arabic-speaking, "Ortadoğu" is discarded with increasing frequency in favor of "Arab world," or "Arab countries." Still rarer are some academics rejecting out of hand generalized conclusions at the zone scale and arguing for a country-by-country analysis.

3. Dal, Emel Parlar, "Entre Précaution et Ambition: Le Néo- ottomanisme de La Nouvelle Politique Extérieure de l'AKP En Question" [Between Caution and Ambition: The Neo-Ottomanism of the AKP New Foreign Policy at Issue], *EurOrient*, 2010, special issue, 35–58.

4. See especially Cook (2011), Garapon (2010), Göle (2011), Hakura (2011), Lundgren (2005), Martin and Keridis (2004), Schmid (2011), Tocci et al. (2011), and K. Öktem, et al. (2012).

5. The use of this term is "trendy" in the academic literature on Turkey (see A. Chenal, "L'AKP et Le Paysage Politique Turc" [The AKP and the Turkish Political Landscape], *Pouvoirs*, 2005, Vol. 115, 41–54). It reflects the heterogeneity of forces claiming for themselves an ideological legacy that supposedly stems from the founder of the Turkish Republic, M. Kemal. On the "new" economic elites that brought the AKP to power and support it, see D. Yankaya, *La nouvelle bourgeoisie islamique: le modèle turc* [The New Islamic Bourgeoisie: The Turkish Model], Paris, PUF, 2012.

6. The Kemalist or secular current—named this way because it combines political forces rejecting any kind of Islamization of political life and institutions—is

often caricatured by the political opposition, reproaching it for denying the deep—Islamic—Turkish identity and vice versa.
7. Some Turks, in the collective imagination and national narrative, consider the Arabs with their nationalist demands in the early twentieth century as having stabbed the Ottoman Empire "in the back." Indeed, at a time when the empire tried to sustain its authority in their lands, the "Great Arab Revolt" broke out under the Hashemite command of Sherif Hussein of Mecca with Great Britain's support. The latter country, great partisan of dismembering the Ottoman Empire, shone again at the Treaty of Sèvres and, from 1919 to 1923, in supporting the Greeks against Turkey's Republican army reconstituted by Mustafa Kemal. The Arabs, for their part, accuse the Turks of having scuttled the Califate and suspect them of never having abandoned their hegemonic aspirations in the Arab Near and Middle East.
8. Pierre Grosser, "De l'usage de l'histoire dans les politiques étrangères" [The Use of History in Foreign Policies], in F. Charillon (ed.), *Politique étrangère. Nouveaux regards* [Foreign Policy. New Insights], Paris, Presses de Sciences Po, 2002, p. 361.
9. *Ibid.,* p. 365.
10. In Turkey, the Ottoman past for a long time had been presented by the Kemalist elite and Republican historiography as "decadent" or even "obscurantist" to the extent that the supposedly tight grip that religion had on politics and society is seen as antithetical to the idea of economic and social progress and therefore Western-style "modernity." See E. Copeaux, *Espaces et temps de la nation turque. Analyse d'une historiographie nationaliste, 1931–1993* [Spaces and Times of the Turkish Nation. Analyzing a Nationalist Historiography, 1931–1993], Paris, CNRS-Éditions, 1997.
11. O. Baskın, *Türk Dış Politikası: Kurtuluş Savaşindan Bugüne* [Turkish Foreign Policy: The War of Independence Today], Vol. 1: 1919–1989, Istanbul, İletişim, 2001, pp. 781–96.
12. The Democratic Party, created when multipartyism was allowed in 1946, quickly opposed the Kemalists (CHP). It won the 1947 legislative elections.
13. Turkey's joining the Atlantic Pact that became NATO signaled not only the country's integration into the Western strategic alliance, but also the final rejection of the socialist society political model promoted by the Soviet "big Brother."
14. Turkey was in the van of the Baghdad Pact—an initiative that consisted of integrating other countries into the Western defensive system (by way of a

"treaty annex"), including Turkey, Iraq, Pakistan, and Iran. However, this pact was short-lived.

15. Allied with Germany in the First World War, the Ottoman Empire was dismembered after its defeat (Treaty of Sèvres, 1920), provoking the Turkish war of independence against the Western powers, Italy, and Greece. Not wanting to risk a commitment that it had paid dearly for, the Turkish Republic remained neutral in 1939 when the Second World War broke out.
16. It involved the regimes of Abdul al-Karim Qassim in Iraq and Hafez al-Assad in Syria.
17. Such as, for example, the death of the Egyptian leader Nasser, champion of Pan-Arabism, succeeded by President Sadat who embarked progressively on the road to peace with Israel and alignment with the United States; the Israeli-Arab war of 1973 and the ensuring oil shock; or again the invasion of Cyprus by the Turkish army in 1974.
18. Necmettin Erbakan (1926–2011) becomes the principal political voice of Turkey's Islamists starting in the 1970s. According to the MSP party's ideology tinged by nationalism, the pacification of societal and communitarian tensions and the country's economic development pass through the reIslamization of political institutions and of society. The MSP is considered as the "founding" branch of R. T. Erdoğan's AKP, from which it separated in the late 1990s on the grounds that the confrontational and "anti" attitude of the party was prejudicial to its integration in politics.
19. This is how Ankara hopes to counterbalance the Soviet support, but also to be credited by the Arab world for mobilizing on behalf of the Palestinian cause.
20. U. Kürt, "The Doctrine of 'Turkish-Islamic Synthesis' as Official Ideology of September 12 and the 'Intellectuals Hearth-Aydinlar Ocagi' as the Ideological Apparatus of the State," *European Journal of Economic and Political Studies*, 2010, Vol. 3, no. 2, 111–25.
21. This movement, started in Turkey during the 1960s by Fethullah Gülen, aims to train Muslim youth in "rationality" and "modern" knowledge through courses in Arabic, history, and civilization, while making sure that it keeps an Islamic identity.
22. B. Balci, *Missionnaires de l'Islam en Asie centrale. Les écoles turques de Fethullah Gülen* [Islam's Missionaries in Central Asia. The Turkish Schools of Fethullah Gülen], Paris, IFEA–Maisonneuve & Larose, 1996.
23. Intervention by the Turkish army's high command (MGK) in the political

arena in 1997 is often called the "post-modern coup d'état" because the MGK published a "warning" on its Internet site threatening the government.
24. This heading is adapted from the work by B. Badie and M. C. Smouts, *Le bouleversement du monde. Sociologie de la scène internationale* [The World Turned Upside Down. Sociology of the International Scene], Paris, Presses de Sciences Po/Dalloz, 1999.
25. This aspect is underlined by J. Marcou in his article "La place du monde arabe dans la nouvelle politique étrangère d'Ahmet Davutoğlu" [The Place of the Arab World in the New Foreign Policy of Ahmet Davutoğlu], in D. Schmid (ed.), *La Turquie au Moyen-Orient. Le retour d'une puissance régionale?* [Turkey in the Middle East. Return of a Regional Power?], Paris, CNRS, 2011.
26. The United States wanted to make Ankara NATO's fulcrum in the region for facing the rising political instability in the Caucasus, as well as the renewed demands of the former Soviet republics in Central Asia for integration with NATO. The purpose was to remove these regions from Iran's potential influence by attaching them to a Turkish sphere of influence traditionally more linked to the West but also more secular and democratic. In reality, Turkey could not really establish leadership but at least it would contribute to training civilian and military personnel of the new NATO members. See M. Benli-Altunisik, "La question du 'modèle turc' ou le *soft power* de la Turquie au Moyen-Orient" [The Question of the 'Turkish Model' or the Soft Power of Turkey in the Middle East], in D. Schmid (dir.), *op. cit.*
27. For Washington, henceforth obsessed by the fight against al-Qaeda, the AKP Government was part of the model embodying a "moderate Islam" able to ally "tradition" and "modernity," "democracy" and "Muslim religion"—a model that would be likely to fight effectively against violent jihadist groups.
28. PKK: Partiya Karkeren Kurdistan in the Kurdish language, that is, the Kurdistan Workers' Party. See H. Bozarslan, *La question kurde* [The Kurdish Question], Paris, Presses de Sciences Po, 1997. See also A. Mango, *Turkey and the War on Terror. For Forty Years We Fought Alone*, London/New York, Routledge, 2005.
29. Ö. Taşpinar, "La relation turco-américaine à l'épreuve du Moyen-Orient" [Turkish–American Relations Put to the Test in the Middle East], in D. Schmid (sub. ed.), *op. cit.*, p. 152.
30. Philippe Droz-Vincent, *Vertiges de la puissance. Le moment américain au Moyen-Orient* [Giddy with Power. The American Moment in the Middle East]

Paris, La Découverte, 2007 and "Le moment américain au Moyen-Orient" [The American Moment in the Middle East], *Esprit*, 2005, no. 5, 150–63.

31. As far as Turkish public opinion is concerned, the United States having turned "pro-Kurd" is henceforth supporting their enemy.
32. With the Cold War over and following the Gulf War (1990–1), the rigidity of the Turkish authorities in refusing to recognize the cultural identity and administrative autonomy of the country's approximately 20 million Kurds incited many young people to join the PKK and relaunch the guerilla conflict.
33. Other than abolishing the death penalty, the AKP quickly moved to reduce the army's role in political life. This party also sought to reform the judicial institution by, for example, suppressing special jurisdictions, and launching a reform of the criminal code.
34. Two major elements contributed to sustain a deteriorated climate between Turkey and the EU: Cyprus and the Kurdish question. On the one hand, the recurring tensions between the Cypriot, but also Turkish and Greek governments, reached a climax during the Cypriot presidency of the European Union (in the second trimester of 2012). On the other hand, the AKP Government's policy toward the Kurds, called the "outstretched hand" initiated in 2006, aimed to open negotiations with the PKK and to envisage a political resolution to the armed conflict. This approach fizzled and hostilities resumed from 2011 to 2013 before opening new talks, "the Imrali process," named after the prison where Abdullah Öcalan was being held. The whole initiative was nevertheless aborted in the aftermath of the Syrian crisis. Ankora's regional policy seems to be majorly determined by its will to annihilate the PKK and avoid the consolidation of a unfied Kurdish territory on its borders with Syria and Turkey.
35. One of thirty-five chapters was concluded and eight were blocked, by reason notably of the Turkish refusal to sign a free trade agreement with the Twenty-Seven, which would have included Cyprus.
36. Until the AKP came to power, cultural diplomacy was more or less the privilege of Islamist opposition groups and Brotherhoods that sought to link up with Arabo-Muslim countries in counterpoint to the "pro-Western" policy pursued by the political leadership (emerging from the secular current) and the army.
37. D. Battistella, "L'intérêt national: une notion, trois discourse" [National Interest: One Notion, Three Discourses], in Charillon, *op. cit.*, p. 153.
38. According to A. Wendt, *Social Theory of International Politics*, 1999, p. 233, quoted in D. Battistella, *op. cit.*, p. 155.

39. After a decade of violent political strife, the Turkish economy is drained. Imitating the American model and in order to escape the deflationary spiral, the Özal Government decides to make a "neo-liberal" change of direction in economic policy—which the army's high command approves. See J.F. Pérouse, *La Turquie en marche, les grandes mutations depuis 1980* [Turkey on the March, the Great Changes since 1980], Paris, La Martinière, 2004.
40. D. Battistella, *op. cit.*, p. 155.
41. *Ibid.*, p. 157.
42. I. W. Zartman, "La politique étrangère et le règlement des conflits" [Foreign Policy and Conflict Resolution], in F. Charillon (ss. ed.), *Politique étrangère. Nouveaux regards, op. cit.* [Foreign Policy. New Looks], p. 275; emphasis added.
43. After A. Wendt, quoted in D. Battistella, *op. cit.*, pp. 152–3.
44. See A. Davutoğlu, *Stratejik Derinlik* [Strategic Depth], 1st edition, Istanbul: Küre Yayınları, 2001.
45. This book was reprinted in fourteens editions in Turkey and translated into numerous languages, including Arabic, but not into English or French.
46. Ahmet Davutoğlu was the Turkish minister of foreign affairs from 2009 to 2014. Before that, he was special advisor to Prime Minister R. T. Erdoğan, from 2000 to 2003. A former professor of international relations at the University of Marmara (Istanbul), he is also one of the founding members of the University of Şehir (Istanbul) and Science and Culture Foundation (a kind of after-hours university mainly attended by young students from conservative circles). See J. B. Le Moulec, "Le Professeur qui a voulu révolutionner la politique étrangère turque" [The Professor who Wanted to Revolutionize Turkish Foreign Policy], April 4, 2013, http://ovipot.hypotheses.org/8642 and also G. Zengin, *Hoca: Türk Dış Politikasında "Davutoğlu Etkisi"* [Professor: The "Davutoğlu Effect" on Turkish Foreign Policy], Istanbul, İnkilâp, 2012.
47. In Turkish: *Psikolojik arkaplan.*
48. C. Karakas, *Turkey: Islam and Laïcism between the Interests of State, Politics and Society*, Frankfurt, PRIF (Peace Research Institute Frankfurt), 2007.
49. Leonore Martin in Lenore G. Martin and Dimitris Keridis, *The Future of Turkish Foreign Policy*, Cambridge, MA, MIT Press, 2004, p. 41.
50. This especially concerns the Alevi. For the Kurds, the collective demands for political autonomy, even self-determination, are organized later, at about the start of the 1960s in Iraq and after 1978 and the creation of the PKK relative to Turkey.

51. The post of secretary general of the Organization of the Islamic Conference, given to Ekmeleddin Ihsanoğlu in 2004, also is a symbolic event in this regard.
52. S. Magued, *La politique arabe de la Turquie depuis 2002 comme une dimension de sa gestion régionale au Moyen-Orient* [Turkey's Arab Policy since 2002 as a Dimension of its Managing the Middle East], PhD thesis in political science (spv. dir. G. Groc), Sciences Po Aix-en-Provence, 2012.
53. Interview with S. E. Özdem Sanberk, Istanbul, April 2013.
54. This is the case in certain academic enclaves: G. Zengin, *Hoca: Türk Dış Politikasında "Davutoğlu Etkisi"* [Mentor: The "Davutoğlu Effect" in Turkish Foreign Policy], Istanbul, Inkilâp, 2012, p. 81.
55. By doing this, they defy the prohibition on Arab language courses that the military high command issues at the start of the "postmodern coup d'état" of February 1997. See A. Sencer, "Changes in the Domestic Politics and the Foreign Policy Orientation of the AK Party," in M. Lenore and D. Keridis, *op. cit.*, pp. 243–75.
56. A. Davutoğlu, *Stratejik Derinlik* [Strategic Depth], 1st edition, Istanbul, Küre Yayınları, 2001, p. 453.
57. The first grants for Arab world research were distributed by Tübitak, the equivalent of the Belgian National Research Fund (FNR), and date from 2005.
58. Interview with Nuray Mert, Istanbul, November 2012, Burcu Gültekin Puntsmann, Ankara, January 2013.
59. However, there can be no talk, in our opinion, of a "new Orientalism" regarding the Turkish knowledge-production enterprise for the Middle East and the Ottoman past, so much so are the attempts at a mental re-appropriation of the Middle East region and of the Ottoman past by means of an effective policy of presence, which are two dimensions of the same policy that the AKP did not manage to reconcile. Certainly, there is an editorial mode effect, by virtue of which scientific and literary publications, as well as televised productions on the subject of the Ottoman empire, "pollute." In addition, the AKP elites often use geographic terms used during the Ottoman empire to name geographic spaces taken over under the heading of the party's "new" foreign policy without taking into account that they glorify the Ottoman past during official trips that they make to their immediate neighbors. But rewriting Ottoman history for public opinion is debatable—and not just inside the university community—and it is suddenly far from appearing to be consensual.
60. TESEV (Turkish Foundation for Political and Economic Studies), SETA (Foundation for Research in Politics, Economy, and Society), USAK

(Foundation for International Strategic Research), ORSAM (Middle East Research Center), and SDE (Institute for Strategic Thinking).
61. The multiplying places for Turkish knowledge of the Arab world lead to a veritable publishing phenomenon. Academics, research groups, think-tank cadres, journalists, and/or pundits publish works on the Middle East, ranging from career narratives (for example, Cengiz Çandar, a reporter for *Radikal*, considered a "center-left" weekly, occasional advisor to chiefs of state and Turkish governments dating back to T. Özal; see C. Candar, *Mezopotamya Ekxpresi, Bir Tarih Yolculuğu* [Mesopotamia Express: A Voyage into History], Istanbul, İlestişim, 2012, to regional histories (for example, K. İnat, M. Ataman, and B. Duran, *Ortadoğu Yıllığı 2008* [*Middle East Annals 2008*], Istanbul, Küre Yayınları, 2009. It is interesting to note that the Küre publishing house belongs to the Foundation for Science and Culture founded by A. Davutoğlu. Other annals have been published by the SETA and USAK think tanks, ranging from works devoted to a single country or a particular problematic (water, the Kurds, and so forth). The Arab revolts and realignments have accentuated the phenomenon, if only by the tone adopted, which is no longer that of a triumphant optimism, but verges more on a worry if not fear of contagion (for example, H. Mahalli, *Ortadoğu'da Kanlı Bahar* [Bloody Springtime in the Middle East] Istanbul, Destek Yayınları, 2012. The author comes from Syria. From the start of the Syrian conflict, he pronounced himself in favor of the B. Al-Assad regime, convinced that the rebellion would lead to civil war and not the departure of the Alawite oligarchy).
62. Such is the case with the more dynamic organizations like SETA and USAK, mostly financed by the Ministry of Foreign Affairs and the Presidency of the Republic.
63. MÜSIAD: Association of Independent Turkish Industrialists and Businessmen (close to theAKP). This employer's association has not yet set up a permanent representation in the Arab world, it appears, although it has branched out to Europe and the United States for several years now.
64. TÜSKON: Confederation of Turkish Industrialists and Businessmen (emerged from the Gülenist movement).
65. See especially H. R. Ebaugh, *The Gülen Movement: A Sociological Analysis of a Civic Movement Rooted in Moderate Islam*, New York, Springer, 2010.
66. TÜSIAD: Association of Turkish Industrialists and Businessmen, created in 1971 (close to the secular current).
67. It is what A. Davutoğlu calls the "geocultural" dimension. A. Davutoğlu,

Stratejik Derinlik [Deep Strategy], 1st edition, Istanbul, Küre Yayınları, 2001, pp. 327–32 and pp. 452–3. The multidimensional aspect also implies the development of links between civil societies and pushing a policy of cultural influence via the media.

68. Understood by this term, which is close to that of "soft power," is the spread of a state's national culture to a foreign society by means of cultural acts and institutions (including the media) and people-to-people exchanges.
69. A. Sever, "Turquie/Syrie: de rapprochements en désillusions" [Turkey/Syria: From Rapprochement to Disillusion], in D. Schmid, *op. cit.*, pp. 174–5.
70. L. Mallet, "Les ambiguïtés des relations turco-israéliennes" [The Ambiguities of Turco-Israeli Relations], Sécurité mondiale [Global security], 40, ISI, Université de Laval, http://www.psi.ulaval.ca/fileadmin/psi/documents/Documents/Securite_mondiale/relations_turco-israeliennes_no_40.pdf
71. A. Sever, "Turquie/Syrie: de rapprochements en désillusions" [Turkey/Syria: From Rapprochement to Disillusion], *op. cit.*, p. 171.
72. The Gulf Cooperation Council condemned Turkey and instead lent its support to Syria at the time of the GAP project. For Syria, the idea is for the PKK to destabilize Turkey, which would lead this state to make concessions on resolving the problem of the water as well as Hatay.
73. It involved President Süleyman Demirel and his prime minister, Mesut Yilmaz.
74. Shortly thereafter, the Kurdish leader was expelled from Syrian territory and arrested when he fled to Kenya.
75. Attendance by the Turkish president Ahmet Necdet Sezer at the funeral for President Hafez al-Assad in 2000 augured a change of course in bilateral Turco-Syrian relations.
76. In 2005, the newly adopted Iraqi constitution made it a federal state and instituted the Regional Government of Kurdistan in northern Iraq.
77. The Kirkuk region is hydrocarbon-rich (containing 13 percent of Iraq's petroleum reserves). Taking control of it would let the Iraqi Kurds have the financial means for the independence that some among them wish for.
78. The difference on this point stemmed from the fact that Turkey considers the waters of the Tigris, Euphrates, and Orontes (in Hatay) as cross-border waters over which it exercises total sovereignty, but that it must share slightly with its neighbors downstream; Syria and Iraq, in contrast, consider them to be international waters, that is, over which they also are also able to exercise sovereignty.
79. This council brings together the ministers of trade and economy of both coun-

tries on a regular schedule. It envisions constructing a high-speed trans-border rail line and a joint bank (two projects practically still-born) or yet, more modestly, setting up Syrian consulates in Turkey—including at Gaziantep, in the Hatay region (until then rather marginalized) to develop commercial ties with the Aleppo region (especially in textiles).

80. A. Sever, "Turkey/Syria: From Rapprochement to Disillusion," *op. cit.*, pp. 179–80. The volume of trade between Turkey and Syria rose from in the region of 773 million dollars in 2002 to approximately 797 million dollars in 2006, and then to about 1.2 billion dollars in 2007, and approximately 1.8 billion in 2009. Turkey imports a small amount of energy, agricultural produce, and textiles, and it exports more technology, metals, chemical products, minerals, electronics, and vehicles.

81. A. Sever, "Turkey/Syria: From Rapprochement to Disillusion," *op. cit.*, p. 177.

82. The US Congress passed the Syria Accountability and Lebanese Sovereignty Restoration Act in 2003, which called for the Syrian regime to withdraw from Lebanon and to cease its political, financial, and military support to the Lebanese Hezbollah faction.

83. O. Baskın, *Türk Dış Politikası: Kurtuluş Savaşindan Bugüne* [Turkish Foreign Policy: The War of Independence Today] *op. cit.*, pp. 793–4.

84. D. Yankaya, *La nouvelle bourgeoisie islamique* [The New Islamic Bourgeoisie], *op. cit.*

85. After the Turkish refusal to aid the American military invasion of Iraq when it opened a second front in 2003, Turco-American relations were imprinted by distrust concerning the Iraqi dossier until 2007. The Turks accused the United States of letting the PKK operate widely in the north of Iraq in parallel with the political autonomy that they granted to the Kurds settled in this part of the country. Starting in 2007, the Turks revisited their attitude regarding the Kurdish Regional Government (KRG) set up in 2005, thinking that the Iraqi Kurds constituted an unavoidable political force in the post-Saddam context (by the fact that they won 26 percent of the vote in the 2005 legislative elections). They therefore played the political-economic rapprochement card with the Kurds in Iraq, expecting that this would let them negotiate a political "opening" with the Kurds in Turkey. In 2008, several official visits took place on both sides, which amounted to a recognition of the KRG by the Turkish Government. A Turkish consulate was opened in Erbil, the KRG capital, in 2010. J. Cécillon, "L'Irak, nouvel espace de déploiement de la puissance turque" [Iraq, New Space for Deployment of Turkish Power], in Schmid, *op. cit.*

86. The development of partnership agreements that concluded with several Sub-Saharan African countries was in response to the same need for diversifying export terrains and markets for national goods in return for access to natural resources and raw materials. The first Turco-African summit thus was organized in 2012 in Istanbul, with the aim of stimulating economic exchanges and to accompany the opening of F. Gülen schools just about everywhere in Africa. The creation of direct air connections between Istanbul and numerous African capitals by the national air carrier Turkish Airlines during the second half of the first decade of the twenty-first century as well as of many Turkish embassies in Africa and African ones in Turkey witnessed to the AKP's political voluntarism in this regard. See the doctoral thesis by Francis Boulou on the Turkish actors in foreign policy in Francophone Sub-Saharan Africa (spv. M. Tozy and A. Signoles), University of Galatasaray–Sciences Po Aix-en-Provence (in preparation).
87. The AKP economic policy resulted in a ripple effect that brought a relatively strong decline in trade during the second half of the 2000 decade, despite the EU remaining Ankara's number one economic partner. See the statistics by MOCI (Moniteur du Commerce International) (International Commerce Monitor), a French magazine that collects and puts out a weekly summary of all import–export related information). (http://www.lemoci.com/0122-412-EXCLUSIF-Les-statistiques-completes-du-commerce-exterieur-turc.html)
88. R. Bourgeot, "Une réorientation de l'économie turque vers le Moyen-Orient?" [A Reorientation of the Turkish Economy toward the Middle East], in D. Schmid, *La Turquie au Moyen-Orient* [Turkey in the Middle East) *op. cit.*
89. *Ibid.* and S. Magued, *La politique arabe de la Turquie depuis 2002* [Turkey's Arab Policy since 2002], *op. cit.*
90. *Ibid.*
91. For C. Sitzenstuhl, *La diplomatie turque au Moyen-Orient. Héritages et ambitions du gouvernement de l'AKP 2002–2010* [Turkish Middle East Diplomacy. Legacies and Ambitions of the AKP 2002–2010], Paris, L'Harmattan, 2011, these two strategies allow distinctions to be drawn between relations woven by Turkey with bordering states for one, and, for another, with those that tie it to non-bordering states. While this distinction has the virtue of clarity, it is not entirely relevant for the case of Iraq, to the extent that this frontier state is the object of a dual Turkish strategy since 2003 that is both political and economic.
92. I. W. Zartman, *op. cit.*, p. 275, in F. Charillon, *Politique étrangère. Nouveaux regards* [Foreign Policy. New Looks], *op. cit.*

93. International Crisis Group, *Turkey and the Middle East: Ambitions and Constraints*, April 7, 2012, http://www.crisisgroup.org, last accessed March 16, 2013.
94. A. Signoles, "Lendemains de guerre dans les Territoires palestiniens" [Aftermaths of War in the Palestinian Territories], in F. Charillon and A. Dieckhoff (eds), *Afrique du Nord-Moyen-Orient*, Paris, La Documentation française, 2010–11, pp. 49–63.
95. B. Rougier, "La guerre d'Israël contre le Hezbollah et la défaite de l'État libanais" [Israel's War against Hezbollah and the Defeat of the Lebanese State], in F. Charillon and A. Dieckhoff (eds), *Afrique du Nord/Moyen-Orient*, Paris, La Documentation Française, 2006–7, pp. 67–94.
96. O. Baskın, *Türk Dış Politikası: Kurtuluş Savaşindan Bugüne, op. cit.* [Turkish Foreign Policy: Independence Wars Today], pp. 781–96.
97. From 2007 on, two rival governments existed side by side in Palestine: Hamas, which controlled all of the Gaza Strip, and Fatah, its power base in the West Bank. See A. Signoles, "Territoires palestiniens: la lutte Fatah-Hamas" [The Palestinian Territories: The Fatah–Hamas Conflict], in F. Charillon and A. Dieckhoff (eds), *Afrique du Nord/Moyen-Orient*, Paris, La Documentation Française, 2007–8, pp. 57–70.
98. The "Gaza flotilla" was a humanitarian action carried out by international militant networks to transport by sea construction materials and food supplies to the Gaza Strip population as a way of breaking the economic blockade imposed on this territory since 2006. On the Turkish side, the humanitarian operation of the *Mavi Marmara* is supported by a humanitarian NGO, IHH (Insan Hak ve Hüriyetleri Insanı Yardım Vakfı) (Human Rights, Freedoms and Humanitarian Relief Foundation) that came out of the Islamic-conservative current. The Israeli attack, which took place in international waters, is widely condemned by the international community. It led to Turkish reprisals: The Israeli ambassador to Ankara was expelled and the military cooperation accords signed between the two countries in 1996 were suspended.
99. Israeli prime minister B. Netanyahu publicly apologized to Turkey three years later, in March 2003.
100. International Crisis Group, *Turkey and the Middle East, op. cit.*
101. O. Baskın (ed.), *Türk Dış Politikası: Kurtuluş Savaşindan Bugüne* [Turkish Foreign Policy: Independence Wars Today], *op. cit.*, pp. 781–96.
102. The G5 is made up of five permanent UN Security Council members, sometimes with the addition of Germany, in which case, it becomes the G5 + 1.

103. The Sadrist party favors the unitary state to the extent that its electoral strongholds are situated around Baghdad and that this region is poor in hydrocarbons.
104. On Turkey's involvement in Iraqi politics, see J. Cécillon, "L'Irak, nouvel espace de déploiement de la puissance turque" [Iraq, New Space for Deploying Turkish Power], in Schmid, *op. cit.,* pp. 185–204.
105. The "zero problem" policy with the neighbors openly flouted the dictatorial character of the partner regime.
106. M. B. Altunisik, in D. Schmid, *La Turquie au Moyen-Orient* [Turkey in the Middle East]. *op. cit.,* pp. 130–1.
107. B. Montabone, "Droit à la ville et contestation de l'ordre moral urbain en Turquie" [Law in the City and Challenges to the Urban Moral Order in Turkey]," *EchoGéo*, October 10, 2013, http://www.echogeo.revues.org/13567, last accessed April 11, 2015; J. F. Pérouse, "Le parc Gezi: dessous d'une transformation très politique" [Gezi Park: Under a Very Political Transformation], *Métropolitiques*, June 24, 2013, http://www.metropolitiques.eu/Le-parc-Gezi-dessous-d-une.html, last accessed April 9, 2015; S. Weber, "Looking from the Side Lines: retours sur la Turquie de Angry nation et de Another Empire" [Returns to the Turkey of the Angry Nation and of Another Empire], *EchoGéo*, Vol. 25, October 10, 2013, http://echogeo.revues.org/13575, last accessed March 17, 2015.
108. Additions: Kadri Gürsel (the author is also a commentator in the anti-government centrist daily *Milliyet*), "Turkey, Lonely Man of the Middle East," *Al-Monitor.com*, July 15, 2013, http://www.al-monitor.com, last accessed October 2, 2012. Akın Kenan, "İktidarın iflas eden Orta Doğu politikası! (La politique moyen-orientale du gouvernement en faillite)" [The Government's Failing Middle East Policy], *Yeniçağ* (a daily coming out of the Kemalist Ataturkist movement), September 2, 2013, http://www.yg.yenicaggazetesi.com.tr, accessed September 5, 2013. Ekrem, Mahmut, "AKP politikalarının iflası, İsrail'in ekmeğine yağ sürüyor! (La faillite de la politique étrangère de l'AKP, du miel pour Israël)" [The Failure of the AKP Foreign Policy is Honey for Israel], posted on the blog "Muhalefet demokrasiye geliştirir" (L'opposition renforce la démocratie) [The Opposition Strengthens Democracy], August 16, 2013, http://blog.milliyet.com.tr/profilimaspx, accessed September 5, 2013. Halkarin Demokratik Kongesi (a political association with socialist and pro-Kurd leanings), in a communique dated October 5, 2013, association undertook to note in article 2 of its declaration of "the failure of the AKP government's Middle East policy," including its "inability to promote democratic

values." http://www.halklarindemokratikkongresi.net, accessed December 2, 2013.
109. Interview with T. Özhan, president of SETA (Foundation for Political, Economic, and Social Research, Ankara), January 2013. Interview with T. Küçükcan, director of foreign policy studies at SETA, December 2012, Istanbul.

Bibliography

Chapter 1

Abo-Kazleh, M. (2006) "Rethinking IR Theory in Islam: Towards a More Adequate Approach," *Turkish Journal of International Relations*, Vol. 5, no. 4, 41.

Acharya, A. and Buzan, B. (2009) *Non-Western International Relations Theory* (London: Routledge).

Adiong, N., Mauriello, R., and Abdelkader. D. (eds) (2016) *Islam and International Relations: Contributions to Theory and Practice* (Basingstoke: Palgrave Macmillan).

Adiong, N., Mauriello, R., and Abdelkader. D. (eds) (forthcoming) *Islam in International Affairs: Politics and Paradigms* (New York: Routledge).

Adraoui, Mohamed-Ali (2017) "Borders and Sovereignty in Islamist and Jihadist Thought. Past and Present," *International Affairs*, Vol. 93, no. 4, 917–35.

Adraoui, Mohamed-Ali (ed.) (2015) *Les islamistes et le monde. Islam politique et relations internationales* (Paris: L'Harmattan).

Amghar, Samir (ed.) (2012) *Les islamistes au défi du pouvoir. Evolutions d'une idéologie* [The Islamist Challenge to Power. Evolutions of an Ideology] (Paris: Michalon).

al-Banna, Hassan (1984) *Majmu'at rasa'il al-imam al-shahid Hassan al-Banna* [Anthology of the Epistles of the Martyr Imam Hassan al-Banna] (Beirut: al-Mu'assasa al-Islamiyya). Translation by Mohamed-Ali Adraoui.

Badie, Bertrand and Smouts, Marie-Claude (1999) *Le retournement du monde. Sociologie de la scène international* [The World Turned Upside Down. Sociology of the International Scene] (Paris: Presses de Sciences Po).

Battistella, Dario (2012) *Théories des relations internationales* [Theories of International Relations] (Presses de Sciences Po, Références).

Bayat, Asef (2005) "Islamism and Social Movement Theory," *Third World Quarterly*, Vol. 26, no. 6, 891–908.

Berger, Peter and Luckmann, Thomas (1966) *The Social Construction of Reality* (New York: Anchor Books).

Buzan, Barry and Little, Richard (2000) *The Idea of International Systems in World History* (Oxford: Oxford University Press).

Cornell, Svante E. (2006) *Islam and Foreign Policy* (Boston: MIT Press).

Durkheim, Émile (1961 [1925]) "What is a Social Fact?" in *The Rules of Sociological Method* (Ann Arbor: Michigan University Press).

Hallaq, Wael B. (2012) *The Impossible State: Islam, Politics, and Modernity's Moral Predicament* (New York: Columbia University Press).

Hourani, Albert (1983) "Conclusion," in Adeed Dawsiha (ed.), *Islam and Foreign Policy* (Cambridge: Cambridge University Press), pp. 176–91.

Husserl, Edmund (1970) *The Crisis of European Sciences and Transcendental Phenomenology* (Northwestern University Press).

Macleod, Alex, Dufault, Evelyne, Dufour, F. Guillaume, and Morin, David (2008) *Relations internationales. Théories et concepts* [International Relations. Theories and Concepts] (Athéna Editions).

Osiander, A. (2001) "Sovereignty, International Relations, and the Westphalian Myth," *International Organization*, Vol. 55, no. 2, 251–87.

Reus-Smit, Christian and Snidal, Duncan (eds) (2010) *The Oxford Handbook of International Relations*.

Roy, Olivier (1994) *The Failure of Political Islam* (Cambridge, MA: Harvard University Press).

Roy, O. (2004) *Globalized Islam: The Search for a New Ummah* (New York: Columbia University Press).

Chapter 2

Abdelnasser, Walid M. (1994) *The Islamic Movement in Egypt. Perceptions of International Relations 1967–1981*. (London/New York: The Graduate Institute of International Studies).

Akesbi, Najib (2008) "L'Accord de libre-échange Maroc-USA: un acte éminemment politique," in Najib Akesbi (dir.), *Accord de libre-échange Maroc-USA* (Rabat: Critique économique no. 21), pp. 3–8.

Al-banna, Hassan (2005) *L'Ensemble des Épîtres (en arabe)*, collected by Al-Shahhât Ahmad al-Tahhân (Egypt: Dâr al-Kalîma li al-nashr wa al-tawzî').

Belhaj, Abdessamad (2006) "L'usage politique de l'islam: l'universel au service d'un État. Le cas du Maroc," *Recherches sociologiques et anthropologiques*, Vol. 37, no. 2, http://rsa.revues.org/575

Benkirane, Abdelillah, (1999) *Le mouvement islamiste et la problématique de la méthode (en arabe)* (Casablanca: Al-najâh al-jadîda).

Bourdieu, Pierre (1980) *Questions de sociologie* (Paris: Éditions de Minuit).

Devin, Guillaume (2007) *Sociologie des relations internationales* (Paris: Repères/La découverte).

Fernandez Molina, Irène (2007) *Le PJD et la politique étrangère du Maroc. Entre l'idéologie et le pragmatisme* (Barcelona: Edicions Bellaterra, Fundacion CIDOB, Documentos CIDOB).

Garaudy, Roger (1996) *Les Mythes fondateurs de la politique israélienne* (Pithiviers: Samisdzat, 1996).

Hassan II (1993) *La Mémoire d'un Roi, entretiens avec Éric Laurent* (Paris: Plon).

Lia, Brynar (1998) *Society of the Muslim Brother in Egypt. The Rise of an Islamic Movement 1928–1942* (Liban: Ithaca Press).

Mohsen-Finan, Khadija and Zeghal, Malika (2006) "Opposition islamiste et pouvoir monarchique au Maroc. Le cas du Parti de la Justice et du Développement," *RFSP*, Vol. 56, no. 1, 79–119.

Perrault, Gilles (1990) *Notre ami le roi* (Paris: Éditions Gallimard).

Roy, Olivier (1992) *L'échec de l'islam politique* (Paris: Seuil/Esprit).

Tarrow, Sydney (2000) "La contestation transnationale," *Cultures & Conflicts*, Vols 38–9, http://conflits.revues.org/276, last accessed November 29, 2013.

Tozy, Mohamed (1999) *Monarchie et islam politique au Maroc* (Paris: Presses de Sciences Po).

Zeghal, Malika (2005) *Les islamistes marocains. Le défi à la monarchie* (Casablanca: Éditions Le Fennec).

Website References

http://archive.constantcontact.com/fs093/110208448196/archive/1102128623072.htlm, last accessed on September 22, 2013.

http://www.attajdid.ma/index.php?info=6700, last accessed on September 22, 2013.

http://www.attajdid.ma/?info=7857, last accessed on September 22, 2013.

Aujourd'hui le Maroc, "Lahjouji courtise le PJD," May 24, 2004, https://www.csidonline.org/, last accessed on September 22, 2013.

http://www.bmaq.org/fre/page/al-quds-commitee, last accessed on September 17, 2013.

http://carnegieendowment.org/experts/?fa=273, last accessed on September 22, 2013.

"Compétitivité des exportations marocaines: quel bilan?," Royaume du Maroc, Ministère de l'Économie et des Finances, Direction des études et des prévisions financières, May 2013, document personnel, http://www.yabiladi.com/articles/details/18632/parlement-l-istiqlal-tacle-normalisation-relations.htlm last accessed on September 22, 2013.

http://www.diplomatie.ma/ActionduMaroc/LeComitéAlQods/tabid/104/language/fr-FR/Defaukt.aspx, last accessed on September 17, 2013.

http://www.diplomatie.ma/ActionduMaroc/LeComitéAlQods/tabid/104/vw/1/ItemID/3261/language/fr-FR/Default.aspx, last accessed on September 17, 2013.

http://www.diplomatie.ma/SearchResults/tabid/42/language/fr-FR/Default.aspx?Search=agressions+israéliennes, last accessed on September 17, 2013.

http://www.diplomatie.ma/SearchResults/tabid/42/language/fr-FR/Default.aspx?Search=palestine, last accessed on September 17, 2013.

Hassan II, *La Mémoire d'un Roi*, interviews with Éric Laurent, Paris, Plon, 1993, http://www.slateafrique.com/37555/economie-maroc-le-partenaire-discret-d-israel, last accessed on September 19, 2013.

PJD. La charte doctrinale et le programme général (en arabe), Rabat, PJD, La politique étrangère du PJD: Principes et orientations, Rabat, Tûb Barîs, 2008.

PJD. Le terrorisme, positions, leçons et enseignements, Rabat, http://www.leconomiste.com/article/886827-le-11-septembre-10-ans-apresbrla-loi-antiterroriste-liberticide-mais-pas-tellement, last accessed on September 21, 2013.

Al-Tajdîd, "Abû Zayd al-Muqrî' al-Idrisî: on veut qu'on oublie et qu'on efface la Palestine de notre mémoire," April 10, 2012.

http://www.slateafrique.com/91355/maroc-les-islamistes-accueillent-les-israeliens-a-bras-ouverts, last accessed on September 24, 2013.

Chapter 3

Belhaj, Abdessamad (2009) *La dimension islamique dans la politique étrangère du Maroc* (Louvain: Presses universitaires de Louvain).

Ben Salem, Maryam (2013) *Le militantisme en contexte répressif. Cas du mouvement islamiste tunisien*, PhD thesis in political science, under the direction of Daniel Gaxie, Université Paris 1 Panthéon Sorbonne.

Chennoufi, Anouar (2012) "Ennahdha réfute les accusations du porte-parole du parti algérien le Front de Libération Nationale (FLN)," Tunivisions, May 12, https://www.turess.com/fr/tunivisions/34660, last accessed October 9, 2016.

Chérif Ferjani, Mohamed (2012) "Révolution, élections et évolution du champ politique tunisien," *Confluences Méditerranée*, Vol. 3, no. 82, 107–16.

Courbot, Cécilia (1999) "De l'acculturation aux processus d'acculturation, de l'anthropologie à l'histoire. Petite histoire d'un terme connoté," *Hypothèses*, no. 1, 121–9.

Hermassi, Mohammed Elbaki (1984) "La société tunisienne au miroir islamiste," *Maghreb Machrek*, no. 103, January–March, 39–56.

Sadri, Khiari (2003) *Tunisie. Le délitement de la cité. Coercition, consentement, résistance* (Paris: Karthala).

Séguy, Jean (1980) "La socialisation aux valeurs utopiques," *Archives des Sciences Sociales de la Religion*, Vol. 50, no. 1, 7–21.

Sources

Constitutive rules of the movement after revision (9th Congress), July 2012.
Constitutive statement of the Islamic Tendency Movement (MTI), June 1981.
Ennahdha's electoral program for the elections of October 23, 2011.
Interview of the Tunisian Minister of Foreign affairs, *al Ahram*, September 11, 2016.
Interviews with sources from the Tunisian Ministry of Foreign Affairs.

Chapter 4

Abdal Fattah, Nabil (2013) *al nukhba wa-l thawra: al dawla wa-l islam al siyasi wa-l qawmiyya wa-l libiraliya* (Cairo: GEBO).

Abū Khalīl, Haytham (2012) *ikhwāān islāhiyyūn* (Cairo: dâār dūn).

Achour, Omar (2015) *Collusion to Breakdown, Islamist Military Relations in Egypt*, https://www.brookings.edu/wp-content/uploads/2016/06/collusion-to-crackdown-english.pdf

Aclimandos, Tewfik (2012) "Les Frères musulmans égyptiens," in Samir Amghar (ed.), *Les islamistes au défi du pouvoir: évolutions d'une idéologie* (Paris: Michalon), pp. 175–201.

Aclimandos, Tewfik (2017) "Les Frères musulmans égyptiens, pour une critique des vœux pieux," *Politique Africaine*, vol. 108, December, 25–46.

Anani, Khalil al (2007) *al ikhwan an muslimun, shaykhukha tusari' al zaman* (Cairo: Dar al Shuruq).

Ben Nefissa, Sara and Abo El-Kasem, Mahmoud Hamdi (2015) "L'organisation des Frères musulmans égyptiens à l'aune de l'hypothèse qutbiste," *Revue Tiers Monde*, June, 103–22.

Gerges, Fawwaz (2012) *Obama and the Middle East: The End of America's Moment?* (New York: Palgrave Macmillan).

Goldberg, Ellis (2012) "Reflections on Egypt's Draft Constitution," http://www.jadaliyya.com/pages/index/8172/reflections-on-egypts-draftconstitution

Hilal, Aliyy al Din, Hasan, Mazin and Mujib, May (2013) *al sira' min ajl nizam siyasi jadid: Misr ba'da al thawrat* (Cairo: al Daar al misriyya al lubnaaniyya).

Imam, Hamada (2012) *Al Saud wa-l ikhwan an muslimun* (Cairo: Kunuz).

Al Khirbāwī, Tharwat (2012) *sirr al ma'bad, al asrār al khafiyya li jamā'at al ikhwāān al muslimīn,* 3rd edition (Cairo: Dār Nahdat Misr).

Lia, Brynar (1998) *Society of the Muslim Brother in Egypt. The Rise of an Islamic Movement 1928–1942* (Reading: Ithaca Press).

Markaz dirâsat al wihda al 'arabiyya (2013) *al din wa-l dawla fi-l watan al arabi* (Beirut).

Masri, Charles Fouad al (2012) *al abb al ruhi, asrar hayat Yusuf Nasa al mufawwid al siyasi li-l ikhwan al muslimin* (Cairo: dar Nahdat Misr).

Milījī, al Sayyid 'Abd al Sattār al (2009) *tajrubati ma' al ikhwān* (Cairo: al Zahrāā' li-l i'lām al 'arabī).

Piquemal, Leslie (2012) *Les Frères musulmans égyptiens à la fin de l'ère Moubarak (2005–2010). Identité et projet politique* [The Egyptian Muslim Brotherhood of the late Mubarak era (2005–2010). Identity and Political Project], PhD thesis, IEP Paris.

Rajab, Iman (2016) *Hamas wa Hizbullah, ta'thir al hawiyya wa-l maslaha 'ala al' fā'ilin al 'anifiyn min ghayr al duwal fi-l sharq al awsat* (al Ahram).

Shuhayyib, Abdal Qadir (2013) *al saat al akhira fi hukm Mursi* (Cairo: Dar al Hilal).

Shuhayyib, Abdal Qadir (2015) *ightiyal Misr, muamara al ikhwan wa-l amrikan,* Vol. 1 (Cairo: Dar al Hilal).

Stork, Joe (2012) 'Egypt: New Constitution Mixed on Support of Rights', http://www.hrw.org/news/2012/11/29/egypt-new-constitution-mixed-supportrightshttp://www.hrw.org/news/2012/11/29/egypt-new-constitution-mixed-supportrights

Tammam, Husam (2010) *tahawullat al ikhwan al muslimin* (Cairo: Madbuli).

Tammam, Husam (2012) *Al ikhwan al muslimun, sanawat ma qabla al thawra* (Cairo: Dar al Shruruq).

Vannetzel, Marie (2016) *les frères musulmans égyptiens: enquête sur un secret public,* Paris: Karthala

Chapter 5

Caridi, Paola (2012) *Hamas, from Resistance to Government* (New York: Seven Stories Press).
Catori, Silvia (2010) *Al-Sabeel*, July, Afro-Middle East Centre–AMEC.
Charillon, Frédéric (ed.) (2002) *Politique étrangère: Nouveaux regards* [Foreign Policy. New Insights] (Paris: Presses de Sciences Po).
Dupret, Baudouin (2012) *La charia aujourd'hui: usages de la référence au droit islamique* (Paris: La Découverte).
Gunning, Jeroen (2007) *Hamas in Politics: Democracy, Religion, Violence* (London: Hurst and Company).
Halevi, Jonathan (2012) *Power Dynamics Inside Hamas*, vol. 11, no. 4 (Jerusalem Center for Public Affairs).
Karabell, Zachary (1996/7) "Fundamental Misconceptions: Islamic Foreign Policy," *Foreign Policy*, winter, no. 105, 76–90.
Khroub, Khaled (2000) *Hamas, Political Thought and Practice* (Washington, DC: Institute for Palestine Studies).
Legrain, Jean-François (1991) "A Defining Moment, Palestinian Islamic Fundamentalism," in James Piscatori (ed.), *Islamic Fundamentalism and the Gulf Crisis* (Chicago: American Academy of Arts and Sciences), pp. 131–53.
Litvak, Meir (1996) *The Islamization of Palestinian Identity: The Case of Hamas* (Tel Aviv: Moshe Dayan Center for Middle Eastern and African Studies).
Mishal, Shaul and Sela, Avraham (2000) *The Palestinian Hamas: Vision, Violence and Coexistence* (New York; Columbia University Press).
Signoles, Aude (2006) *Le Hamas au pouvoir et après?* (Toulouse: Milan, collection Milan actu).
Walt, Stephen (1990) *The Origins of Alliances* (London: Cornell University Press).

Chapter 6

Daher, Aurélie (2014) *Hezbollah, Mobilisation et pouvoir* (Paris: PUF), *Proche-Orient* collection. (Translated in English (2017) under the title: *Hezbollah. Mobilisation and Power* (London: Hurst/New York: Oxford University Press).)
Jaber, Hala (1997) *Hezbollah, Born with a Vengeance* (New York: Columbia University Press).
Picard, Elizabeth (1988) *Liban, État de discorde* (Paris: Flammarion).

Chapter 7

Badie B. and Smouts, M. C. (1999) *Le bouleversement du monde. Sociologie de la scène internationale* [The World Turned Upside Down. Sociology of the International Scene] (Paris: Presses de Sciences Po/Dalloz).

Balci, B. (1996) *Missionnaires de l'Islam en Asie centrale. Les écoles turques de Fethullah Gülen* [Islam's Missionaries in Central Asia. The Turkish Schools of Fethullah Gülen] (Paris: IFEA–Maisonneuve & Larose).

Baskın, O. (2001) *Türk Dış Politikası: Kurtuluş Savaşindan Bugüne* [Turkish Foreign Policy: The War of Independence Today], Vol. 1: 1919–1989 (Istanbul: İletişim).

Bozarslan, H. (1997) *La question kurde* [The Kurdish question] (Paris: Presses de Sciences Po).

Candar, C. (2012) *Mezopotamya Ekxpresi, Bir Tarih Yolculuğu* [Mesopotamia Express: A Voyage into History] (Istanbul: İlestişim).

Charillon, F. (ed.) (2002) *La politique étrangère: nouveaux regards* [Foreign Policy: New Outlooks] (Paris: Presses de Sciences Po).

Chenal, A. (2005) "L'AKP et Le Paysage Politique Turc," [The AKP and the Turkish Political Landscape], *Pouvoirs,* no. 115, 41–54.

Cook, S. A. (2011) "The USA, Turkey, and the Middle East: Continuities, Challenges, and Opportunities," *Turkish Studies*, Vol. 12, no. 4, December, 717–26.

Davutoğlu, A. (2001) *Stratejik Derinlik* [Strategic Depth], 1st edition (Istanbul: Küre Yayınları).

Droz-Vincent, P. (2005) "Le moment américain au Moyen-Orient" [The American Moment in the Middle East], *Esprit*, no. 5, 150–63.

Droz-Vincent, P. (2007) *Vertiges de la puissance. Le moment américain au Moyen-Orient* [Giddy with Power. The American Moment in the Middle East] (Paris: La Découverte, 2007).

Ebaugh, H. R. (2010) *The Gülen Movement: A Sociological Analysis of a Civic Movement Rooted in Moderate Islam* (New York: Springer).

Garapon, B. (2010) "La politique arabe de la Turquie depuis 2003 à la lumière de la 'doctrine' Davutoğlu" [Turkey's Arab Policy since 2003 in the Light of the Davutoğlu "Doctrine"], *Averoès*, no. 3, spring–summer.

Göle, N. (2001/4) "La Turquie, le Printemps arabe et la post-européanéité" [Turkey, the Arab Sprins and Post-Europeanity], *Confluences Méditerranée,* Vol. 4, no. 79, 47–56.

Hakura, F. (2011) "Turkey and the Middle East: Internal Confidence, External

Assertiveness," *Chatham House Briefing Papers*, November, http://www.chathamhouse.org/publications/papers/view/179761

İnat, K, Ataman, M., and Duran B. (eds) (2009) *Ortadoğu Yıllığı 2008* [Middle East Annals 2008] (Istanbul: Küre Yayınları).

International Crisis Group (2012) *Turkey and the Middle East: Ambitions and Constraints*, April 7, http://www.crisisgroup.org, last accessed March 16, 2013.

Karakas, C. (2007) *Turkey: Islam and Laïcism between the Interests of State, Politics and Society* (Frankfurt: Peace Research Institute Frankfurt (PRIF)).

Kürt, U. (2010) "The Doctrine of 'Turkish–Islamic Synthesis' as Official Ideology of September 12 and the 'Intellectuals Hearth-Aydinlar Ocagi' as the Ideological Apparatus of the State," *European Journal of Economic and Political Studies*, Vol. 3, no. 2, 111–25.

Le Moulec, J.-B. (2013) "Le Professeur qui a voulu révolutionner la politique étrangère turque" [The Professor Who Wanted to Revolutionize Turkish Foreign Policy], April 4, http://ovipot.hypotheses.org/8642.

Lundgren, A. (2005) "La politique turque de la frontière,". *Confluences Méditerranée*, no. 53, February, 79–90.

Magued, S. (2012) *La politique arabe de la Turquie depuis 2002 comme une dimension de sa gestion régionale au Moyen-Orient* [Turkey's Arab Policy since 2002 as a Dimension of its Managing the Middle East], PhD thesis in political science, Sciences Po Aix-en-Provence.

Mahalli, H. (2012) *Ortadoğu'da Kanlı Bahar* [Bloody Springtime in the Middle East] (Istanbul: Destek Yayınları).

Mallet, L. (2009) "Les ambiguïtés des relations turco-israéliennes" [The Ambiguities of Turco-Israeli Relations], Sécurité mondiale [Global security], 40, ISI, Université de Laval, http://www.psi.ulaval.ca.

Mango, A. (2005) *Turkey and the War on Terror. For Forty Years We Fought Alone* (London/New York: Routledge).

Martin, L. and Keridis, D. (2004) *The Future of Turkish Foreign Policy* (Cambridge, MA: MIT Press).

Montabone, B. (2013)"Droit à la ville et contestation de l'ordre moral urbain en Turquie" [Law in the City and Challenges to the Urban Moral Order in Turkey], *EchoGéo*, http://www.echogeo.revues.org/13567.

Öktem, K., Kadioglu, A., and Karli, M. (eds) (2012) *Another Empire. A Decade of Foreign Policy under the Justice and Development Party* (Istanbul: Bilgi University Press).

Parlar Dal, E. (2010) "Entre Précaution et Ambition: Le Néo- ottomanisme de La

Nouvelle Politique Extérieure de l'AKP En Question" [Between Caution and Ambition: The Neo-Ottomanism of the AKP New Foreign Policy at Issue], *EurOrient* special issue number, 35–58.

Pérouse, J.-F. (2013) "Le parc Gezi: dessous d'une transformation très politique" [Gezi Park: Under a Very Political Transformation], *Métropolitiques*, June 24, http://www.metropolitiques.eu/Le-parc-Gezi-dessous-d-une.html, last accessed April 9, 2015.

Rougier, B. (2007) "La guerre d'Israël contre le Hezbollah et la défaite de l'État libanais" [Israel's War against Hezbollah and the Defeat of the Lebanese State], in F. Charillon and B. Rougier (eds), *Afrique du Nord/Moyen-Orient* (Paris: La Documentation Française), pp. 67–94.

Signoles, A. (2007) "Lendemains de guerre dans les Territoires palestiniens" [Aftermaths of War in the Palestinian Territories], in F. Charillon, and and A. Dieckhoff (eds), *Afrique du Nord-Moyen-Orient* (Paris: La Documentation Française), pp. 49–63.

Sitzenstuhl, C. (2011) *La diplomatie turque au Moyen-Orient. Héritages et ambitions du gouvernement de l'AKP 2002–2010* [Turkish Middle East Diplomacy. Legacies and Ambitions of the AKP 2002–2010] (Paris: L'Harmattan).

Tocci, N., Taşpınar, Ö., Barkey, H. J., Soler y Lecha, E., and Nafaa, H. (2011) "Turkey and the Arab Spring: Implications for Turkish Foreign Policy from a Transatlantic Perspective," Mediterranean Paper Series. The German Marshall Fund of the United States, http://www.iai.it/pdf/mediterraneo/GMF-IAI/Mediterranean-paper_13.pdf.

Weber, S. (2013) "Looking from the side lines: retours sur la Turquie de Angry nation et de Another Empire" [Returns to the Turkey of the Angry Nation and of Another Empire], *EchoGéo*, vol. 25, http://echogeo.revues.org/1357.

Yankaya, D. (2012) *La nouvelle bourgeoisie islamique: le modèle turc* [The New Islamic Bourgeoisie: The Turkish Model] (Paris: PUF).

Zengin, G. (2012) *Hoca: Türk Dış Politikasında "Davutoğlu Etkisi"* [Mentor: The "Davutoğlu Effect" on Turkish Foreign Policy] (Istanbul: İnkilâp).

INDEX

Abbas, Mahmoud, 116, 168
Abdelnasser, Walid M., 28
Abdesselem, Rafik Ben, 56–7
AKP (Justice and Development Party) *see* Justice and Development Party (AKP)
Amar, Ali, 27–8
Al-Aqsa Mosque, 23, 24
Arab Spring, 60, 75, 106, 114–15, 118–19

al-Banna, Hassan
  on the independence of the al-Umma, 29
  Islamist ideology of, 3–5, 9, 21, 28
  Palestine as sacred site, 29–30
  promotion of secrecy, 71
Belhaj, Abdessamad, 23
Benkirane, Abdellillah, 31–3, 42
Bettayeb, Ridha, 50–1
Brigades of the Lebanese Resistance (AMAL), 130
Bush, George W., 38, 39

the Califate
  Muslim Brotherhood's conception of, 29, 30, 71–2, 83–4, 94
  PJD's stance on, 30–1
  within political Islam, 29
Center for the Study of Islam and Democracy (CSID), 40
Chari'ati, Ali, 54
constructivism
  applied to Turkey, 144
  and international relations, 11–12
  in relation to Islamism, 13–14

Davutoğlu, Ahmet
  knowledge production for Turco-Arab ties, 158
  re-alignment of Turkey towards the Arab world, 160, 171
  on regime change in Syria, 170
  Strategic Depth (*Stratejik Derinlik*), 153–6, 157, 159
democracy
  and the Ennahdha movement, 48
  and the Muslim Brotherhood, 74–5, 81
  post-Islamic conversion to, 8–9, 13–14
  and the Turkish model, 152

Egypt
  failure of the Morsi presidency, 73–4
  foreign policy under Hosni Mubarak, 90–1
  foreign policy under Mohamed Mursi, 91
  Islamic Guidance Society (IGS), 90, 92
  see also Muslim Brotherhood
Ennahdha movement
  anti-Western attitudes and family socialization, 49–50
  bilateral relations with Gulf countries, 59–61
  breaks with traditional diplomatic traditions, 58–9
  coalition with Nidaa Tounes, 62–3
  coming to power of, 47–8, 56–7
  demarcation from society's dominant values, 51–2
  democracy/societal Islamization tensions, 48
  desecration of Islamist militancy, 64–5
  early position towards the West, 48–55, 57

exiled activists and Western ideals, 55–6
foreign policies, 48–9, 66
impact of the Iranian revolution, 54–5
Islamization of the Marxist referential, 52–4
militarization of members of, 49–56
parallels with the AKP (Justice and Development Party), 66
partisan diplomacy, 57
reformulated anti-Westernism of, 57–8
relations with France, 58–9, 66
relations with Iran, 60–1
relations with Israel, proposed normalization of, 61–2
relations with Qatar, 56, 60, 61
relations with Syria, break in, 61
relations with the USA, 59
religiosity and militancy, 51–2, 64
stance on the Palestinian problem, 61
Erdoğan, R. T., 157, 167, 168; *see also* Justice and Development Party (AKP)

Faisal bin Abdulaziz Al Saud, 23
al-Fassi, Allal, 22, 23
Ferjani, Said, 52–3, 54
France
  Hezbollah's stance on, 132
  relations with the Ennahdha movement, 58–9, 66

Ghanouchi, Rached, 62, 64
Giraud, Roger, 34–5

al-Haddād, Isām, 91
Hamas (Movement of Islamic Resistance)
  dispersal of the Political Section (*maktab siyassi*), 105, 109
  foreign policy of, 105, 117–19
  interior/exterior decision-making authorities, 109–10, 113, 116–17, 118
  Islamic ideological status of, 106–7
  limited ideological discourse against Israel, 110–11
  Marj al-Zouhour incident, 108
  as non-state actor, 104–5
  normative discourse on Israel, 111–13, 118
  post-Arab Spring foreign policy, 114–15, 118–19
  pragmatic, non-ideological approach, 107–9
  Qatari funding of, 92
  relations with Iran, 112, 115
  relations with the Egyptian Muslim Brotherhood, 85, 92
  stance on the Syrian uprising, 115–16, 118–19
  transnationalism of, 105

united resistance front concept, 112–13, 114–15, 118
Haniyeh, Ismaël, 113, 114–15, 117
Hariri, Rafik, 135, 163, 166, 167
Hassan II
  accommodation of anti-terrorism rhetoric, 38–9
  early opposition to political Islam, 26
  early stance on Israel, 26–7
  the monarchy and foreign relations, 21–2
  and the Palestinian problem, 23–4
  pan-Arab/Islamic initiatives, 22, 24, 42
  presidency of the Al-Qods Committee, 24
  "Sherifness" of, 21–2
Hezbollah
  foreign policies of, 127–8
  foreign policy and the defense of the IRL, 131, 133–4
  formation of, 131
  internal decision-making on foreign policy, 132–3
  parliamentary presence and the IRL, 134–5
  the principle of *wilāyat al-Faqīh*, 128–9
  relations with France, 132
  relations with Iran, 128–9
  relations with Syria, 129–30, 136–9
  stance on Israel, 131–2
  state relations, post-2006 Lebanon War, 135–6
  Tunisian classification as terrorist organization, 63–4
  see also Islamic Resistance in Lebanon (IRL)

international relations
  constructivist approaches, 11–12
  Islamist view of, 2–3
Iran
  energy supplies to Turkey, 165
  interests in Syria, 138
  relations with Hamas, 112, 115
  relations with Hezbollah, 128–9
  relations with the Ennahdha movement, 60–1
  relations with the Muslim Brotherhood, 89–90, 94–5
  Turkey's role in nuclear discussion with, 168–9
Iranian revolution, 54–5
Iraq
  energy supplies to Turkey, 165
  invasion of Kuwait, 91, 108
  Kurdish population, 162
  relations with Turkey, historical, 146, 147, 149
  Turkey's interest in territorial integrity of, 149–50, 152, 153, 160
  Turkey's mediator role in, 169

Islamic Resistance in Lebanon (IRL)
　complementarity relationship with Hezbollah, 131
　Hezbollah's parliamentary presence and, 134–5
　interests of and Hezbollah's foreign policy, 133–4
　involvement in Syria, 136–9
　see also Hezbollah
Islamic Youth, 26, 28, 30
Islamism
　defined, 6–7
　and Hassan al-Banna's guiding principles, 3–5, 21
　as an ideocracy, 12
　legalist/protesting logic dual discourse of, 47
　and a Muslim nation, 2–3
　at the national level, 9–11, 16
　plurality of implementation of, 15, 16
　within the political system, 15–17
　rejection of the term "Islamist," 65–6
　as Salafist, 6–7
　and the wider Islamic identity, 3
　see also post-Islamism
Islamite Movement of Islamic Tendency (MTI), 51–2
Israel
　diplomatic relations with Morocco, 27–8
　Hamas's discourses on, 110–13, 118
　Hassan II's early stance on, 26–7
　Hezbollah's stance on, 131–2
　invasion of Lebanon (1982), 131
　PJD's confessionalization discourse on, 32–5, 41–2
　PJD's rationalization discourse on, 35–8
　PJD's stance on, 28
　proposed normalization of relations with the Ennahdha Government, 61–2
　stance of the Muslim Brotherhood on, 84–5
　trade with Morocco, 41
　Turkey and Israeli-Syrian negotiations, 166–7
　Turkey's role in Israeli–Palestinian negotiations, 167–8
　2006 Lebanon War, 135
　withdrawal from Lebanon (2000), 130

Justice and Development Party (AKP)
　Arab-focussed foreign policy, 142–3
　autonomisation vis-a-vis the West, 149–50
　break with Atlanticism, 142–3, 146, 148, 150, 152–3
　Davutoğlu Doctrine of Foreign Policy, 153–6
　economic policies, 164–5
　energy supplies and foreign policy, 164–6
　EU membership negotiations for, 150, 169–70
　evocation of Ottoman heritage, 145–6
　expansion of regional influence, 155–6
　foreign policies, 170–1
　"Gezi Park" protests, 171
　Iraqi territorial integrity and the US invasion, 2003, 149–50, 152, 153, 160
　Islam in political discourse, historical, 146–8
　as Islamist government, 142–3
　as key regional state, 160, 166–9
　knowledge producers for foreign policy, 157–8
　the Kurdish problem and relations with Syria, 161–2
　mediator role in Iraq, 169
　neo-Ottomanism, 142, 143, 145–6, 161
　parallels with the Ennahdha movement, 66
　regional economic partnerships, 158–9
　regional status, 153
　relations with Lebanon, 166
　relations with the US, post-9/11, 148–50
　relations with the USSR/Russia, 146, 148
　relationship with the Muslim Brotherhood, 82
　restoration of Turco-Arab relations, 145–8, 157–9, 160, 165–6
　role in Iran–the West nuclear discussions, 168–9
　role in Israeli–Palestinian negotiations, 167–8
　role in Israeli-Syrian negotiations, 166–7
　role of the military, 152, 156
　secular current's opposition to, 143, 155, 159, 170, 171
　state identity, 2000s onwards, 151–3
　structural transformations (the Turkish model), 170
　Turco-Islamic synthesis, 147
　Turco-Syrian rapprochement, 160–1, 162–4, 170

al-Khalfi, Mustafa, 40
Khatami, Mohammad, 129
Khomeini, Ruhollah, 54–5

Laariadh, Ali, 51–2
Lebanon
　Israeli invasion (1982), 131
　Israeli withdrawal (2000), 130
　relations with Turkey, 166
　2006 Lebanon War, 135
　see also Hezbollah; Islamic Resistance in Lebanon (IRL)
Libya, 165
Lourimi, Ajmi, 54–5

Mechaal, Khaled
　Fatah–Hamas Doha Agreement, 116

as leader of Hamas, 109
meeting with Dimitri Medvedev, 112
non-ratification of reconciliation document, 113
post-Arab Spring foreign policy, 114
during the second Intifada, 110
visits to Iran, 112
and Youssef al-Qardawi's sermon, 117
Menderes, Adnan, 146
Mohammed V, 22
Mohammed VI, 24, 27
Molina Fernandez, Irene, 21–2
Morocco
 Al-Tajdīd magazine, 41–2
 anti-terrorism law, 38–9
 diplomacy and the Israeli-Palestinian conflict, 25
 diplomatic relations with Israel, 27–8
 Green March, 1975, 22, 35
 Islamic Youth, 26, 28, 30
 Islamist/monarchy relations, 22, 28
 local/global Islam interactions, 22–3
 the monarchy and foreign relations, 21–2
 Popular Forces Party, 39
 trade with Israel, 41
 US–Morocco Free Trade Agreement, 39–40
 see also Party of Justice and Development (PJD)
Morsi, Mohamed, 74, 83, 90; *see also* Muslim Brotherhood
Mubarak, Hosni, 90
MÜSIAD, 158–9
Muslim Brotherhood
 and the army, 92–3
 as broad Islamist coalition, 89
 conception of the Califate, 29, 30, 71–2, 83–4, 94
 connections with jihadists, 87–9
 connections with Salafist movements, 85–8, 89
 constitution of whilst in power, 76
 culture of clandestinity, 71, 76–7
 democratic transition paradigm, 74–5, 81
 failure of the Morsi presidency, 73–4
 foreign investment in Egypt, 93–4
 foreign policies, 91, 94–6
 foundation of, 7, 29
 great narrative of, 77–8, 90
 ideology of, 80
 inapplicability of post-Islamism to, 72
 inconsistencies within, 72–3
 international arm of, 91–2
 nationalism of, 82–3
 Palestine as sacred site, 29–30
 and the PJD, 30
 pragmatism of, 72, 78

principles for the Muslim nation, 3–6
 Qutbism, 71, 77–9, 86
 relations with Hamas, 85, 92
 relations with Iran, 89–90, 94–5
 relations with Saudi Arabia, 75–6, 84
 relations with the AKP, 82
 relations with the Islamic Guidance Society (IGS), 92
 relations with the USA, 80–1, 94
 sources of knowledge about, 77–80
 stance on Israel, 84–5
Muslim nation, 3–6
Muslim World League, 23

Nasser, Gamal Abdel, 26
nation states
 Islamist action at level of, 9–11, 12–13
 in relation to the global *Umma*, 12–13

Organisation of Islamic Cooperation (OIC), 23–4
Organization of the Islamic Conference, 23

Palestine
 and the Al-Qods Committee, 24–5
 Ennahdha movement's stance on, 61
 glorification of the intifada, 32–3
 within Islamist foreign policy, 22
 Moroccan diplomacy and, 25
 the Organisation of Islamic Coperation's stance on, 23–4
 PJD's confessionalization discourse on, 32–5, 41–2
 PJD's rationalization discourse on, 35–8
 as sacred site for the Muslim Brotherhood, 29–30
 Al-Tajdīd magazine texts on, 41–2
 Turkey's role in Israeli–Palestinian negotiations, 167–8
Party of Justice and Development (PJD)
 accommodation of anti-terrorism rhetoric, 38–9
 alignment with the Popular Forces Party, 39
 and the Califate, 30–1
 confessionalization period, 31–5
 declining anti-American rhetoric, 39–41
 economic policies, 39, 41
 evolution of, 30
 externalization of anti-establishment discourse, 38–42
 ideology of the Muslim Brotherhood and, 30
 ideology/pragmatism tensions, 20
 international relations conception of, 30–1
 Islam vs. the West dualism, 31–2
 normalization of, 42–3

Party of Justice and Development (PJD) *(cont.)*
  rationalization of discourse, 35–8
  stance on Israel, 28, 32–8, 41–2
  stance on the Palestinian problem, 32–8, 41–2
  and US–Morocco Free Trade Agreement, 39–40
  see also Morocco
Piquemal, Leslie, 75, 77
post-Islamism
  and conversion to democratic norms, 8–9, 13–14
  inapplicability of to the Muslim Brotherhood, 72
  revisionism and redefinition of the international order, 8, 15

al-Qaeda, 85
al-Qardawi, Youssef, 117
Qatar
  funding to Hamas, 92
  relations with the Ennahdha movement, 56, 60, 61
  relations with Tunisia, 63
Al-Qods Committee, 24–5
Qutb, Sayyid, 71, 77–9, 86

Rafsanjani, Akbar Hashemi, 129
Russia, 146

al-Sadat, Anwar, 26, 42
Salafism
  within Islamism, 6–7
  and the Muslim Brotherhood, 85–8, 89
Saudi Arabia
  and the Organization of the Islamic Conference, 23
  relations with Tunisia, 60, 63
  stance on the Muslim Brotherhood, 75–6, 84
al-Shātir, Khayrat, 91, 92
social identities, 13–14
Soviet Union (USSR), 146
Syria
  Ennahdha movement's break in diplomatic relations with, 61
  Hamas's stance on, 115–16, 118–19
  the Kurdish problem and relations with Turkey, 161–2
  relations with Hezbollah, 129–30, 136–9
  relations with the USA, 162
  relations with Tunisia, 63

Turco-Syrian rapprochement, 160–1, 162–4, 170
Turkey and Israeli–Syrian negotiations, 166–7

Tunisia
  Bourguiba regime, 48, 50–1
  classification of Hezbollah as terrorist organization, 63–4
  elections, 2011, 47
  foreign policy, post-2014, 62–4
  Islamite Movement of Islamic Tendency (MTI), 51–2
  Nidaa Tounes (Call for Tunisia), 62
  perceived moral decline and anti-Western sentiments, 50
  relations with Qatar, 63
  relations with Saudi Arabia, 60, 63
  relations with Syria, 63
  relations with the USA, 59
  separation of the political from the religious, 64
  see also Ennahdha movement
Turkey
  structural transformations (the Turkish model), 151–2
  see also Justice and Development Party (AKP)
TÜSKON, 158–9

al-Umma, 2, 8, 12–13, 29, 33, 48, 50
United States of America (USA)
  foreign policy in the Middle East, post-9/11, 149
  relations with Syria, 162
  relations with Tunisia, 59
  relations with Turkey, post-9/11, 148–50
  relationship with the Muslim Brotherhood, 80–1, 94
  USA Patriot Act, 39
  US–Morocco Free Trade Agreement, 39–40
  war on terrorism, 38–9

the West
  attitudes towards of the Ennahdha movement, 48–50
  Ennahdha's position towards, 48–9
  Islam vs. the West dualism, 31–2
  nuclear discussions with Iran, 168–9
  Turkey's autonomisation away from, 31–2

Yassine, Sheikh Ahmed, 27, 32, 108, 109, 110

EU representative:
Easy Access System Europe
Mustamäe tee 50, 10621 Tallinn, Estonia
Gpsr.requests@easproject.com

www.ingramcontent.com/pod-product-compliance
Lightning Source LLC
Chambersburg PA
CBHW051117230426
43667CB00014B/2615